Divine Self, Human Self

Divine Self, Human Self

The Philosophy of Being in Two *Gītā* Commentaries

Chakravarthi Ram-Prasad

B L O O M S B U R Y
LONDON • NEW DELHI • NEW YORK • SYDNEY

Bloomsbury Academic
An imprint of Bloomsbury Publishing Plc

1385 Broadway
New York
NY 10018
USA

50 Bedford Square
London
WC1B 3DP
UK

www.bloomsbury.com

First published 2013

Library of Congress Cataloging-in-Publication Data
A catalogue record for this book is available from the Library of Congress.

ISBN: HB: 978-1-4411-8265-4
PB: 978-1-4411-5464-4
ePub: 978-1-4411-4042-5
ePDF: 978-1-4411-7681-3

Typeset by Fakenham Prepress Solutions, Fakenham, Norfolk NR21 8NN
Printed and bound in the United States of America

For Julius Lipner

Contents

Preface

This book is one of the outputs of a major research grant, 2008–11, from the Arts and Humanities Research Council, UK, of which I was the PI. I would like to thank the AHRC for its support of the study of classical Sanskrit thought.

I would like to thank Irina Kuznetsova, who was Research Associate on the AHRC project, for her careful and deeply scholarly editorial help; this book would have taken far longer to complete without her assistance. Sections of this book were presented at different places, and I would like to thank the audiences at the Dahlem Humanities Centre at Free University, Berlin, The Oxford Centre for Hindu Studies, and Lambeth Palace for their interest and comments. I would particularly like to thank the participants of a discussion group at The Centre for the Study of World Religions, Harvard, for their sympathetic yet rigorous and highly informed response to a draft of over half of this book. Various people have discussed ideas that have gone into this book, or read sections of it, and I am deeply grateful to them: Frank Clooney, Gwen Griffith-Dickson, Gavin Hyman, Parimal Patil, Laurie Patton, and Kate Wharton. Frank Clooney invited me to Harvard to give the inaugural Comparative Theology Lecture, where I first outlined the idea of this book; he also organised the discussion group from which I benefitted a great deal. Gavin Hyman long ago encouraged me to look carefully at postmodern Christian theology, and conversations with him for well over a decade have informed many of my ideas.

My uncle, K. Sudarsan has always followed my interest in these philosophical materials, and gifted me Sanskrit texts across the years.

Insightful and wise remarks by Rowan Williams, and the experience of working with him at a meeting with Hindu *ācāryas* in Bangalore, had a deep impact on my thinking about the central issues with which I have dealt here.

Since the very beginning of my career, Julius Lipner has been an unfailingly encouraging and supportive senior colleague. His book on Rāmānuja was the first thing I read that made me understand the contemporary possibilities of the philosophical tradition into which I had been born. I dedicate this book to him.

Lancaster University has been a supportive place, and I would particularly like to thank Tony Mcenery and Emma Rose.

As ever, my parents, brother, father-in-law and children have provided a constant and warm environment for my work. And as always, nothing would be possible for me without Judith.

Introduction

This book is an essay in constructive theology. Let me approach what I mean by that through the timeworn tactic of saying what this book is not. It is not a study of the *Bhagavad Gītā* (c. first century CE) in any way: historical, philological or even theological. In much of this introduction, I do outline the *Gītā*'s structure, textual location, and reception history, as well as the contemporary secondary literature on it; but this is primarily to offer the full context of the commentaries on which I work thereafter, especially for those not familiar with Hindu traditions and Sanskrit. But this book is not a study of Śaṅkara's (c. eighth-ninth century CE) and Rāmānuja's (eleventh-twelfth century CE) commentaries (*bhāṣyas*) either, in the strict sense of systematically going through these commentaries and offering a sort of sub-commentary within a textual-historical study. Nor is this book an overarching comparison of Śaṅkara's Advaita (Non-Dualism) and Rāmānuja's Viśiṣṭādvaita (Qualified Non-Dualism); that is to say, their competing interpretations of the meaning of the ancient *Upaniṣad* texts (called the Vedānta or end portions of the Vedas) and other sacred materials.

It should not need saying – although, sadly, it usually does – that a theologian of Christianity would not need to make any such preliminary declaration. Contemporary Christian theology, in whatever different ways writers within it characterise themselves, is a living tradition in which the works of the great Christian thinkers of the past become the source of new thinking and re-thinking; and this is seen as a perfectly legitimate undertaking in the academy, along with historical, philological and other forms of study. There is no doubt that Hindu thought must come to terms with a hermeneutic rupture created in its history. Nevertheless, for some time now, it has been widely recognised in the Western academy, where constructive Christian theology flourishes as a discipline, that there can be neither moral nor intellectual grounds for denying that constructive theology is perfectly possible in different traditions.[1] (That various hegemonies of thought still hold on tenaciously to strictures on what is permissible in the study of Hindu thought and culture is another matter. I propose to ignore them – they aren't worth the bother of engaging in asymptotic approaches to the overcoming of prejudices.) The reality is that some sort of context-setting is required for a work that seeks to do constructive Hindu theology: there is no established field as such, and the precise nature of my engagement with the Sanskrit material requires some clarification, since it does not follow standard Indological disciplines.

Some of the most creative work in Hindu theology has actually emerged within recent developments in comparative theology, especially Hindu-Christian studies, where several scholars have worked across and between the traditions, usually from a Christian perspective. The growing area of 'Dharma Studies' has also seen scholars approaching such issues as gender and politics from Hindu perspectives. This book is not, strictly speaking, a comparison across 'religions'. Rather, it can be called 'inter-cultural', a theological equivalent of what the philosopher Mark Siderits has called 'fusion philosophy'. Following from the very fact that it is in English, this book has to acknowledge that theological language has to make sense in the idiom of English-language theology, for otherwise it will lapse into a hybrid idiolect that leaves behind the Sanskrit, with nothing to show for its translational effort. But I do not take this conceptual effort as merely a linguistic necessity. There is a rigorous, vigorous, densely populated history of analysis and exploration in modern and post-modern Christian theology that is rich with interpretive potential; it provides a disciplinary vocabulary for any sort of contemporary theology, of whatever tradition and with whatever hermeneutic challenges. If Hindu theology is to flourish (again), it must do so in a world that it did not make but may yet enrich, a world in which a global discourse is becoming possible without being merely rendered so by the cultural fiat of Western hegemony. It will be a very different world from the classical and medieval spaces within which Śaṅkara and Rāmānuja lived, but new ways of re-establishing a living connection with them have to be explored. So, in this book, I draw freely from a wide range of Christian theological writing, always acknowledging those sources and seeking to engage with them from my perspective, formed as it is by the objective of understanding Śaṅkara and Rāmānuja on the *Gītā* in terms that I find relevant. But this is only one side of the fusion. As I read, I find again and yet again how extraordinarily rich and creative, how filled with the potential for re-interpretation across the ages, are the thoughts of these great Vedāntic figures. Unless one rejects outright the possibility of learning from another tradition, one will find discussions originally articulated in Christian theology illuminated and perhaps even re-shaped by the spiritual force of their ideas.

Earlier, I said that this book is neither a straightforward study of the two *Gītā* commentaries nor of the *Gītā* itself. Let me say a little more on this issue, by way of indicating more clearly the task I have set myself. One way of engaging with the commentaries has been to remark on whether or not they somehow adhere to what the *Gītā* actually means: this is most evident in Zaehner's classic, scholarly and influential translation,[2] which is also, indirectly, a form of Christian apologetic (at a time when comparative theology was a much more agonistic enterprise than it has perhaps tended to be in recent times). Arvind Sharma's *The Hindu Gītā*,[3] one of the very few books to compare Vedānta commentaries, also follows Zaehner quite closely, despite emphatically not being committed to a Christian perspective. The underlying assumption is that the contemporary scholar ought to look beyond the specific commitments of the Hindu traditions and recover the original meaning. Of course, the traditions themselves usually claim to be doing the same thing: a thoroughly engaging but deeply sectarian English-language example is S. M. Srinivasa Chari's *Philosophy of the Bhagavadgītā*,[4] which presents Rāmānuja's interpretation as the most persuasive, compared to Śaṅkara and Madhva. By contrast, I approach the two commentaries as creative and profound texts in themselves, the variations in interpretations all the more interesting for being constrained by the very specific aspects of the text – especially Kṛṣṇa's declarative presence. So there is no attempt to determine what the *Gītā* 'really' means.

Am I trying instead to say what Śaṅkara and Rāmānuja 'really' mean? To a certain extent, yes. This book does contain exegesis, founding its claims at every stage on a close reading of the commentaries and offering extensive translations (with the Sanskrit text in footnotes for those interested). The whole book proceeds through such reading, and my aim is to establish that the ideas presented here are found in the commentaries themselves. But this is nevertheless not a linear sub-commentary on the commentaries; I make no attempt to present the sequence of the *Gītā* to which commentaries have to adhere. Here, in overall form, I take leave of the structure of both the *Gītā* and the *bhāṣyas*. My primary interest is in presenting coherent accounts of an Advaitic and a Viśiṣṭādvaitic theory of divinity, being and self, as they emerge from the two commentaries considered as wholes. It is here that the constructive (or, in a more intellectually conservative sense, systematic) theological nature of this book becomes obvious. The theories I present range across the commentaries according to my organisation of concepts. In that sense, I am explicitly not making a claim to have brought out the meaning of the commentaries. Instead, I wish to present two ways of conceiving the nature of, and relationship between, the notions of divinity, selfhood, and being. Each, I hope, will offer a contemporary Hindu theology that can engage with questions that appear to be asked similarly in recent Western thought.

There are reasons why I have chosen to look at two commentaries and only two; some reasons are pragmatic, others more conceptual. Pragmatically, the challenge of entering into the third great Vedānta tradition, Madhva's Dvaita (Dualism) is formidable, both in terms of the tradition's own complex requirements for entry into its intellectual heritage and in terms of my own lack of knowledge of Madhva's very specific sectarian concerns. Going beyond that to other commentaries – most provocatively, Abhinavagupta's mystical re-reading within the Kaśmiri Śaiva tradition – would not only have meant a whole new branch of scholarship, given the esoteric demands of that tradition, but also a shallowing out of the project itself.

As someone from Rāmānuja's Śri Vaiṣṇava community who has worked on Śaṅkara for half a lifetime, I felt that pragmatically, such a dual-focus study was possible. Practical considerations of scholarship and booklength and depth out of the way, the advantages of this dual focus also became evident. The dialectical tension between the two readings of the *Gītā* is fruitful. Śaṅkara strives to reach beyond the theologically rich presence of Kṛṣṇa to a metaphysics of being (or perhaps, a metaphysics beyond being, or yet again, a transmetaphysics of being, depending on your Heideggerian taste), while Rāmānuja sees all the *Gītā*'s metaphysics as subserving the theology of a gracious God. Within that contrast – which, of course, is a vastly simplified summing up – are complementary challenges, which this book sets out to explain and in some small measure, meet. All in all, this great contrast says something of use to contemporary Christian and comparative philosophical theology, namely, that a fundamental choice (and yet a subtle one) has to be made between whether explanation should seek the limits of an understanding that encompasses God or whether God explains everything else. Of course, Śaṅkara and Rāmānuja do not treat it as quite the intellectual exercise I appear to present here; rather, they suggest different answers to the question of where we should rest our understanding the better to continue our existential journey. For Śaṅkara, God is a vital component of our self-realization; for Rāmānuja, self-realization is merely a movement towards our reception of God's grace. This immediately indicates that their accounts also pertain to who the 'we' are; and that is because the *Gītā* does too. Indeed, for the *Gītā*, it is the human predicament that is the proximal cause of the text's own existence, in the course of whose unfolding, much else – divinity, being, the relationship between divine and human – is revealed. And here too, the great teachers have different conceptions of the nature of the human self, and therefore of its relationship with the divine and with reality. In a purely intellectual sense, there is piquancy in the fact that they end up so far from each other while starting from the same place – the deceptively simple Sanskrit verses of the *Gītā*. Reading Śaṅkara and Rāmānuja beside and against each other allows for a sharper analysis of where they cleave and why, thereby delineating each of my theological reconstructions more clearly. Reading these two commentaries for this book seemed the right thing to do: to offer a binocular study, albeit not one in any way synoptic.

The organisation of this book, to repeat, does not follow the linear structure of the *Gītā*. In two relatively self-contained chapters, I present what I hope will be two coherent systems of thought, each grappling with the question of the nature and meaning of *brahman*, the significance of the first-personal presence and declarations of Kṛṣṇa, and above all, the conceptual relationship between the two – for the *Gītā* itself offers no easy conclusion. In effect, these chapters present the nature of the divine, in relation to an exploration of being, in Śaṅkara and Rāmānuja respectively. These chapters are only relatively self-contained for, of course, I refer in each to the other. Perhaps there is more on Śaṅkara in the chapter on Rāmānuja, since he often explicitly responds to the Advaitic interpretation of the *Gītā* that must have become quite famous in the intervening two or three centuries. In the final chapter, however, I bring the theological and metaphysical theories presented in the first two chapters to bear on a comparative study of the two teachers on the relationship between human and divine self. I compare what each says of the relationship between the concrete human person – in the *Gītā*, Prince Arjuna – and the core, metaphysical self (*ātman*) to which Kṛṣṇa adverts from the beginning of his teaching. This chapter, while it takes a philosophical look at the nature of self, nevertheless focuses on the specific theological context of the *Gītā*, where the meaning of selfhood makes sense only within a larger exploration of *brahman* and Kṛṣṇa.

I would hope that this book was interesting to those studying the *Gītā* and its significance, and to those studying medieval Hindu thought, despite the fact that it is not a disquisition on (let alone an introduction to) *Gītā* commentaries. But certainly, the real intent of this book is to contribute to the global discipline of comparative theology, by offering systematic re/constructions of two interacting, contesting, complementing, and contrasting ways of tackling fundamental questions of existence. I would hope too that it had some appeal to those trained in Western and Christian traditions, who were willing to engage reciprocally in an understanding of intellectual positions whose sources were in non-Western and non-Christian traditions. Only in that willingness does hope lie of a global discourse beyond cultural hegemonies. (I do not, for a moment, deny that there are other hegemonies that this work is utterly useless in addressing – gender and caste/class being the most significant.)

In some ways, the context of the *Gītā* is relatively well-known even outside Indology. It is found within the magnificently long poetic composition, the *Mahābhārata*, which has long been called, together with the Rāmāyaṇa, an Indian 'epic';[5] its embeddedness is brought out in van Buitenen's translation, which explicitly treats it as 'the sixty-third of the Hundred Minor Books of the Mahābhārata, and…the third episode of…the

Book of Bhīṣma, the sixth of the Eighteen Major Books'.[6] It is divided into eighteen chapters, and traditionally comprises 700 verses in total. (Although there is a further convention that most classical and medieval commentators follow, of dividing the eighteen chapters into three hexads, this plays no role in the numbering of the *Gītā* verses (which is Chapter.Verse). And although the commentators disagree on what the subject-matter of each hexad is, that textual disagreement is not part of my philosophical and theological reading in this book.)

The *Bhagavad Gītā* is a conversation. Looking across the battlefield, the warrior, Prince Arjuna, one of the five Pāṇḍava brothers, sees his teachers and uncles, as well as his hostile cousins and their followers. It has come to this because his eldest brother has been denied a kingdom, his wife has been humiliated, his mother marginalised, he and his brothers harassed. His wife wants revenge, and his eldest brother the kingdom. His cousins' father (his uncle) is nominally the rightful king, and with infinite sorrow and reluctance, his great-uncle and his beloved teachers have bound themselves in duty to the king to fight against the Pāṇḍavas. That, in its barest bones, is the *Mahābhārata* context of the *Gītā* (for, of course, the *Mahābhārata* has vastly more to its compendious story-telling). Arjuna is the foremost warrior on his side. But should he fight, knowing what horror and suffering the battle will bring? He throws down his great bow, expressing his despair to his charioteer (and cousin to both sides), Kṛṣṇa. The *Gītā* is Kṛṣṇa's response to Arjuna's deep despondence. Its narrative arc is provided by Kṛṣṇa's effort to make Arjuna take up his bow and fight, in the course of which he reveals himself as God in human form. Kṛṣṇa is successful in this regard, and the eighteen-day battle commences, full of moral ambiguity on both sides, with exactly the sort of slaughter that Arjuna had anticipated. Even the ultimate victory of his side is contaminated by the death of the sons of the Pāṇḍava brothers, as well as their eldest half-brother who had fought for the Kaurava cousins on the other side. The rest of the *Mahābhārata* includes the fifteen discontented years of rule by Arjuna's eldest brother, Yuddhiṣṭhira, and the eventual deaths of most of the survivors of the battle, including Kṛṣṇa himself. The Pāṇḍava brothers and their wife Draupadī finally set off to the mountains, gradually dying away one by one, until Yuddhiṣṭhira alone, having faced stern tests to his moral nature, enters the celestial realm. The epic peters out with the challenges faced by the sole surviving Pāṇḍava scion, Arjuna's grandson Parikṣit and his progeny. The *Mahābhārata* is as capacious, multiform, open-ended and ambiguous as life itself. As such, in its endless forms, it has been part of the warp and weft of culture wherever it has travelled.

The *Gītā* partakes of the historical and compositional complexities of the vast text within which it was finally redacted, and yet stands apart as a self-contained unit. Its narrative drive, which locates it at that particular point of the clash between the two sides, does not exhaust its intrinsic conceptual density; and this is clear in its subsequent reception by the tradition. Assuming the general contemporary consensus that it was composed either side of the start of the Common Era, and finally redacted within the *Mahābhārata* around the fourth to the fifth century, clearly by Śaṅkara's time around the 8th century, it had gained sufficient significance for him to write a commentary on it; the recension of 700 verses on which his commentary is based became, due to the influence of the commentary itself, the standard version on which subsequent commentaries were based. The commentarial reception history of the *Gītā* shows that it was understood as a unified and distinct text, with a sacrality not associated with the *Mahābhārata* as a whole. Doubtless the commentators on the *Gītā* took their audience to be familiar with the epic context and characters, as is evident from their references to other parts of the *Mahābhārata*; but from Śaṅkara onwards, it is clear that there is a categorical difference between the two.

The independent status of the *Gītā* made it a focus of modern scholarship from the late eighteenth century, when it came to the attention of Enlightenment Europe.[7] It should be noted too that by this time, the Sanskrit scholarship of the *paṇḍits*, while continuing to flourish in many philosophical areas, appears to have suffered a hermeneutic rupture with the commentarial tradition. As Angelika Malinar points out, the modern and contemporary scholarship (initially only by Westerners but, with the establishment of a British pattern of university education in the Raj, by Indian scholars too, and now in universities globally) shows two dominant approaches. One is what she calls 'analytic', which is text-critical and historical in its aim of establishing the textual history of the *Gītā*; the other is 'unitary', treating the text holistically and seeking to interpret it through different theoretical perspectives (especially philosophical/theological).[8] These are not necessarily antithetical, as she points out (and as her own work demonstrates). In the meantime, from the mid-nineteenth century onwards, Hindus began to go back to the *Gītā* and read it in the radically changed context of colonial modernity.[9] A sequence of politically, socially and spiritually significant figures engaged with the *Gītā*, with concerns distinctively different from that of the classical commentators; where the earlier thinkers had worked within an established, highly structured, epistemically familiar Sanskritic culture, the modern Hindus worked in an intellectual world often not of their making, in its language, socio-political power and terms of cultural reference. In recent decades, the divide between the systematic scholarly approaches to the *Gītā* and the urgent, existential engagement with it no longer has the mainly ethno-racial divide it may once have had, when

Europeans took the former attitude and Indian Hindus adopted the latter. (Not that this divide was ever absolute.) The *Gītā* is a spiritual and religious text for people from different cultures around the world, while it is also studied in scholarly fashion by people of Hindu background.

I have very quickly outlined this history only to contextualise what follows; as mentioned already, this is not a book about the *Gītā*. I will now turn to an equally brief contextualisation of Śaṅkara and Rāmānuja, on whose *Gītā* commentaries I focus on in this book, as well as the famous schools of thought they established; brief because, again, this is not a work on either the commentators or on Advaita and Viśiṣṭādvaita.

Despite the vast hagiography on Śaṅkara, very little is known about him; his dates remain vaguely between 650–800 CE and he is generally acknowledged to have been born in present-day Kerala, into a family of the highest sub-class of brahmin priests in the region, the Nambudripad.[10] Śaṅkara drew on a variety of non-dualist thought, especially the linguistic reading of reality by Bartṛhari (sixth century), the perhaps Buddhist-inspired idealism of Gauḍapāda (probably two generations before Śaṅkara), and the reconciliation of a metaphysics of non-dualism with Vedic ritualism by Maṇḍanamiśra, Śaṅkara's older contemporary. He is generally taken to be the founder of the system of Advaita (non-dualism) specifically, as an interpretation of the *Upaniṣads* which, because they form the 'end' or 'final' portion of the sacred Veda corpus, are called Vedānta.[11] Although a vast number of works are traditionally attributed to Śaṅkara, Paul Hacker's analytic method established for certain that Śaṅkara was the author of a commentary on the 1st century summary of the *Upaniṣads* (the *Brahmasūtra*), called the *Brahmasūtrabhāṣya*, and commentaries on at least ten of the major *Upaniṣads*. The short treatise, the *Upadeśasāhasrī*, is also now firmly attributed to him. Finally (and necessary for the very existence of this book), Sengaku Mayeda established that Śaṅkara was the author of the *Gītābhāṣya*.[12] There remain two or three other commentaries and several poetic cycles that seem attributable to Śaṅkara. What is not debatable is that, within the two centuries or so of his writing, his thought gained wide currency in the intellectual landscape of India. A stream of sub-commentaries and glosses, usually in one of two competing sub-schools, were written on his work, especially the *Brahmasūtrabhāṣya*. From the 19th century onwards, Advaita became a dominant vehicle for newfound Hindu self-representation, although ideas attributed to Śaṅkara were seldom textually grounded in his own work, to such an extent that scholars usually talk of a wholly modern Neo-Vedānta (which, in fact, is specifically Neo-Advaita rather than any other system of Vedānta).

The next significant interpretation of the Vedānta occurred some three hundred years later, in the work of Rāmānuja. Although there are competing theories about how and why he is traditionally assigned the extraordinarily long life span of 120 years (1017–1137) and what a more realistic dating might be, a great deal more is known about his life than Śaṅkara's. This is because Rāmānuja was born in the Tamil country amongst those who had already coalesced in the previous three hundred years into a mainly Brahmin community devoted to the worship of Viṣṇu and his consort Śrī (and therefore called Śrīvaiṣṇavas). The community also ensured that his works were carefully noted, and there is only some controversy about Rāmānuja's œuvre: his key works are his commentary on the *Brahmasūtra*, the *Śrībhāṣ ya*; an independent summary of his views, the *Vedārthasaṃgraha*; and the *Gītābhāṣya*. He is generally supposed to have written two shorter commentaries on the *Brahmasūtra*, the *Vedāntadīpa* and the *Vedāntasāra*. There is some controversy over whether he wrote the rather different prose hymns, the *Gadya Traya*, which introduce ideas not found in the acknowledged works.[13] Unlike Śaṅkara, whose teachings appear not to have had an immediate effect on the community that he left behind on becoming a renunciate, Rāmānuja continued to work amongst his own community even after renunciation, and strengthened their theological identity immeasurably. Although competing interpretations of his views fed into the formation of two sub-groups within the community, there continues to be a close association between the philosophical theology he developed called Viśiṣṭādvaita – Qualified Non-Duality – and the Śrīvaiṣṇava community.[14]

By contrast, the link between doctrine and religious community is more oblique in the case of Śaṅkara. Today, there are several pontifical cloisters (*maṭhas*) which are said to have been established by Śaṅkara himself, although it is likely that they were founded only from the 14th century onwards. While it is a matter of dispute as to whether Śaṅkara himself was a worshipper of Viṣṇu,[15] most of these centres associated with him are strongly Śaiva in cast. For example, in the Tamil context, whereas Rāmānuja is at the heart of the theology and practices of the Śrīvaiṣṇavas, the *maṭha* at Kanchipuram that is said to have been founded by Śaṅkara is authoritative for orthodox Tamil Smārta Brahmins, who are Śaiva in their ultimate theological commitment. But the conflation of sectarian and theological commitments that we see here is quite beside the point when we consider the *Gītā* commentaries, which naturally both focus on the presence and significance of Kṛṣṇa, understood by Śaṅkara's time as a form of Viṣṇu. (It should, however, be mentioned that this is not a fundamental doctrinal problem for present-day Smārtas, since Śaivism is not as exclusivist about Viṣṇu as Śrīvaiṣṇavism is about Śiva.)

I would like to end this introduction with a very brief sketch of the Vedāntic positions developed by Śaṅkara and Rāmānuja, so that the reader can appreciate the exegetical challenges presented by the *Gītā*. Nothing, however, turns on this, since this book deliberately studies the *Gītā* commentaries as self-contained sources for competing visions of the relationship between metaphysics and theology. The *Upaniṣads* have a range of concerns that can seem surprising from the viewpoint of subsequent (and contemporary) perceptions of Vedānta. It is not often appreciated that they contain, for example, guidance on sexual conduct when seeking different types of offspring. They also offer, for the contemporary scholar, insights into the power structures of ancient society and the dynamics of gender. But they have, as their leitmotif, the intricate relationship between the inmost sense of human existence, *ātman*, and the utmost explanatory principle of all reality, *brahman*.

The *Brahmasūtra* or *Vedāntasūtra* text, composed perhaps some two or three hundred years after the latest of the dozen or so of the earliest and most authoritative *Upaniṣads*, plays the central historical role in presenting the *Upaniṣads* as being primarily about the relationship between *ātman* and *brahman*. The text presents in laconic phrases – the *sūtras*, which together must have functioned as an *aide memoire* for teaching and learning – what it takes to be the core teachings of the *Upaniṣads*, namely, the inquiry into *brahman* and all that it encompasses. These two terms, *ātman* and *brahman*, function as formal vehicles for a variety of sometimes incompatible and sometimes complementary concepts, and the relationship between them is repeatedly and variously explored in the *Upaniṣads*; the *Brahmasūtras* present most of these divergent views. The *ātman* can be anything from body to breath to mental activity to the functions of consciousness to some deeper principle of reflexive awareness. Likewise, *brahman* can be a universal consciousness or an abstract limit to all explanation, a mysterious presence or a robustly personal deity. To say that the *Upaniṣads* posit an identity between *ātman* and *brahman* is to say very little, because – as the widely divergent interpretations of the multitude of Vedāntic schools amply demonstrate – the content and implications of that identification can be understood in many different ways.

In a profound sense, even the veriest outline of a position is an interpretation, and this is particularly the case with Śaṅkara; for that reason, I shall have to take recourse in terminology that is general (and therefore vague) enough to encompass different readings of him. For Śaṅkara, as we find across his various works, *brahman* is primarily the absolute ontological source and epistemological basis for the very possibility of all understanding of reality. This rigorously abstract and formal principle of explanation is identifiable only obliquely, definitively rather than attributively,[16] through the Upaniṣadic formula that it is truth (*satya*), knowledge (*jñāna*) and infinitude (*ananta*) (or in the terms favoured in later Vedānta, existence (*sat*), consciousness (*cit*) and bliss (*ānanda*)). Strictly speaking, there is only the self-defeating description of *brahman* as without qualities (*nirguṇa*), all qualities being projections of our understanding. However, the *Brahmasūtras* also talk of *brahman* in more personalistic terms, and Śaṅkara reads this substantive and qualitied (*saguṇa*) *brahman* as God (*īśvara*). The all-pervasive explanatory function of *brahman* and its ultimately irreducible foundational role mean that statements on the identity of *brahman* with *x* have to be read carefully, for they are asymmetrical. To say that *brahman* is God (and *brahman* is self) is not to say that Śaṅkara takes *brahman* to be God (God is *brahman*) or *brahman* to be *ātman*. Of course, much also turns on what 'God' means here: it would be difficult for any scholar to maintain that Śaṅkara takes *īśvara* to be *brahman*, but it has been possible for radical comparative theologians like Sara Grant to take Śaṅkara's *brahman* to be the 'Mystery' that Aquinas or Dionysius the Aeropagite thought of as the Christian God.[17] The function of *īśvara* shifts according to context for Śaṅkara, but generally, it appears to be a personalizing term for the absolute *brahman*, through the conceptual apparatus of attribution, which thereby offers an explanation for language-bound religious activity. Śaṅkara also talks of the core reflexivity of consciousness, which is *ātman*; it is the irreducible being, that derives from and is not different from the ground that is *brahman*. The gnoseological task is for this consciousness, which finds itself individuated in 'its own parametrically determined region of reflexive occurrence'[18] as the *jīva*, to regain itself as not different from the universal consciousness which is indirectly a term for *brahman*. Furthermore, just as it is an error for consciousness to take as real its individuation into a plurality of loci, so too is it an error for it to take the plurality of the material world – in which individuated consciousness finds itself – to be existent. All plurality, whether of the subjective loci of consciousness or the objective entities found in consciousness, is ultimately not existent in the way consciousness is. But so long as there is individuation, then so too is there a world. Ontologically, the world is not assimilable into the phenomenal subjectivity of consciousness; but through the guarantee of the sacred *Upaniṣads* (as read by Śaṅkara), all plurality is non-being, only consciousness is being, and *brahman* is the ground of both. If this is at all a reasonable reading of Śaṅkara, then the challenge of the *Gītā* for him is to develop more carefully what exactly *īśvara* is, in the self-declared presence of Kṛṣṇa, within the gnoseological dynamic of *ātman*'s inquiry into its being as *brahman* and its realization of the non-being of the world. Rāmānuja differs radically in his reading of Vedāntic principles. For him, an absolute understanding of *brahman*, the supreme *brahman* (*parabrahman*), always concerns God, in the self-revealed personhood of Nārāyaṇa-with-(his consort)-Śrī.[19] While the austere aspects of the *brahman* of the Vedānta indicate the limits of our understanding of God, we do not quail in the face of mystery, as God has made available an infinite number of ways of understanding and approaching him-and-her, through our understanding of being but also through our devotion to what is not merely being. The self is not a singular abstraction of reflexive consciousness but one of an infinite plurality of entities that partake of God by being portions of divine being. While in this sense identifiable with the divine (thereby fulfilling the Vedāntic assertion of a fundamental relationship between *brahman* and *ātman*), selves are not symmetrically identical with God, for God is inexhaustibly other than the beings selves are. So too the world: the world is another order of multitudinous being, just as selves are. Selves and world are both encompassed by divine being: God takes selves and world to be the body of the divine self, at once becoming available through our reality and transcending it absolutely.[20] Rāmānuja needs to do much less in the *Gītā* as opposed to the *Brahmasūtra* commentary in deriving a dazzlingly personal God from Vedāntic formulae on *brahman*; for in the *Gītā*, God is present in deliberately rich characterfulness. In that sense, commenting on the *Gītā* permits Rāmānuja to articulate a fully personal theology of Kṛṣṇa (the descended form (*avatāra*) of Nārāyaṇa), within which he can locate a metaphysical account of *brahman*.

I would now like to ask the reader to bracket this brief description of the philosophical history of the *Gītā*, of Śaṅkara and Rāmānuja, and their Vedāntic systems – save perhaps the bare outline of the *Gītā* narrative for those who are not familiar with it – and start reading the book on its own terms. I intend in what follows to use the two *Gītā* commentaries as self-contained texts that offer me the opportunity of trying to develop two competing visions of the relationship between metaphysics and theology, and therefore of how one may relate inquiry to faith.

1

The Ground of Being/Non-Being, and the Divine Self: Śaṅkara on *brahman* and Kṛṣṇa

We will now inquire into the nature of *brahman* in Śaṅkara's commentary. The critical hermeneutic point about his commentary is that he chose to do it all: Śaṅkara was perhaps the first to comment on the *Gītā*, and it is striking that he should have engaged with a text that could, if we go by his commentaries on the *Brahmasūtras* and (especially) the *Bṛhadāraṇyaka* and *Chāndogya Upaniṣads*, be at odds with his austere metaphysics. In those texts, he interprets the ancient identification of *brahman* and *ātman* as a fundamental absence of difference between the reflexive consciousness that is the core of *ātman* and the universally constitutive consciousness (*cit*) that is at least one – phenomenologically and gnoseologically significant – characterisation of ineffable *brahman*. His system, then, is to work out the way in which the multitudinous actuality of ordinary experience – the plural loci of consciousness that is humanity and all living creatures, and the physical diversity of the world that they inhabit – can be read in terms of this ultimate non-duality of an all-pervasive and all-constituting consciousness.

Śaṅkara does not give up this overarching metaphysics: we will return to the question of the plurality of beings and the physical presentation of the world in which beings find themselves. But the challenge that is posed to him in undertaking a commentary on the *Gītā* is the presence of Kṛṣṇa at the heart of the narrative. In simple terms, what is God doing here? And of course, those are simple terms indeed, for what 'God' means and how Kṛṣṇa is that 'God' are questions that can be answered only by going through Śaṅkara's actual treatment of the *Gītā*. But the tension between a sweeping metaphysics and an inescapable theology is what provides the hermeneutic energy to his commentary; and furthermore, there is the intriguing fact that he chose to so comment, and indeed, render the *Gītā* one of the three sources (*prasthānatrayī*) of all subsequent Vedānta schools. There could, of course, be historical reasons for why he chose to do so, but I want to argue that, in any case, the result is a subtle and indirect account of God and reality that is not quite ontotheological and only in some respects a form of mystical ontologism. Given this, it would be unwise to start with a translation of '*brahman*', any translation being already an interpretation; so, let the meanings accrete as we look at what he has to say about the nature of *brahman*.

Brahman in excess of being and non-being: On what there is and is not

On how things and being are non-existent (*sensu strictu*)

Śaṅkara first mentions *brahman* at the end of the long commentary on 2.16. This verse says: 'For that which is non-existent (*asat*), no being (*bhāva*) is found; for that which is existent (*sat*), no non-being (*abhāva*) is found. But the core (*antaḥ*) of both of these has indeed been seen by the seers of reality.'[1] Śaṅkara leads up to talk of *brahman* through an exploration of the key terms in this verse. He starts by reading 'being' (*bhāva*) from the root word √bhu, as 'coming into being' (*bhavanaṃ*), as also 'isness' or 'presence' (*astitā*). This way, we get to the meaning of 'the existent' (*sattā*), derived from the root word √*as* from which is generated 'is' (*asti*) and thence, 'isness' (*astitā*). These grammatical moves, of course, indicate the start of his presentation of a radical metaphysics.

The existent – that which is – (*sattā*) is the universal category (*sāmānya*) of generic existence, derived in the Nyāya school in the centuries preceding Śaṅkara; it is what medieval Western thought calls the *ens commune*, the general fact that beings are. Śaṅkara's claim is that for there to be such a general category of isness, is for any entity to be infused by being. So he clearly distinguishes between the isness of beings and being as such, that by which such isness is rendered. In that sense, from the beginning, it is clear that he is aware of the distinction between ontology – the classification of entities based on their isness – and being as such, that by which entities are beings. This is important when we come to what he has to say about Kṛṣṇa's being and Kṛṣṇa as being as such.

Being – which can also be a coming into being, presence, and therefore, that which renders existence – is contrasted with non-being, i.e., those entities which may be called, ultimately, non-existent. But what he calls non-being is startling: for all things are non-being. But this is neither solipsism nor even idealism; for rather, Śaṅkara wants to attach a particular meaning to being, derived from his understanding of being as such. He says of all things present to us that they are changeful (*vikāra*), and whatever is changeful deviates (*vyabhicarati*) from what it appears to be to our awareness. This conclusion, he maintains, is available even through standard epistemological requirements. The means of knowledge (the *pramāṇa* system) like perception and inference, are expected to give us a grasp of what things really are. But such essence of existence (*vastu sat*) is never obtainable … for things constantly change. So epistemological standards direct us to an understanding of epistemic limits. The pot comes out and goes back to earth, and so all things and their material cause shift and change (for earth itself must have a further material cause, and it too shifts and changes in its presentation). So, he asks himself, does this imply nihilism? Could all be non-being (*sarvābhāva*)? No; it can always be understood that there are two apprehensions – the apprehension of existence, and the apprehension of non-existence. That regarding which apprehension does not deviate, exists; that regarding which apprehension deviates, does not exist. Thus, the distinction between existence and non-existence rests on the faculty of apprehension (*buddhitantra*); in all cases, there are two apprehensions.[2]

Śaṅkara goes on to draw out what these two apprehensions are. Objects (*viṣayaḥ*) of apprehension are changeful: in the cognition, '[this is a] blue lotus', the 'blue' is a quality and 'lotus' the qualificand, and both change. In cognitions such as 'the pot exists', existence is not a quality of the pot, so that, while the pot may change, existence as such does not.[3] The apprehension of being does not change in the way apprehension of objects does. Pots (*ghaṭāḥ*) and cloths (*paṭāḥ*) may come and go, and so our apprehension of them ceases when they do. 'But apprehension of existence does not [cease] with the absence of objects' (*na tu sadbuddheḥ viṣayābhāvāt*). He goes on to say: 'Thus of the non-existent, the body and the binaries [such as heat and cold, etc.] together with their causes, it is said that there is no being. Then, the existent is the self, which is not non-being, for it is always non-deviating; this is what we say.'[4] (We will, of course, return to self later in this chapter; and in even greater detail in the chapter on Self).

Śaṅkara here is not seeking to investigate the nature of objects, that is to say, how one distinguishes between different elements of the order of things, or how one uses epistemic instruments to determine the difference between water and mirage. Rather, he brackets the whole question of entities and their individual natures, and attempts to get to the very fact that there are things in all their diversity presented to and in our awareness. That being-there (as pots and bodies and coloured lotuses) of these things is existence itself, while the way they are is not-existence. Consciousness grasps both simultaneously, but to be ever-aware in consciousness of this duality – a strange and virtual duality to be sure – of being and non-being, is the attainment of the seers (*darśinaḥ*) of thatness (*tattva*). For them, the core (*antaḥ*) of the teaching is the certainty (*nirṇayaḥ*) that this is so. 'That (*tat*) is the name of all, all is *brahman*; its name is "That" (*tat*). The manner of being (*tadbhāvaḥ*) of "that" is thatness, the as-it-is-hood (*yāthātmyam*) of *brahman*.'[5] In this swift yet indirect way, Śaṅkara gets to *brahman*. *Brahman* is the way in which beings have their being. What renders being as it is, is *brahman*. We begin to understand that there is an intimate connection between *brahman* and being, given how Śaṅkara interprets being.[6] But *brahman*'s connection is with non-being too; as we will see soon, for Śaṅkara, *brahman* is in excess of both being (that is to say, what is called Being in Christian and Heideggerian writing) and non-being (including the entitative nature of beings in the world). But before we turn to that, let us look a little more closely at the somewhat strange thought that the world as it is found in apprehension is non-existent, i.e., is non-being. We will see later that ontology itself is radically circumscribed for Śaṅkara, as there is nothing other than *brahman*. What is to be noted here is that he draws the line between being and non-being, not by way of subjective and objective states (where a metaphysical realist might say that the latter is being and an idealist that it is the former that is being), but by distinguishing between the changeful and the permanent.

For Śaṅkara, the changeful is perishable, mutation being the destruction of identity. Strictly speaking, every entity whose identity is given by changeable qualities is non-existent. Clearly, Śaṅkara is not talking of non-existence in the terms of an ontology. He is not stating that water is existent and a mirage not, or perception is real and its objects not. Rather, he is talking of ontology *tout court*. All things, being changeful, are non-being, while what is not changeful is being itself. In commenting on 15.16 – which is about selves – he returns to the strict construal of being as that which is imperishable. 15.16 talks of two groups of persons, the perishable and the imperishable, and goes on to say, 'the perishable is all beings (*kṣaraḥ sarvāṇi bhūtāni*); the immutable (*kūṭastha*) is the imperishable'. Śaṅkara's exegesis here ingeniously works in his distinction between being and non-being through the categories of the immutable and the changeful. 'The immutable is a group that is [made up of] a heap, is stable as in a group. Or the heap is an illusion, a deception, crookedness, trickery, which are synonymous … it is called the imperishable because, due to the countless seeds of worldly existence, it does not perish.'[7] Śaṅkara therefore limits existence, in the strict sense, to the constancy of being as such ('Being' – which I hesitate to use, for capitals carry their own implications in contrast to Sanskrit words, where they do not occur), in contrast to changeful beings, presented to themselves (as persons) or in apprehension as objects. The Heideggerian parallel is the distinction between 'presencing' and 'presence'.[8] Later we will see what Śaṅkara means when he says the immutable (the 'presence', as it were) is illusion.

Brahman in excess of being and non-being

So we see that the existent is being as such, not particular beings. Being is the thatness of all, not any particular thing amongst the all. But is thatness – the constancy of being as such – itself *brahman*? It is not easy to come to a simple conclusion about the metaphysical relationship between *brahman* and thatness. If, naturally, we take 'That' to be 'Being' (being as such, as opposed to the being (*bhāva*) of things and persons), we get the formulation that 'Being' is the name of *brahman*. But, having the option of equating *brahman* with Being, we have seen that, under 2.16, Śaṅkara chooses not to. Indeed, in the passage from 15.16 just quoted, he even equates the imperishable – the heap that as a whole is immutable – with the illusory. Later, we will see how he undercuts the metaphysics of what is not *brahman*, so that *brahman* is not other than what it is not. But first, we must look at another of Śaṅkara's moves: *brahman* exceeds both being-as-such/the imperishable/the immutable/the existent/the unmanifest, as well as non-being/the perishable/the changeful/the non-existent/the manifest. Let us look at how, while distinguishing between being and non-being, Śaṅkara also talks of the excession (*paramatva*) of *brahman*.

Śaṅkara draws on the *Gītā*'s repeated use of the distinction between the unmanifest (*avyakta*) and the manifest (*vyakta*) and maps them on to the binary of being and non-being – being is the unmanifest, non-being is the manifest. This equation is not puzzling. Being as such is never individuated in awareness, never manifests itself, while what is manifest is always the particularity of beings. In that context, he notes 8.18's statement that all manifest things emerge (*prabhavanti*) from the unmanifest at the break of cosmic day; this is the source of beings in this world, into which the multitude of beings (*bhūtagrāmaḥ*) dissolve (*pralīyante*) in the cosmic night. Then he points to the next verse: 'But exceeding this is the other eternal, unmanifest state of being, unmanifest of the unmanifest; and that, when all beings are lost, is not destroyed.'[9] Its exceeding the unmanifest he glosses as its being distinct (*vyatiriktaḥ*) and different (*bhinnaḥ*) from the unmanifest. This state of being (*bhāvaḥ*) is the imperishable (*akṣara*), *brahman in excelsis* (*paraṃ brahman*). The unmanifest state of being is the seed of the multitude of beings (*bhūtagrāmabījabhūta*). *Brahman* contains – or rather, is – the possibility of being, and therefore it is beyond both the unmanifest from which the manifest arises, and the manifest that does so arise. Śaṅkara recognises that it is necessary to both (i) indicate *brahman*'s exceeding being and non-being, and (ii) take being as such (or Being) to derive from it. Commenting on the chapter on the Vision of the Cosmic Form, he notes Arjuna's saying of Kṛṣṇa in the midst of the theophanic event, at 11.37, 'You are the imperishable, existent, non-existent, and what exceeds that.'[10] On this,

Śaṅkara says, the existent and the non-existent are merely a contingency (*upādhi*) of *brahman*, and therefore it comes to be referred to metaphorically (*upacārāt*) as existent/non-existent. In the ultimate sense, it exceeds existence/non-existence (*paramārthastu sadasatoḥ paraṃ*).

Even while offering a metaphysics – being and non-being, what count as one or the other, and why – Śaṅkara strives towards what may be called a transmetaphysics, an exhaustion of the limits of discursive understanding of our phenomenological being so that what lies beyond our own being is realized in our being.

We have, then, two movements by Śaṅkara with regard to *brahman* and being. The first is that *brahman* is other than both the manifest (non-being) and unmanifest (being), i.e., different not only from the strictly non-existent world represented in apprehension, and also from its seed or that from which being comes into such representation in apprehension. The second move is to maintain, however, that all is *brahman* and that *brahman* is not other than the manifest and the unmanifest. We have, then, the world of beings which is not-being as such; and we have being as such under all the changing world of beings. The former is not real, the latter is indicative of the real. *Brahman* is neither of them, yet there is nothing other than *brahman*. For now, I hope we can begin to see why choosing a translational term for *brahman* is neither easy nor sensible.

Speaking of Kṛṣṇa and Kṛṣṇa speaking of Himself

Now we must turn to the very framing of the *Gītā*, for it is a curious locale for an exploration of *brahman* as Śaṅkara conceives it. For Kṛṣṇa, who is a specific being in this world, the enigmatic charioteer and cousin who speaks to Arjuna, the person present on the battlefield, also says that that *brahman* is his 'support' (*pratiṣṭha*). How so?

This is the central theological challenge of Śaṅkara's reading of the *Gītā*: the inescapability of a divine person who speaks and is spoken to throughout. In other commentaries, Śaṅkara has the freedom to sustain an inquiry into *brahman* as the metaphysical exploration of all dimensions of the existence of consciousness. The *Gītā* centres on Kṛṣṇa – not only what is said to and of him by Arjuna and of him by Sañjaya, but in a significant sense, what is said by Kṛṣṇa to Arjuna (and us). We will see in the next chapter how theologically effective Rāmānuja found this divine directness, but for Śaṅkara it presents a different challenge. As we have just seen, there is a vast and complex task on hand for him, namely, an exploration of how *brahman* is to be understood in all and as all. But this is to be approached only through the persona of Kṛṣṇa in the *Gītā*. No quick answer is available as to what Śaṅkara does in his commentary in response to this exegetical situation. The quick answer that we must not be tempted by is that Śaṅkara, uninterested in the divine person who is Kṛṣṇa, sought to simply subordinate theology to philosophical metaphysics, leaving a personal god as a prop for the gnoseologically challenged, while all the while striving for an understanding of an impersonal absolute. Perhaps this is true of other commentaries; perhaps there is a germ of truth in it with regard to this commentary. But no more than a germ, for given many opportunities to simply read Kṛṣṇa as a formal symbol of limited understanding, Śaṅkara does not quite do so. In other words, we should not think that the task before Śaṅkara is somehow to get around the fact of Kṛṣṇa's first-personal presence in order that he can work out the universality of *brahman*. The more painstaking task that Śaṅkara takes up is to read the former in such a way as to make it an integral part of the latter.

Kṛṣṇa first invokes divinity in first-personal terms at 3.22, 'In all the three worlds, Pārtha [Arjuna], there is nothing at all yet to be done by me; nothing remains unachieved or to be achieved, and yet I continue to act'.[11] From then on, he gradually discloses himself in the *Gītā*, becoming ever-clearer about his divine selfhood in chapter 10, preparatory to the cosmic vision he provides in chapter 11. Thereafter, while he continues his teaching, its reception is imbued with our knowledge that Arjuna has been transformed by his vision. In comparativist perspective, this disclosure could not be more radically different than the Mosaic God of the burning bush who is said to say at Exodus 3.14: *'ehyeh 'asher 'ehyeh* (I am the Being, I am who I am, I will be that I will be, I am that I am). Now, Śaṅkara does not face the direct and deep mystery of what an aniconic God's apparently tautological first-personal description can mean. In the *Gītā*, the first-personal speaker says at great length – rather than in an enigmatic pinpoint – what 'I' am. Rather than permitting description to collapse into the mystery of divine self-proclamation, the *Gītā* allows it to flourish exuberantly, seeking to exhaust language in order to indicate the divine presence Who is in excess of language. In this, it more naturally follows the *via eminentiae*, relating qualities that spring from the human – in the automatic sense that they are expressed in language, pre-eminently or perfectly in Kṛṣṇa.[12] The striking point, in comparativist terms, is not so much that Arjuna so approaches Kṛṣṇa but that the text takes Kṛṣṇa to describe himself in this manner. And the more detailed this descriptions, the more challenging it may seem for Śaṅkara to relate this proliferation – naturally personalistic, because derived by definition from qualities understandable only by virtue of being human – to *brahman*.

Śaṅkara has to work out how Kṛṣṇa – robustly limited as the very specific being at the heart of the narrative, using language (even at its limits), necessarily structured in his disclosure through the grammatical imperative of the first person – can yet advert to *brahman* as Śaṅkara understands it. How to handle this being who speaks not just of being but what permits being as such, to be – and identifies himself thus?

The *Gītā* does not – whether problematically or helpfully – allow easy identification of Kṛṣṇa and *brahman* or smooth passage between (the confusing if conventional categories of) the personal and the impersonal. Where Kṛṣṇa declares anything about himself in relation to *brahman*, much depends on how he is read; and indeed, the vivid contrasts between Śaṅkara and Rāmānuja on the divine self turn on such exegetical divergence. But Kṛṣṇa does not call himself *brahman* as such in the *Gītā* itself; of course, saying that Kṛṣṇa is *brahman* is nothing notable, for *brahman* is all. So what he means in relation to *brahman* is something Śaṅkara has to bring out through his glossing of relational terms. Śaṅkara uses a range of names for Kṛṣṇa, some directly found in the *Gītā* which he uses freely, and others derived from the tradition that developed in the intervening centuries, by which Kṛṣṇa was identified with Viṣṇu/Nārāyaṇa. Kṛṣṇa is *īśvara*, a term drawing on root meanings of capability and sovereignty, and therefore most familiarly translated as 'God'; and also, *maheśvara*, 'great God' – sometimes implying a distinction from other (smaller) gods but, dominantly, indicating maximal ownership of divine qualities. He is also *bhagavat* (a term used earlier for the Buddha), with a root meaning of 'the dispenser' or 'patron', and usually translated as 'the Lord'. Then there are the epithets for Kṛṣṇa that arise from the narrative surrounding the *Gītā*, where he is Vāsudeva (the son of Vāsudeva) and the like. There is, then, not only the task of interpreting the first-personal uses of Kṛṣṇa about himself where he adverts to his divinity, but also the second-personal uses by Arjuna in describing him. Kṛṣṇa speaking of himself and Arjuna speaking of Kṛṣṇa, both provide opportunities for talking of God (or rather, translationally, what 'God' means); the question is how such talk relates to the *brahman* with which Śaṅkara is concerned.

Generally, Śaṅkara uses two hermeneutical tactics to get to *brahman* via Kṛṣṇa's first-personally articulate presence. First, he notes the rare occasions on which Kṛṣṇa says he is the *ātman*; and much more often, emphasises many of Kṛṣṇa's self-declarations by identifying him with *ātman* or the supreme self (*paramātman*). Second, he often uses a locution when talking of Kṛṣṇa – 'God, called Nārāyaṇa' (*nārāyaṇākhyaṃ*) or '*brahman*, called Vāsudeva (*brahmavāsudevākhyaṃ*) – that inserts an awareness of the necessary limitation of language in the usage of a name (*nāma*), even the name of God. Let us look at these in turn.

Let us provisionally understand the 'self' as the abstract, core or inner consciousness. It is the linguistic signifier of the subject that renders inquiry meaningful and possible. It is through there being self that there is both the misunderstanding of the nature of being and the capacity for realizing the way that there is being at all. It is, to start with, who is. In 7.18, Kṛṣṇa declares that the cognisant one (*jñāni*) is 'verily self' (*ātmaiva*). Here Śaṅkara explicates the implicit reflexivity: he glosses it as 'not another' (*nānyaḥ*). This would be emptily tautological, if we did not consider the import of 'self' here. The cognisant one, he explains, focuses on the thought, 'I myself am the Lord Vāsudeva, none else'.[13] Therefore, the true implication of self – the only self that is self – is Kṛṣṇa. Seen this way, Kṛṣṇa's statement in the following verse, that the cognisant one realizes that 'Vāsudeva is all (*sarvaṃ*)' indicates that such a one 'realises me as the self of all'.[14] Later, at 10.20, Kṛṣṇa says, 'I am self, Guḍākeśa [The Thick-Haired One, Arjuna], dwelling as the resting-place of all beings.'[15] Śaṅkara reads *ātman* here as the innermost self (*pratyagātma*), by which time we have become habituated to his repeated (and anticipatory) equation of Kṛṣṇa with *ātman*. As we explore the use and range of *ātman*, we will gradually come to see the universal scope of this equation.

The rigorous selfhood of Kṛṣṇa is driven home in the brief commentary on 7.20, where Kṛṣṇa says that people deprived of wisdom 'resort to other deities' (*prapadyante 'nyadevatāḥ*): Śaṅkara expands this as 'resort to deities other than (*anyāt*) Vāsudeva who is self (*vāsudevād ātmanaḥ*)'. The hierarchy of deities emerging in the composition of the *Gītā* is not the point here for Śaṅkara;[16] the distinction between the gods of ritual worship and Kṛṣṇa comes through the latter's identity with the selfhood of all who worship in the first place. The source of the possibility of worship is the subject who worships; and that subject is – although not in any experientially or linguistically transparent way – Kṛṣṇa. All other deities (*devatāḥ*) are objects of worship, and therefore elements of that world, different from and yet not-other than *brahman*/self/Kṛṣṇa.

Kṛṣṇa, then, is centred by Śaṅkara through the identification with self, so that Kṛṣṇa's 'I' preserves layers of meaning that peel away to reveal the very notion of self – the self of all. Śaṅkara's tactic is to take Kṛṣṇa's speaking of himself at face value, not challenging the routine self-proclamation of a personal God but reading it as the mapping of self on self. Kṛṣṇa as self becomes the key that unlocks Kṛṣṇa's self-statement of divinity. At 7.24, Kṛṣṇa says, 'The unintelligent think of me as having become manifest even thought I am unmanifest, not knowing of my being in the highest, which is immutable and unsurpassable.'[17] Śaṅkara explains this as the undiscriminating (*avivekinaḥ*) not being aware of my being in the highest, that is, my being of 'the very form of the highest self' (*paramātmasvarūpaṃ*) – free of mutability (*vyayarahita*), none more eminent (*niratiśaya*) – taking me to be the hidden (*aprakāśa*) that has become the revealed now (*prakāśaṃ gatam idānīṃ*), although I am 'the ever-established' (*nityaprasiddha*) God (*īśvara*). Śaṅkara therefore asserts the greatest intimacy possible between us and another – that of identity. Dull-wittedly, people interpret the physical presence of Kṛṣṇa in that time as a manifestation of the hidden God, an interpretation in whose narrative sequence the ontological distance of otherness between divine and human is always preserved. But the God who is in excess of both visible and invisible being (as we have already noted in the first section) is the supreme construal of selfhood, for self is nothing to become known – as in the third-personal story of a manifest God hitherto hidden – but that which is always and unquestionably established for itself.

There is one wrinkle that Śaṅkara has to iron out. Śaṅkara in other works argues that *ātman* is not picked out by 'I' (*ahaṃ*), as all such linguistic usage generates mistaken identification with something which is mine (*mama*), so that the sheer subjective presence of unitary consciousness that is *ātman* is ever deferred in its own awareness; this has implications for the conception of self that we will explore in detail in the chapter on Self.[18] Yet, of course, the *Gītā* is full of such usage by Kṛṣṇa, which Śaṅkara ought, for the sake of consistency, to condemn as the proliferation of egoity (literally, the 'I'-maker or *ahaṃkāra*), which generates mistaken conceptions of who one is. Śaṅkara has no option but to explain this (away), in the commentary for 9.5. 'How, again, does he say, "This is my self"? Following worldly understanding, separating the body and other aggregations, and then superimposing egoity, he talks of "my self"; but this is not as if he takes self to be other than self as the worldly ignorant do.'[19] First-personal usage by Kṛṣṇa is a necessary locution to advert to self; this is not a license for us to persist in our mistaken identification of the psychophysical apparatus with self. Kṛṣṇa appears, because of the grammar of teaching, to preserve the individuatedness that limits self-talk to each locus of awareness in our worldliness; but the consciousness in Kṛṣṇa is ever-free of mistaken individuatedness. Once we understand this, we are able to take in his teaching, which is that Kṛṣṇa's self is our self. The individuation is the linguistic consequence of our psychophysical limitation, while Kṛṣṇa's teaching points us towards the liberating awareness of the universality of self. Kṛṣṇa, then, is self, and Kṛṣṇa's expression of self is selfhood *par excellence*. Pre-eminently, Kṛṣṇa's self-talk adverts to what is truly self. In this way, Śaṅkara negotiates the path from the self-proclaimed presence of a personal God to the inquiry into the ways of being, not through any obvious subordination of the former to the latter, but as integral and pedagogically critical aspects of the same gnostic inquiry. Still, this alerts us to the fact that the theologically significant presence of Kṛṣṇa is nevertheless only part of a larger project, and not – as we will see with Rāmānuja – the goal of the project itself.

The second tactic is found in Śaṅkara's curious formulation, 'called Vāsudeva' – one might even say, 'so-called Vāsudeva'. In the Introduction itself (p. 3), he offers a potent précis of how he will approach the whole matter of the *Gītā*. This sacred text, he says, reveals (*abhivyañjayat*) the supreme reality (*paramārthatattvaṃ*), called Vāsudeva (*vāsudevākhyaṃ*), the being that signifies (*abhidheyabhūtaṃ*) *brahman* in the highest (*parabrahman*) as its subject matter (*viśeṣataḥ*). We will explore the relationship between Kṛṣṇa and *brahman* later, in section 6; but for now, let us note the first occurrence of this locution, 'called Vāsudeva'. Why not, we can ask ourselves, just 'Vāsudeva, the supreme reality'? (Rāmānuja conspicuously does not use this locution.) In another instance, at 10.08, Kṛṣṇa declares, 'I am the source of all' (*ahaṃ sarvasya prabhavaḥ*); and Śaṅkara glosses 'I' as 'the supreme *brahman* called Vāsudeva' (p. 150).

At first, we may think that this is indicative of an apophatic move – calling him 'Vāsudeva' does not actually name God, it is only a name that we use for God, as too 'Nārāyaṇa' and the like. So one might think that Śaṅkara is indicating that God escapes naming; God alone properly uses the 'I' (*ahaṃ*),[20] but when we attempt to describe him, we are left with names, which we give. But there is nothing else in what Śaṅkara says that suggests that he was concerned specifically with the unnameability of Kṛṣṇa. This is because of the extremely significant fact that Kṛṣṇa speaks in the first person in the *Gītā*; he has, as it were, named himself for us. It is God's declaration that he is so named; we begin with it. So we must look for some other explanation for Śaṅkara's locution.

My suggestion is that the locution points to something deeper than the limitation of our speaking of God. It points to the limitation of God as that of which we speak. We speak here of God (Kṛṣṇa, Nārāyaṇa, Vāsudeva), so-called. What we speak of is God – for speaking of God is the extent to which we can speak of *brahman*; profoundly, we cannot speak of *brahman* as such. God becomes the way language mediates consciousness' understanding of itself (self that it is) as *brahman*. God is, of course, *brahman*; there is nothing other than *brahman*, a thought to which we will turn in the next section. We may provisionally attach the name of 'God' to *brahman*, but, strictly speaking, we cannot really name and describe *brahman* as such; we can only realize it as self. We must be careful here, as I do not want to lurch back to one conventional understanding of Śaṅkara, namely that he thinks God is a limitation, a distraction, a construct to be transcended – in the *Gītā*, at any rate, he makes no such move. What I am trying to say is that Śaṅkara uses the locution, 'so-called', to indicate how the phenomenological inquiry into *brahman* towards which the exegetical authority of the *Gītā* points (which we will explore in pages 19–28) is made possible only through language, and Kṛṣṇa is the self-signifier of the promise that such inquiry can be undertaken.

In these two ways, then, Śaṅkara indicates how Kṛṣṇa is central to the non-duality of self and *brahman*, of God and *brahman*, and world and *brahman*. It is in the light of these ideas that we can understand an occasion where Śaṅkara brings the two tactics together. At 10.8, where Kṛṣṇa says 'I am the origin (*prabhava*) of all', he glosses the 'I' as 'supreme *brahman*, called Vāsudeva'.[21]

Who and/or what is God? Śaṅkara's Kṛṣṇa theology

The two broad tactics considered in the previous section can therefore be identified as Śaṅkara's reading of Kṛṣṇa within his exposition of *brahman* (*brahmavāda*). They are meant to permit Kṛṣṇa's declarations to be received theologically, but without disturbing Śaṅkara's understanding of *brahman* as the *terminus ad quem* of the non-dualist task. But, for the purposes of enunciating a theory of *brahman* (which is also a guide to the re/attainment of *brahman* by the theorist and his adherents), the *Gītā* is a difficult text. It has to be read, first and foremost, on its own terms as offering a theology of Kṛṣṇa. Śaṅkara does not seek to discard, or even deflect the theological promise on offer. It is only obliquely that we come to see what he does with the theology, in its location within a *brahmavāda*. So, we must first look at how Śaṅkara reads the theology of Kṛṣṇa. Understanding how Śaṅkara understands Kṛṣṇa will help locate Kṛṣṇa within Śaṅkara's theory of *brahman* (*brahmavāda*), not just as something he had to attend to (perhaps for the historical reason that Kṛṣṇa/Viṣṇu and the *Gītā* had become too important to ignore) but as vital to his exploration of reality. In this section, we will discuss various things that Kṛṣṇa says about himself in the *Gītā* and how Śaṅkara receives him theologically.

Śaṅkara does not see Kṛṣṇa as a creator god, a being whole and distinct before there is creation, bringing beings and things into existence *ex nihilo*, and continuing to have a being distinct from all beings thus created. He reads Kṛṣṇa's statements about his power in relation to beings and things in a way that does not challenge Kṛṣṇa's divinity, yet subtly re-presents it within a metaphysics of non-duality. At 7.4–5, Kṛṣṇa talks of his evolutive nature (*prakṛti*)[22] as having an inferior (*aparā*) and a superior (*para*) form. The former is material and includes the elements, as well as the mind (*manas*) and the 'I'-maker (*ahaṃkāra*), which is to say, the physical conditions of individuation. The latter consists in the individual beings (*jīvabhūtāḥ*), by which the world is upheld. Śaṅkara accepts these declarations with only a little exposition. He glosses Kṛṣṇa's mention of 'this other, higher nature of mine' (*tvanyāṃ prakṛtiṃ*) as 'my pure, self-being' (*viśuddhāṃ mamā'tmabhūtām*) (p. 118), so that the individual beings are taken as not other than Kṛṣṇa's own being. This then casts the next verse, in which Kṛṣṇa says he is the womb or origin (*yoni*) of all beings and their birth (*prabhava*) and dissolution (*pralaya*), in a rather different metaphysical light; for what Kṛṣṇa is saying is therefore not to be understood as a story of creation and destruction of beings separate from him, but a cosmogonic narrative of the self-expression of being itself, in its coming forth in a manifold of individuation and its going back to being alone (pure Being, being as such, being beyond the phenomenology of individuated beings).

Kṛṣṇa says soon after, at 7.13–14, that people are deluded by the qualitative diversity of the world in which they find themselves, and this manifold (*māyā*) becomes difficult for them to go beyond; therefore, Kṛṣṇa says, they 'cross over' (*taranti*) by taking refuge in him. Śaṅkara does not here directly take up *māyā*'s metaphysical status according to Advaita, as the phenomenal appearance of changeful things that is less-than-real (*mithyā*), a construal that Rāmānuja, of course, would later explicitly rule out. Here, Śaṅkara's aim is to identify precisely what it is about Kṛṣṇa that prompts our seeking refuge in him; and yet again he does this by saying who and what the Kṛṣṇa is who speaks thus of himself. The 'I' of Kṛṣṇa, he says, refers to 'the conjuring master of *māyā*, the being that is itself the self of all'.[23] (It should also be added that he reads 'to take refuge' (*prapadyante*) to be 'to forsake all ritually enjoined action' (*sarvadharmān parityajya*); its full significance we will explore in the last chapter's consideration of 18.66, but we can see that this austere and disciplinary gloss is an unobvious way to understand the devotional implications of taking refuge.) Without denying Kṛṣṇa's theological claim, Śaṅkara nevertheless presents what is going on in these verses as essentially a gnoseological project of self-realization expressed through the mediating reality of Kṛṣṇa.

Śaṅkara's theology of Kṛṣṇa therefore is not some simple denial or even marginalisation of theology itself: nowhere in the *Gītābhāṣya* does he suggest that God is a conceptual construct driven by human need; he does not even say that God – Kṛṣṇa/Viṣṇu/Nārāyaṇa – is the provisional goal of the cognitively underdeveloped, a sort of culturally conditioned penultimate absolute. At the same time, Kṛṣṇa is not the culminating point of his inquiry; nor is a devotional love of God the ultimate human mode of fulfilment. Let us look further at his treatment of Kṛṣṇa, especially Kṛṣṇa's self-declarations, before we sum up what Śaṅkara takes Kṛṣṇa to be.

Śaṅkara takes no particular pains to articulate or defend a monotheistic conception of Kṛṣṇa, but despite talking easily of the various deities mentioned in the *Gītā*, at one point he makes a brief yet emphatic statement about monotheism. In amidst the great series of overflowing exaltations of the theophany in chapter 11, Arjuna says at 11.43, 'There is no one like you' (*na tvat samo'sti*). Śaṅkara goes beyond just glossing 'like' as 'equal to' (*tulya*):

'It is not possible for there to be two Gods, for worldly doing (*vyavahāra*) would fail if there were many Gods!'[24] This is not in itself an argument for a monotheistic conception of God, but it flows naturally from Śaṅkara's understanding of Kṛṣṇa as being itself of which all beings partake – for there is no sense to the thought of a multiplicity of being as such. As to the multifarious deities of the tradition, Śaṅkara treats them as merely belonging in another category of beings, albeit ones that exemplify the components of sacrifice. So, when Kṛṣṇa says at 9.24, 'I am the only Lord' (*ahaṃ hi prabhur eva*), Śaṅkara says (p. 144) that this means, 'I am the selfhood of the deities (*devatātmatva*) of all the sacrifices', that is to say, their essence. The importance of this affirmation of monotheism to our understanding of Śaṅkara can be gleaned indirectly from an observation made by Etienne Gilson about Hebraic monotheism in comparison to Greek philosophy: none of Plato, Aristotle, the Stoics, or the neo-Platonists posited the existence of a single God, 'because they lacked that clear idea of God which makes it impossible to admit more than one'.[25] Śaṅkara's emphatic rejection of a second God is clearly tied to his developed idea of what and who Kṛṣṇa is.

This one God is to be understood both in the terms of a devotional love for a supreme being and in insightful understanding of being itself. (We will look more closely at how God, thus conceived, is integral to Śaṅkara's doctrine of *brahman*.) In another of the poetic sequences of self-identification that marks Kṛṣṇa's disclosure from the middle of the *Gītā* onwards, he talks at 15.12–15 of being the effulgence (*tejas*) of the sun, the moon and fire, the vitality (*ojas*) in life on earth, and the cooking of food; of being seated in the hearts of all, and in memory, knowing and their loss. Taking all this in, Śaṅkara then proceeds to say, 'In the verses beginning, "that effulgence in the sun which…" (15.12), is given a compendium of the sovereign powers of God – the Lord called Nārāyaṇa – as it is rendered by particular contingent limiting adjuncts. Then, the succeeding verses begin to determine his reality, as without contingency, as simple, as distinct from the contingent limiting adjuncts of the perishable and imperishable.'[26] God understood in the language of prayer and poetry is for Śaṅkara a God described through contingent limiting adjuncts – that is to say, our conceptual capacities, our emotional needs, our cognitive dispositions. Although here he subtly subordinates the worshipped God, through much of the *Gītā* he is much more cautious about, indeed even asks for, such a God. But even when he recognises worship of God, it is always secondary to the gnostic function of self-realization through God, as we will see later.

This subordination leads on (*via* a discussion of mutable non-existence and the immutability of existence, which we have already considered in the opening section) to Kṛṣṇa's statement at 15.17, 'But beyond this is the foremost person (*uttama puruṣa*), who is called the supreme self (*paramātma*)/and entering the three worlds, upholds them, as the unchanging (*avyaya*) God (*īśvara*).' Now Śaṅkara presents his vision of God, in a passage dense with the tactics characteristic of his theological articulation. He glosses 'supreme self' as, 'supreme', compared to bodily selves made from primal unwisdom;[27] and 'self' as 'the innermost consciousness of all beings'.[28] He reads 'upholds' (*bibharti*) as 'bears [the three worlds] purely (*mātra*) through intrinsic (*svarūpa*) real (*sat*) being (*bhāva*), entering [those worlds] through "the power in the energy of consciousness" (*caitanyabalaśakti*).' He concludes, 'The unchanging "God" is the omniscient, called Nārāyana, sovereign by nature'.[29] God is the supreme being, but strictly in the sense of being the true, the only, truly existing core of all beings, their very self. This supremacy is not given through Kṛṣṇa's being the most 'beingful' entity or what is 'most in being' ('*das Seiendste*' in Heidegger's critique of the illusion[30]) but, through being the self of all, that by which beings have being. Kṛṣṇa is a particular being, a subjective presence with maximal qualities; but Kṛṣṇa is also precisely not particular, for he is, instead, the expression of being, as the self of all. In indicating this inwardness, I think that Śaṅkara also clarifies that Kṛṣṇa, as God, is not to be seen – only – as another being, whatsoever the primacy of his being. (But of course, he is also to be seen thus, as the God of loving worship, of both prayer and praise.)

Our sense of self is given in this world by our individuated embodiment, but that world and the body in it are not truly being, nor existent in the ultimate sense – as we have seen before, Śaṅkara argues that they are changeful and thus less than real. But consciousness as such, that which is innermost in our changeful life, is our being – and that being is God. Doubtless we need to examine in greater detail Śaṅkara's topology of the self's being, but again, it suffices at present to see that the self is consciousness given by – indeed not different from – God's being. This being-consciousness that is our very self, is Kṛṣṇa, sovereign in being, because not plagued by the limitations of unwisdom. (Note too, that it is implied that it is this unwisdom that structures our embodied life and therefore provides the adjuncts through which we devoutly take God to be the light, the life, the living and the knowing.) And we call that God, Kṛṣṇa/Nārāyana. 'God' is the term we use to indicate being itself – being which gives us our being – for it is thus that we come to worship and to think theologically in the first place.

It becomes clear that Śaṅkara's avowal of a theological commitment to Kṛṣṇa is based on his mapping of our being onto Kṛṣṇa's. A divine quality that might, to another theologian, signify the greatness of God becomes, for Śaṅkara, an indicator of non-dual being. Kṛṣṇa says at 9.9, 'I am unbound by those actions (*na māṃ tāni karmāṇi nibadhnanti*)' that come of bringing forth, sustaining and dissolving the world, because, he says, 'I sit' (*āsīnāṃ*) as one sitting apart (*udāsīnavat*), free from ties (*asaktaṃ*). Whereas Rāmānuja takes this to imply a theodicy in which God is not tied to consequential action in the way beings in the world are,[31] Śaṅkara explains that Kṛṣṇa is untouched because the self is unchangeable (*ātmano'vikriyatvāt*), having freedom that consists in 'forsaking attachment to fruit, abandoning the possessiveness of the "I do"'.[32] Kṛṣṇa's divinity is therefore expressed through the modular universality of selfhood: to be is to be the self, even though beings are differentially and only partially aware of it. Kṛṣṇa's divinity consists in his being the first self, the always-realized self, the perfect self that never required perfecting, the self of plenitude. While preserving the theological primacy of Kṛṣṇa, Śaṅkara also expresses his primacy in terms of the universal imperative to gnoseological understanding. Kṛṣṇa is the exemplary self, for his self is the self as it is to be realized by us. We may be reminded here of the paradox implicit in Meister Eckhart's words, 'There is between God and the soul neither strangeness nor remoteness, therefore the soul is not only equal with God but it is ... the same that He is.'[33]

This is a careful, but nonetheless emphatic, circumspection of a theology of being, for God's intimacy with us comes out of an ultimate (but only ultimate) non-duality. When Kṛṣṇa tells Arjuna at 2.17 that he should know that 'that' (*tat*) cannot suffer destruction (*vināśa*), Śaṅkara clarifies (p. 18) that 'that' is *brahman* ('called real', *sadākhyaṃ* – to signify our efforts to talk about it). It has nothing of its own, and so it does not cease to have what is its own; thus, it suffers no loss, no mutability that would destroy its being. So *brahman* does not undergo such a loss as Devadatta might undergo a loss of wealth. Śaṅkara once again points to the incoherence of thinking of *brahman* as a particular being or its non-being adjuncts. Now he makes his crucial move: 'Nothing can destroy its own self, not even God. For self is *brahman*.'[34] God-talk is therefore always within self-talk, which ultimately is *brahman*-talk (to the extent that *brahman* can be talked of). God cannot destroy Godself, not because of a theological conception of God's fullness but because of the ultimacy of self-that-is-*brahman*. Even God is *brahman*, and there is no more powerful way for Śaṅkara to signify his location of theology within the transmetaphysics of *brahman*.

It has been suggested in Christian theology that modern theologians find it difficult to make sense of older approaches in which an intensely personal, narrative and dogmatically significant conception of God is reconciled with the God of metaphysics: 'Modern commentators sometimes find this unbelievable, but for Augustine, the God who is Being itself, immutable, incorporeal, and so on, is simultaneously the God who called Abraham, sent Moses, and for that matter revealed his name at the burning bush. There is no need to set metaphysics and salvation history over against one another.'[35] Augustine's distinction is between the God for us (his *nomen misericordiae*) and God in himself (his *nomen substantiae*),[36] but these conceptual distinctions, necessary for our understanding, are not inconsistent and do not imply any division in divine nature. Clearly, for Śaṅkara too, the personal narrative and a theology of being co-exist in the *Gītā*; indeed, the former is the mode of revelation of the latter, while the latter is what provides cosmogonic underpinning for the assurances of the former.

But we cannot pretend that the resolution of the tension between these two conceptions of Kṛṣṇa is an easy one. On occasion, Śaṅkara is keenly aware of the problem that Kṛṣṇa's persona presents to the theology of being, for the *Gītā* itself expresses it clearly. As Kṛṣṇa says at 9.11, when he takes human form (*mānuṣīṃ tanum*) the foolish treat him with contempt, not knowing his highest being (*paraṃ bhāvam*), as the great god of beings (*bhūtamaheśvara*). Śaṅkara reads 'highest being' as supreme selfhood (*paramātmatvaṃ*; p. 140), the self of beings; and yet it is this which is treated as a human person. So, clearly there is a tension between the concrete personhood of the Kṛṣṇa who is teaching him now and the sublime being that sustains all reality. At other places, he strains to overcome this tension by *fiat*. In 14.27, he suggests at one point that the word '*brahman*' is *brahman* as conceptualised by us.[37] But then he puts these words into Kṛṣṇa's mouth: 'Of that *brahman*, I myself, the *brahman* free of all conception – and none else – am the support.'[38] So Kṛṣṇa's words – conception-laden as they are – must, through divine will, be able to tell the truth of what is beyond conception, since all other truths about *brahman* are limited by our conceptions. By permitting Kṛṣṇa to say of himself that he is *brahman*, Śaṅkara wants to blast through our inescapable limitations, for only in that way can we begin to see both Kṛṣṇa and *brahman*. Śaṅkara's resolve is remarkably similar to medieval Christianity; as Richard Kearney notes, 'most scholastics identified God with Being by means of proofs and analogies, seeking some sort of balance between Being's universality and indeterminacy on the one hand, and God's density as a quasi-subject or person (which holds God from descent into infinite dispersion) on the other.'[39] It even resonates, in this particular way, with more modern developments, such as process theism's 'distinction between the abstract essence of God (as absolute, eternal, unchangeable) and God's concrete actuality, which is temporal, relative, changing, and dependent on decisions made by finite actualities.'[40]

Of course, text-historically, it is difficult to know precisely why Śaṅkara seems to move back and forth between different articulations of the relationship between *brahman* and Kṛṣṇa (as *īśvara*). In a study of the *Brahmasūtrabhāṣya*, Paul Hacker surveyed most of the occurrences of *brahman* – both as *paraṃ* or ultimate and *aparam* as lower – and *īśvara*.[41] (Kṛṣṇa is not identified as *īśvara* in that text, but Hacker also wanted to expound the claim that Śaṅkara was, in any case, a Vaiṣṇava.) The textual analysis is wide-ranging and highly instructive, but Hacker's conclusion does not quite bear out his analysis. He points out that Śaṅkara tends to use *brahman* and *īśvara* terms interchangeably, identifying the latter in terms of the lower form of the former when asserting the 'illusory' nature of the world, but at other times identifying the latter even with the ultimate *brahman*; there are times, he notes, when one is reluctant to decide. From this, he concludes that Śaṅkara therefore uses these terms loosely, as was probably the widespread practice in his mainly theistic socio-historical context, so that 'an intuitive theism has joined with an intellectual monism to form an illogical, but for that reason much more lively, combination'.[42] Yet, he also recognises that on Śaṅkara's interpretation *brahman* and *īśvara* are not different; so it is not clear why he thinks Śaṅkara is only speaking loosely or is being illogical. It seems more persuasive to think that, as with medieval Christian scholastics, he too was striving to find the balance between different ways of speaking. Furthermore, the non-duality he expounds has the asymmetrical feature we have already noticed: *brahman* ultimately, is in excess of being and non-being, and even God-as-being-as-such; but it is also not other than non-being, and being, and even God. So Śaṅkara has to speak of God as not-other than *brahman*, while also gesturing at *brahman* being in excess of God. Compared to the *Brahmasūtras*, the *Gītā* has another striking feature, of course, in that Kṛṣṇa is the *īśvara* who speaks directly. And while it may be that Śaṅkara does struggle to keep the two apart, we should draw lessons from the struggle itself – both when he distinguishes them, occasionally sharply; and when he runs them together. My exploration here suggests that, regardless of whether it was a failure on his part to make rigorous distinctions (for historical reasons) or not, we can learn something about the challenge of presenting non-duality, the non-duality of God as being itself, and *brahman* as the ground of being and non-being.

My conclusion is that in the *Gītābhāṣya*, Śaṅkara seeks the balance Kearney talks of, between the personal, quasi-subjective presence of Kṛṣṇa and Kṛṣṇa as the essential self, as being itself. But he has an even more fraught balance to preserve, that between anything that he can say about Kṛṣṇa (and that Kṛṣṇa says about himself) and the *brahman* that is the support of all this. Kṛṣṇa – as the concrete subject, as supreme being, as the self of all – speaks and is therefore identifiable through self-proclamation. Yet this identity and identifiability do not bespeak of anything other than *brahman*, even while *brahman* is not exhausted by such identity. So *brahman* becomes the terminological focus of Śaṅkara's exploration of how we even begin to understand the possibility of reality, including how God renders that reality. I believe that Śaṅkara is highly original in what he has to say here. In order to see that in more detail, we need to examine the relationship between *brahman* and Kṛṣṇa.

Brahman, Kṛṣṇa and being(s): The ontology of non-duality

We now turn to the radical aspect of *brahman* that makes for the very name of Śaṅkara's position – non-dualism (*a-dvaita*). In the first section, we saw how *brahman* is distinguished from both changeful beings and immutable being-as-such. Śaṅkara, however, views this difference as entirely consistent with the non-duality of being and non-being from *brahman*. It is this claim of Śaṅkara's which is probably unique to him. However, in the context of the *Gītā*, he must reach this only through Kṛṣṇa – and what Śaṅkara says of the relationship between being and Kṛṣṇa is important. To anticipate the course of this section, we will see that for Śaṅkara, it is the case that being itself is Kṛṣṇa while Kṛṣṇa is being. This is not a symmetrical identity. To say that being is Kṛṣṇa is to say that the very understanding of self and world is given only through their complex unity with Kṛṣṇa. This asymmetrical identity between Kṛṣṇa and being nevertheless falls short of true realization, for all our talk is of Kṛṣṇa, while *brahman* is beyond.

Let us, then, look more carefully at what Śaṅkara says about Kṛṣṇa and being, *via self*. For Śaṅkara, the key to the understanding of Kṛṣṇa's declaration of being the all (with nothing left over, so to speak) is the recognition of Kṛṣṇa as being self. So when, at 7.19, Kṛṣṇa says that the cognisant one (*jñānavān*) realizes, 'Vāsudeva is all (*sarvaṃ*)', Śaṅkara, as we would expect, answers the question of who is all with the answer, Vāsudeva, who is the innermost self (*pratyagātman*), the self of all (*sarvātman*) (p. 122).

The identity of God and self has implications for the Advaita metaphysics that Śaṅkara reads into the *Gītā*, as the 'all' is made clearer in two verses in chapter 10. At 10.20, Kṛṣṇa says, 'I am the beginning, middle and end of beings' (*aham ādiś ca madhyaṃ bhūtānām anta eva*), and at 10.32, he says, 'Of created things (*sargānāṃ*), I am the beginning, middle and end'. As we will see with Rāmānuja, the 'I am …' permits of different interpretations, of which ontological identity is but one. Śaṅkara treats that interpretation, however, as so obvious as to need no comment. The non-dual ontotheologism is revealed a little later, in 10.39. There, Kṛṣṇa says, 'There is no being, moving or unmoving that can exist without me' (*na syād asti vinā yat syān mayā bhūtaṃ carācaram*). Śaṅkara points out that 'can exist' (*syāt*) is 'can be' (*bhavet*); and then goes on to make the point clear: 'For what is rejected, forsaken, by me, becomes without self, void.'[43] The relationship between God and the world of beings is asymmetrical in the sense that to be is to be self, and to be self is to have Kṛṣṇa as self. God gives beings their self, by being their self.

But it should be kept in mind that God's being is not given by being the world. (So the lazy equation of Advaita with at least one form of the Western doctrine of pantheism, that God and world are identical,[44] should be resisted.) At 9.4, Kṛṣṇa says, 'This whole world is diffused through with me in my unmanifest aspect; all beings stand in me, but I am not established in them.'[45] Śaṅkara seeks in his commentary to preserve both the ontological identity by which the being of beings is given by Kṛṣṇa and the asymmetry of dependence contained in that identity. As ever, Śaṅkara takes 'stand in me' to mean 'established in my own selfhood' (*mayā'tmanā'tmavattvena sthitāni*) (p. 137). He takes Kṛṣṇa to be making this syllogism: No functional (*vyavahāra*) being can be without self (*nirātmakam*), and I am their self, so they are established in me (*mayi sthitāni*). That does not mean that Kṛṣṇa is established in them; Śaṅkara glosses 'established' (*avasthita*) here as 'contained' (*adheya*); so Kṛṣṇa is not contained in them, or confined in their being. Śaṅkara puts this statement on Kṛṣṇa's behalf: 'I am the core of even space' (*ākāśasyāpy antaratamo hy aham*), driving home the asymmetry between him and the beings of the (less-than-real) world. Just in order to reinforce the dynamic interplay of immanence and transcendence, the *Gītā* itself has 9.5, where Kṛṣṇa seems to contradict himself immediately, by saying, 'And yet beings are not established in me' (*na ca matsthāni bhūtāni*). But this latter assertion, Śaṅkara indicates, is not at the same level as the previous one stating the opposite. Whereas the establishment of all beings in Kṛṣṇa is in his unmanifest aspect (the unseen image (*avyakta mūrti*)), which is an understanding of him still within our ken, that still does not exhaust him; beyond even the containment of beings – and therefore beyond our ken – is Kṛṣṇa in his self as it is (*ātmano yāthātmyaṃ*) (p. 138), where beings are not established in him. This asymmetry is an important aspect of non-duality, one to which we will keep returning in the course of the chapter.

Kṛṣṇa therefore says of beings that they come under the category of existence (i.e. ultimately have being) only through him, while his existence is not defined through them. Śaṅkara then explains this through the formulation that Kṛṣṇa is the self of beings, even while beings do not give him his self. Again, at 11.40, when Arjuna hails Kṛṣṇa as encompassing all and therefore being all (*sarva samāpnoṣi tato'si sarvaḥ*), Śaṅkara expands 'encompassing' as 'encompassing wholly, through being the single self',[46] and reads 'being all' as 'without you, no being exists'.[47] God as being gives being; God is therefore not the general category of being, the universal (*sāmānya*) which is dependent on instantiation by particular beings to be their universal.

Going at least back to Rudolf Otto,[48] this position has been compared to Meister Eckhart on the oneness of God and self. (I will not go into the contentious argument from Paul Hacker over whether the comparison is about the true nature of being (as Otto claimed) or whether it was purely about the notion of consciousness as reality.[49]) The complication of understanding Kṛṣṇa as both being-as-such, which gives beings their being, and as the conscious self of all, is resonant of Eckhart's saying both that 'Existence is God' (*Esse Deus est*),[50] and that creatures are nothing in themselves since they possess their being in the divine existence, which is pure intelligence or understanding (prior, in fact, to existence).[51] But this seems to imply that God is the existence of beings as a whole; and while Śaṅkara, whether he held it or not, would not have had to worry about being seen as advocating pantheism, Eckhart was charged with heresy. As Colledge and McGinn point out, Eckhart might not have given a good defence of himself, but theologically, he could not be seen as advocating pantheism, because he sought to maintain the transcendence of God.[52] He did this by distinguishing between the 'formally inherent existence' of creatures and the 'absolute existence' of God.[53] If being is what particular beings have, then God is not such being: to quote them on Eckhart's position, 'God is the existence of all things (*esse omnium*) in an absolute sense, but not as formally inhering in them'. This could virtually be a commentary on the *Gītā* verses we have considered above.

The absolute term for transcendence that Eckhart uses is 'Unity' (*unum*), an indication of a dialectical relationship between God and beings, where God is simultaneously distinct and indistinct, set off against beings and yet not to be distinguished from them. Given, further, that consciousness or intelligence (*intelligere*) for Eckhart is another way of understanding divine nature – for 'what is to understand other than to become one or be one with what is understood?'[54] – one can see why his view of Being can be called 'mystical ontologism'.[55] The absolute oneness of God combined with the capacity of the human being to understand this oneness makes for a powerful interpretation of the relationship between the mystical experience that transcends difference and the ontology of the transcendental that permits the overcoming of such difference (for never having been absolutely different at all). Śaṅkara's account of such realization comes in a passage that reads divine unity in Kṛṣṇa's statement about his supervisory power. At 9.10, Kṛṣṇa says that the world of moving and unmoving things is born of material nature (*prakṛti*) under his supervision (*adhyakṣa*). Śaṅkara reads (pp. 139–40) this supervisory power only as the self's intrinsic form (of self) as pure witness (*dṛśimātrasvarūpa*), which is unchangeable (*avikriya*). But there are no other conscious beings (*anyasya cetanā*), no other experiences (*anyasya bhokturabhāvāt*); there is only one deity (*eka deva*), which is the absolute consciousness (*paramārtha caitanya*). Here, Kṛṣṇa – as the one deity – is explicitly read as the consciousness in and of all beings, the consciousness that is in itself all.

We must not, of course, over-stress the parallel with Eckhart, for it may be the case that Eckhart's concept of unity, as oneness of God and self, could lend itself just as much to a theology of union compatible with Rāmānuja's account of the being-together of God and beings (although I am not sufficiently persuaded of that possibility to advocate that myself). But we can find mutually illuminating Śaṅkara's and Eckhart's strategy of understanding our own existence through seeing existence as essentially God; Śaṅkara explains being – and especially, our being – through Kṛṣṇa. This does resonate with Eckhart's saying that God is more intimate to all things than they are to themselves, so that, as Jean Greisch notes, the same task is both spiritual and ontological.[56]

Richard Kearney has made the interesting point that the ontology of the divine self-statement at Exodus 3.14, 'I am that I am', which we have looked at before, was interpreted in two polar ways by medieval thinkers bringing Greek philosophy to bear on the Biblical God: either as an ontotheology of God as being (indeed, a category of substance) or as a mystical ontologism in which divine and human consciousness are conflated in the 'I am'.[57] We have just seen that, reading Śaṅkara through Eckhart, we do find a mystical ontologism in the former. Not only does Śaṅkara see being or existence as God (i.e., the world of being as consisting in God's being), but he also sees God as being – indeed, as supremely being (i.e. taking the being of the self as indicative of the supreme plenitude of God's being).

Admittedly, he is less interested in this understanding of Kṛṣṇa as supremely being; we must see this only through his brief and matter-of-fact re-description of the *Gītā*'s approach to God *via eminentiae*, its repeated exaltation of Kṛṣṇa (whether self-declared or stated by Arjuna) through the infinite extension of all the virtues when talking of him. This is strikingly the case in both Kṛṣṇa's preparatory self-description in chapter 10, and Arjuna's (and Sañjaya's) description of the cosmic vision in chapter 11. Śaṅkara simply re-describes the *Gītā*'s verses, and draws very little from them; we will see how Rāmānuja uses the opportunity to read considerably more theologically significant meaning into them. For example, where Rāmānuja reads Kṛṣṇa's 'Of the Vṛṣṇi clan, I am Vāsudeva' at 10.37 as indicating that the son of Vāsudeva is the sovereign manifestation (*vibhūti*) of God

(p. 350), Śaṅkara glosses it as 'I myself, who am your friend' (*ayam eva ahaṃ tvatsakhaḥ*) (p. 157). At the same time, Śaṅkara makes no effort to read away the awesome theological lesson of these two chapters, the presentation of the God who exhausts description – description, especially, that locates him as the pre-eminent presence in all forms of being, from earth and fire to weapons and horses, from gods and sages to prayers and seasons. This is the God of light and death, time and destruction. All that is already in the *Gītā* and Śaṅkara leaves it as it is, in the main. Nevertheless, of all beings, Śaṅkara is content to leave Kṛṣṇa supreme. Kṛṣṇa's supremacy, for Śaṅkara, lies in the fact that he alone provides beings with their being.[58] Hence my suggestion that Śaṅkara combines ontotheology with mystical ontologism. This combination is perhaps unique to him, and sharpens the nomenclatural point that his position is non-dualist and not monist.

What we see in Śaṅkara is that God is other than beings, while also not-other to them. At 13.18, Kṛṣṇa summarises his teachings on *brahman* by saying that by understanding his teachings, his devotee 'attains my state of being' (*madbhāvāyopapadyate*). Śaṅkara glosses 'my state of being' as 'the state of being the supreme self' (*paramātmabhāvaḥ*) (p. 202). This is in keeping with his consistent reading of Kṛṣṇa as the self of all beings (hence his supremacy qua self). Yet, at 13.27, when Kṛṣṇa says that 'he sees [truly] who sees the supreme god (*parameśvaraṃ*) abiding (*tiṣṭhantaṃ*) alike in all beings (*sarveśu bhūteśu*)', as the 'imperishable among the perishable' (*vinaśyatsv avinaśyantaṃ*), Śaṅkara takes this opportunity to say that 'this is meant to show the utter difference of beings from the supreme god'.[59] How so? The modification described as 'birth' (*bhāvavikārāṇāṃ janilakṣaṇaḥ*) is the root (*mūla*) of all other modifications; and all modifications end in destruction (*sarve bhāvavikārāḥ vināśāntāḥ*). Beyond death (*vināśāt paraḥ*) there is no modification. By saying that this final modification (*antyabhāvavikāra*) is absent in the supreme god, all modification is denied (*pratiṣiddha*) of him. 'Therefore, it is established that the supreme god is completely other to all beings, is without particularity, and is singular.'[60] The otherness of God here, however utter, is otherness from what is not truly being, for what is other to God is not being at all, but non-being. So it is that the one who sees the supreme god thus truly sees; and the one who truly sees, sees the *ātman* as one, undivided (*ekam avibhaktaṃ*) in and as God.

The otherness of this godself consists in its singular reality, while the divided and modified are metaphysically less-than-real. The otherness is not between God and the being of beings. Alterity is therefore merely the non-dualist otherness of the one real to the less-than-real.

It should be realized, however, that this is not Śaṅkara's final move. We will now turn to his argument that the non-otherness of God to all being is itself part of the non-otherness of *brahman* to both being **and** non-being. This is evident in the celebrated exegesis of 13.12, where Śaṅkara indicates an alternative gloss which he rejects, and which is later adopted by Rāmānuja in pointed disagreement. Kṛṣṇa first says, 'I shall speak of that which is to be cognised, knowing which one attains immortality.' This is not controversial. In the next line, he goes on, '*anādimat paraṃ brahma na sat tan nāsad ucyate*'. The latter part of it means, 'it is neither said that it is nor that it is not'; the significance of which will be clear soon. The crucial interpretive move is to read the first half as '*anādimatparaṃ brahma*': 'the *brahman* beyond is without beginning'. The line would then read, 'the *brahman* beyond is that which is without beginning; it is said neither that it is nor that it is not'. Śaṅkara goes on (p. 197) to say, *anādimat* is one without beginning; and who is that one? That which is beyond (*param*), that is, the unsurpassed (*niratiśaya*) *brahman*. He then acknowledges that some split the phrase (*padaṃ chindanti*) as '*anādi matparaṃ brahma*': *brahman*, which is without beginning (*anādi*) is 'that which has me beyond it' (*matparam*), that of which, I, Vāsudeva, am the 'supreme power' (*parāśakti*). Rāmānuja will later take precisely that reading, with significant theological consequences, for on that reading, beginingless *brahman*, whatever it is, is distinct from Kṛṣṇa and subject to him, having him beyond it. Śaṅkara is aware that, on his reading, the '*mat*' suffix appears redundant, since '*anādi paraṃ brahma*' – 'the *brahman* beyond is without beginning' – seems sufficient to convey the meaning, without having to add another phrase to convey the same possessive qualifier. Śaṅkara concludes that its purpose is to complete the verse (*ślokapūrṇārthaḥ*).

More importantly, Śaṅkara argues, the alternative reading is untenable because it would then contradict the following claim, namely, that it neither is nor is not. Kṛṣṇa would engage in a contradiction (*vipratiṣedha*) if he were first to point out the possession of a distinctive power (*viśiṣṭaśaktimattvapradarśana*) on his part – his being beyond *brahman* – only to then go on to say, as the last part of the line definitely shows, that *brahman* is to be known only through the denial of all distinguishing attributes (*sarvaviśeṣapratiṣedha*). But if Śaṅkara's interpretation is taken, then it is consistent to say that beginingless *brahman* is beyond, its beyondness characterised by noting that it is said of it that it neither is nor is not (p. 198). Here we go back to the start of our study of Śaṅkara: the critical aspect of approaching *brahman* – what structures the entire inquiry – is that *brahman* is not being as such, and therefore is not available through a (howsoever demanding) phenomenological focus by consciousness on its own being. Of course, consciousness – the presencing self that is *ātman* – can indeed realize its non-difference from *brahman* only through rigorous inquiry; but in the intellectual process of characterising the subject of our inquiring cognition (*jñeya*) through our reading of sacred text, what we have to realize is that *brahman* is not being as such, even at its purest or in its supremacy.

Śaṅkara now has to face up to the standard objection that he must always face when he says that *brahman* is neither being nor non-being but yet is to be realized. He considers the following objection: If a thing cannot be talked of by the phrase, 'x is', then it is not [existent].[61] So too with the thing called 'the realisable' (*jñeya*). All judgements (*sarvāḥ buddhyah*) must involve the judgement of existence or non-existence (*astināstibuddhyanugatāḥ eva*). So, that which is to be realized (*jñeya*) must be either an object of an awareness involving the judgement that it is[62] or of one involving the judgement that it is not. To this, he replies that this is not the case when *brahman* is the *jñeya*. With sensory things like pots (*indriyagamyaṃ vastu ghaṭādikaṃ*) this is indeed the case. But *brahman* is beyond the senses (*atīndriya*), and is associated with sacred testimony as a means of knowledge (*śabdakapramāṇagamyatva*) alone. 'The two forms of judgement do not apply to it, and thus it is said of it that it neither is nor is not. The sacred texts, on that [*brahman*] which is other than what is to be known or not known, are for the purpose of attaining that which must be realised.'[63]

He expands further (p. 199) on why *brahman* cannot be spoken of through the expressions, 'is' and 'is not'. Words about objects convey meaning through the use of genus (*jāti*), action (*kriya*), quality (*guṇa*) or relationship (*saṃbandha*); e.g. cow/horse, cooking/reading, white/black, wealthy/owner of cows respectively. But *brahman* is not a genus (as we have already seen, not even the genus 'existence'), and so cannot be expressed by '…is' and the like; this is what it means to say that it is 'without qualities' (*nirguṇa*). It is without action (*niṣkriya*); and as it is unitary (*ekatva*) it has no relationships. It is non-dual (*advaya*), not an object (*aviṣaya*); it is selfhood (*ātmatva*). So it is said that it cannot be talked about through any word.[64] It should be noted that the *via negativa* adopted by Śaṅkara here, as elsewhere when talking about *brahman*, does not much fit into a comparison with the dominant strands of medieval Christian scholasticism: the insistence on the non-objectivity of *brahman*, and its non-dual non-relationality, indicate the uniquely non-realist metaphysics of Śaṅkara, wherein the ontology of the experienced world, while left untouched philosophically, is nevertheless circumscribed radically by consigning it to the ultimate category of changeful non-being.[65] Without that move, Śaṅkara could simply be seen as proffering an incoherent idealist metaphysics.

One specific comparison that does bear up is his notion of *brahman* as unitary or one, that is to say – in the language of Christian scholasticism, and Aquinas particularly – simple.[66] Conceptually, as Fergus Kerr points out,[67] unitary nature relates to not being a genus. However, crucially, the Thomistic conception of divine simplicity derives from the idea of God as pure being, that is, one whose essential nature does not differ from his existence; for only where there is such difference can there be the complex qualifications that make up an individual. But *brahman* is not even being-as-such but rather, the way there is both being and non-being; so Śaṅkara is striving here towards a notion of unitariness shorn even of considerations about the nature of being. The unitariness of *brahman* seems here to be a way of indicating the import of the *via negativa*, namely, that all names require linguistic proliferation to capture the differentiated structure that permits qualities, and unitariness is nothing other than a place-holder for the incapacity of qualification to advert to *brahman*. For Śaṅkara, the pure beingness of God is itself somehow still within our conceptual compass, due to the fortunate circumstance of the self-presentation of Kṛṣṇa; while what is beyond, as that which we call *brahman*, is that from which both being and non-being come.

On the basis of this examination, I suggest that things are exactly the opposite of what Richard De Smet says in his religiously-inspired reading of Śaṅkara on Kṛṣṇa. De Smet is insightful on what he calls the 'open man' of the *Gītā*, arguing that a highly personalistic conception is found in it, despite an abstract, Sāṃkhya-based starting point for the conception of self. In the chapters on Self, we will see how this is only partially true, and how a sophisticated interaction between abstract and personalistic conception of self is key to both the metaphysics and the ethics of the non-dualist reading of the *Gītā*. But De Smet also goes on to assert that this exalted personalism marks even the *Gītā*'s conception of the Deity. 'None of the great teachings of the Upaniṣads concerning the absolute *Brahman* is neglected but the notion of *Brahman* or even *Paramātman* is itself transcended insofar as it is said to have a basis. This basis is Kṛṣṇa as the supreme *Puruṣa* (*Puruṣottama*), the Absolute as Person, *Bhagavān*, Dispenser of grace, not only love but Lover in the eternal union of perfect mutual *bhakti*.'[68] My point is that, on the contrary, it is precisely this personalism that is exceeded by Kṛṣṇa himself, on the way to what is realized of *brahman*.

If somehow we still choose to call *brahman*, thus adverted to by Śaṅkara, 'God', it would be something like Eckhart's God beyond God; but we must be guided by the fact that Śaṅkara himself chooses not to cease using both the godly terms regarding Kṛṣṇa and the trans-godly terminology of *brahman*. The striking comparison here is probably Cusanus who, in the mid-15th century most interestingly explored the possibilities opened up by Eckhart. Cusanus too talks of God, but also of Godhead, as the negation of the relationship between being and non-being; as Burkhard Mojsisch notes, 'one can know the pure negation of … godly unity … only when one occupies the standpoint of this unity itself and expresses it in a godly manner'.[69] Here we approach a comparison that requires a great deal more systematic work as a task in itself, something I am not able to undertake in the context of this book. In Cusanus we find the move to Godhead that is not through being, even at its purest. Ignoring the Aristotelian requirement that a definition proceed through the predication of a genus and the specific difference of the species – in a manner carefully set aside above by Śaṅkara too (probably in reference to the Nyāya rules of definition available to him) – Cusanus famously talks of the Godhead thus: 'the "not-other" is not other than the not-other'.[70] In this way, Mojsisch points out, the not-other defines itself through itself, being oppositionless. Even 'being', 'true' and 'one' are what they are only through the not-other. 'On the other hand, however, since the not-other is not everything other, or is different from all others, inasmuch as it is not other than the not-other, it transcends all others'.[71] Conceived thus, Mojsisch says, Godhead 'as oppositionless opposition guarantees movement forth from itself and back to itself and not as movement beyond itself'.[72] Here we have a summing up that could apply to Śaṅkara's *brahman*: it is not-other, i.e., not-different, i.e., not-dual. It stands in opposition to being and non-being, but without opposition, since there is nothing other than it. And it is realized only by itself, in the self realizing itself as *brahman*.

We begin to see what Śaṅkara is doing by preserving both God (called Kṛṣṇa, Vāsudeva) and *brahman* in his account, despite their not being different. I have already commented that, for Śaṅkara, Kṛṣṇa is not a creator God; at 13.19, Kṛṣṇa himself says that nature and self – that is to say, both orders of being – are beginingless (*anādi*). Śaṅkara explains that beings are not creation (*kṛtaṃ*), that is, beings wholly existent yet distinct from the being that created them. He dismisses an opponent's anxiety to assert that the world is God's creation (*īśvarasya jagataḥ kartṛtvaṃ*; p. 202). If God were defined as creator, before the emergence (*utpattaḥ*) of nature and self at the point of creation, God would be no God, he expatiates. That leaves intact his view, which we have explored, of Kṛṣṇa as the supreme being whose supremacy of being gives being to all other things but which does not consist in being the greatest instantiation of being amongst beings.[73]

In this, we have a parallel to the Christological phenomenology that seeks, as Orrin Summerell does, for example, to develop a theology out of Heidegger's rather impatient observation that any 'metaphysics that determines God as the perfect causal ground of beings' is 'an ungodly God', while 'the God of being is definable solely in terms of the figuration of being as such'.[74] So, beings are uncaused by God, but have their being through God.

As Summerell summarises his Hedeggerian position, in freedom, 'God is God not as God, in the sameness of deity, but rather as the identity of being; as another subjectivity or as one's own subjectivity; as the wholeness of experience that is the relation of these three terms; or as the nothing that is the negation of all of them'.[75] Śaṅkara's Kṛṣṇa too is aptly described thus, as the self of all, as the identity of being. But, of course, the comparison rather depends on one's interpretation of Heidegger and what Heidegger said. Heidegger said in a later work that 'being is further than all entity, be it a rock, an animal, an artwork, a machine, be it an angel or God', listing God among those entities that have being, while being is not God.[76] Clearly, while preserving that concrete subject who is Kṛṣṇa, Śaṅkara also sees the *Gītā* as understanding the relationship between Kṛṣṇa and being quite differently. If one considered, instead, the Heidegger who said that 'the divine itself lies outside the field of Being and outside metaphysics'[77] – metaphysics understood in the self-serving way in which Heidegger uses it – then it would seem that the Heideggerian divine is more properly comparable to Śaṅkara's *brahman*, for *brahman* clearly is not the unmanifest being as such (although being is also *brahman*). Yet there is no difference between Kṛṣṇa (both as the foremost being and as being which gives being to all) and *brahman* (who is the ground of being and non-being as such). It is that paradox which invites ultimately no further words but only the realization of *brahman*.

Worshipping Kṛṣṇa, attaining *brahman*: Self-realization and theology

So, we find that there is no simple answer to the question of the relationship between Kṛṣṇa and *brahman* in Śaṅkara's commentary. Taking the commentary as a whole, or at least, across many passages in many chapters, we gain the impression of a struggle to maintain a balance between widely differing conceptions of ultimate meaning (and this is not just an issue about the layers of the *Gītā* itself). But some sort of an answer, howsoever hedged in by elusive restrictions on meaning, emerges. Kṛṣṇa is the subject of worship, the person with maximal qualities, the vibrantly relational recipient of worship and source of grace; but also the abstract presence in all, the supreme being understood as being itself out of which being is found. And this is because Kṛṣṇa is self; while he is the supreme self and the self of all, the self as self is the essence in all beings; and the significance of this is that *brahman* is the self of all, is not other than beings, and is not other than God. This is so because *brahman* is not other than being and non-being, but that whereby both are possible.

All this leaves us with a question: What is the role of a theology of Kṛṣṇa for Śaṅkara? We can say, broadly, that his answer clusters around two types of answers. One concerns loving devotion (*bhakti*) towards the self-declared God who is found in the person of Kṛṣṇa, and is interesting because of the way Śaṅkara takes such passages in the *Gītā* and makes them point to something else, even while never denying devotion and the complex of ritual life. The other concerns a theme familiar to us by now, which is the invocation of Kṛṣṇa's selfhood that Śaṅkara sees as key to the rationality of spiritual life, what we might call, in a cumbersome way, a gnoseo-phenomenology of consciousness. Let us look at each in turn.

Śaṅkara's location of devotion within a larger spiritual project of inquiry is not a simple denigration of the former. The second chapter of the *Gītā* is given over to gnostic discipline (*jñāna yoga*) and the discipline of ethico-ritual action (*karma yoga*). Kṛṣṇa says at 2.39 that, having taught of the discernment (*buddhi*) that comes from Sāṃkhya (the early school of metaphysics, which here stands for the path of knowledge, and therefore for gnostic discipline), he will now talk of what comes from Yoga (here, the school of consciousness-controlling practice, and implying the path of action, and therefore of ritual and worship), which will lead to freedom from bondage. But Śaṅkara goes out of his way to say (p. 30) that disciplined action (*karma yoga*) is not only the discipline of spiritual absorption (*samādhi yoga*) but also the performance (*anuṣṭhāna*) of rites (*karma*) with detachment (*niḥsaṅga*), for 'the adoration of God' (*īśvara-ārādhana*). This act of adoration leads to the discarding of all action itself, by the attainment of 'the gnosis caused by God's grace'.[78] Such gnosis is, of course, the realization in consciousness of the non-duality of self, God and *brahman*. Śaṅkara therefore maintains that the gnostic path is also a devotional one.

But for all that, the devotional path is more importantly also a gnostic one. Śaṅkara reconstructs as gnoseology Kṛṣṇa's teaching at 8.22 that the supreme person (*paraḥ puruṣa*) 'within whom stand all beings' (*antaḥsthāni bhūtāni*), is reached through singular (*ananyayā*) devotion (p. 133). First, he analyses '*puruṣa*' – 'person' – as '*puri śayanāt pūrṇatvāt*' – 'residing/resting in the whole of the fortress (of the body, or heart or intellect – i.e., the human being)'. In other words, the supreme person (God) is that which is, supremely, the self of beings. Second, he crisply states that the singular 'devotion' (*bhakti*) encouraged here is that which is characterised as gnosis (*jñānalakṣaṇa*). So the love of God is a signifier of insight into non-duality. That is its true and ultimate function. One role for the theology of Kṛṣṇa is to transmute devotion into gnosis: the presence and promise of Kṛṣṇa permits the human response of love to become a path to self-realization, while Kṛṣṇa's grace is itself to be understood as the prompt for that realization.

This gnoseological re-reading of devotion permits Śaṅkara to discipline all loving worship within that inquiry into *brahman* that brings about the realization of non-duality. The worship that he takes to be of greatest value can be framed as a gnostic undertaking. He reads 9.15 as 'Others do homage to me by offering the sacrifice of the knowledge of oneness; [others worship my] diversity; [yet others, worship me] variously [as] facing in all directions.'[79] (As a contrast, in Laurie Patton's translation of this verse, we have: 'And others, through the sacrifice of wisdom, worship me as the oneness which is multiple, placed in many ways, facing all sides.'[80] In other words, this can be read quite naturally as a single, cumulative description, whereas Śaṅkara takes Kṛṣṇa to be talking of three classes of worshippers.) The three classes of worshippers are: those whose sacrificial performance is the attainment of the knowledge that '*brahman* is one'; those whose worship takes the form, 'Lord Viṣṇu alone abides (*avasthitaḥ*) in all the distinct (*bheda*) forms, like the Sun, the Moon, etc.'; and those who worship in many ways (*bahuprakārena*), thinking, 'Lord Viṣṇu alone resides variously in His omni-directional (*sarvatomukha*) cosmic form (*viśvarūpa*)' (p. 141). So, the most exalted form of worship is one in which it is taken that *brahman* is one; in the next level down, it is taken that Viṣṇu abides in all; and finally (i.e., at the most accessible and the least spiritually valuable level), there is the belief that Viṣṇu abides in many forms. While preserving the monotheism that we have noted before (which is not his concern), Sankara hierarchizes the forms of worship according to their cognitive sophistication, as he sees it.

Another striking example of his view that worshipful action directed at Kṛṣṇa should only be taken to lead to insight into non-duality comes in his commentary on 12.12. There, Kṛṣṇa says that intellectual gnosis (*jñāna*) is superior (*śreyaḥ*) to permanent exercise (*abhyāsa*); sustained reflection (*dhyāna*) surpasses gnosis; renunciation of the fruit of action (*karmaphalatyāga*) is better than reflection; and from such renunciation comes peace (*śānti*). The verse's apparent assertion of the renunciation of the fruit of action as the culminating form of the spiritual life (superior, as it were, to gnosis), should be understood (p. 180) as the most powerful path, in the sense that it is the one that is to be followed by those who are not able to do anything else. The power of the path does not lie in its spiritual exaltation, but rather in its being the most accessible and easily enabling. In the preceding verses, 8-11, Kṛṣṇa talks of those who fix their mind on him alone; advises those who cannot do that to strive for him through disciplined action; and finally, if they are unable even to discipline their action, then to at least renounce the fruit of their action.

In the exegesis relevant for our present purpose, Śaṅkara maintains that intellectual gnosis accompanied by reflection surpasses gnosis alone. In the commentary, he argues that the disciplinary practice 'characterised by focussing thought on the cosmic form of God'[81] and the performance of actions with God as objective (*īśvarārthaṃ karmānuṣṭhā*) are premised on 'a difference between self and God' (*ātmaiśvarabheda*). So the discipline of action (*karmayoga*) is the result of unwisdom (*ajñāna*) and its practitioner is incapable of seeing non-difference (*abheda*). The discipline of action is unsuitable for the one who meditates on the imperishable (*akṣara*).

So, when, at 12.7, Kṛṣṇa says 'I am their saviour' (*teṣāmahaṃ samuddhartā*), he is talking of those who are dependent (*paratantra*) on God. Those who have become Godself (*īśvarsyā'tmabhūtā*) should be considered as having the form of the imperishable (*akṣarasvarūpa*) since they would have seen the non-difference between God and self. In that case, it would not be sensible to talk of their being objects of the saving act (*samuddharaṇakarmaviṣaya*) of God. In this superbly imaginative passage, Śaṅkara demonstrates that a rigorous and uncompromising form of mystical ontologism or unitive mysticism is central to his theology. He neither rejects theological value in the spiritual life nor expounds a theology of salvific grace that sits within an unquestioned ontotheological framework. Śaṅkara's Kṛṣṇa is the God through (and, given ultimate non-duality, with) whom *ātman/brahman*-realization is sought.

This brings us to the other role that Śaṅkara discerns for a theology of Kṛṣṇa, namely, the attainment of non-duality rendered possible (only?) through Kṛṣṇa's universal selfhood. Kṛṣṇa's grace is attained through gnostic realization and is expressed non-dualistically. At 9.22, Kṛṣṇa promises '*yogakṣema*' to those who worship him while 'thinking of none else but me' (*ananyāścintayanto māṃ*). Śaṅkara interprets (p. 144) *yogakṣema* as two interrelated things; '*yoga* is attaining the unattained, and *kṣema* is the protection of it'. The attainment, of course, is non-duality, since 'thinking of none else but me' means, for Śaṅkara, 'becoming non-separate, having realised the supreme deity, Nārāyaṇa, as the very self'.[82] We have already seen that Śaṅkara by no means denies the role of worship and divine grace, albeit within a gnostic teleology. We also see now how these two things, while in apparent tension with each other, actually fit together: the gnosis is that confluence of consciousness – guarded and guaranteed by Kṛṣṇa for the worshipper – that is the realization of non-duality.

The connection between examination of the self and the exploration of being is, of course, an integral part of Christian theology's assimilation of Greek philosophy; in fact, it is one of the dominant characteristics of onto-theology – ontotheology understood, not necessarily in the way Heidegger did in order to establish his own self-proclaimed originality, but plainly as the conception of an intimate connection between God and being, of at least an understanding of being in and through God (although not necessarily taking Being to name God). 'The idea of God as Spirit, pure Being without material parts, led classical Christian authors to approach the understanding of God largely through reflection on the self. In his *On Free Choice of the Will*, Augustine holds that human intelligence is the highest and best of human attributes. This intelligence is dependent upon a reality that is higher than itself, the spiritual, eternal and unchanging God (2:37–15:39). The soul's knowledge of itself leads to knowledge of God, and to a true idea of being', point out Fiorenza and Kaufman.[83]

Understood in this way, later Christian developments appear to point to a deepening of this methodology. In Aquinas, it seems plausible to think that there is a worked-out doctrine of theosis, a mystical union that is the final goal of the human being.[84] As Anna Williams says, for him the love that brings about union with God is meditation on God's nature, a theological activity that is sharing in God's being. (Of course, this union is between the human and God through God's self-giving, a theme we will see much more appropriately comparable to Rāmānuja's vision of God's love, although he permits inquiry into being as no more than preparation for a loving relationship with God.) Two things strike us here in relation to what we have been learning about Śaṅkara: one is the idea that loving devotion (*bhakti*) is noetic, the thinking of God by the worshipper, and therefore directed towards gnosis on the worshipper's part; the other is that such a relationship is possible because of the mapping of self and God through being.

Even while pointing out the centrality of this theosis to Thomism, Laurence Hemming has argued that, for a Heideggerian, there might well be a problem with the enquiry into the being of oneself becoming the inquiry into God's being. Such an attempt is metaphysical, for it 'makes the being of God the ground of the being of being human'. If so, this 'displaces the ground of the being of being human from the very self that I am, whose being I can then enquire into, onto a being whose being is not transparently interrogable for me, namely God'.[85] The response to this (although perhaps not by a Thomist) has to be, I think, that the success of the inquiry lies not in the attainment of a metaphysical grasp of God's being, but in God's self-giving. However, we have a very different situation with Śaṅkara. It is not so much that Śaṅkara rules out Kṛṣṇa's grace as playing a role in realization: the *Gītā*'s communication of Kṛṣṇa's declarations of gracious giving are too many for that line of interpretation to be sustainable. And it is certainly the case that our love of Kṛṣṇa is, at any rate, noetic for Śaṅkara; we have seen that often enough. What is important is that Śaṅkara is not talking of a union of God's being and the self, but the non-duality of the two.

The inquiry, in Advaita, is already rendered possible only because there is no ontological difference between God and self – 'ontological' both in the standard sense of constitutive nature and in the Heideggerian sense of having the nature to comprehend, reflexively and recursively, one's own being. It is precisely gnosis – turning the attention of consciousness to illuminate consciousness itself – that is rendered possible by the fact that the conscious self is also the self that is God. God's selfhood is the self of all being, and that is why, at one and the same time, immediately and without transition, to attain God and to attain gnosis of true selfhood is also to (re-) attain non-duality.

In the middle of the famous commentary on 18.66 concerning Kṛṣṇa's culminating promise of salvation (which will occupy us in the last chapter), Śaṅkara states (p. 285) that freedom from entanglement with the less-than-real world of action comes to those 'who have taken refuge in the oneness of the Lord's quiddity ('own-form' (*svarūpa*)) and the self'.[86] This, then, is Śaṅkara's theology of Kṛṣṇa, and his account of its role within gnoseology. But it has always to be remembered that theology does not exhaust Śaṅkara's system; there is *brahman*. The *ātman* seeks to realize its non-duality with *brahman*, not (just) with God; but the person prays to God and God is *ātman* is *brahman*. The gnoseological search (*jijñāsa*) is not for God even with a theology, but for *brahman*. This combination, of course, has no Christian parallel. And it is important to keep that in mind, in order to not read him in Christian a/theological terms.

Self, God and *brahman*: Śaṅkara, theology and non-dualist metaphysics

Let us try and bring together the various, intertwined strands of Śaṅkara's thinking on Kṛṣṇa and *brahman* in the *Gītā* commentary. In contrast to his commentaries on the Upaniṣads and on the *Brahmasūtras* (which latter, after all, present themselves as concise *aides memoire* to the teachings of the former), the *Gītā* offers Śaṅkara the unique challenge of interpreting the presence of a robustly immanent, densely subjective and clearly self-declarative being, Kṛṣṇa, whose declarations advert to his supreme divinity. This is because, by contrast, the other texts on which he comments locate *brahman* as the nodal point of all explanation, and permit him to develop his broad theme of the non-duality of conscious presence condensed in the individuated self and the singular, permeating and originary principle that is *brahman*. Since *brahman* clearly occupies a significant position in the *Gītā*, it is not as if Śaṅkara is unable to extend his non-dualist conceptual vocabulary to it, but he has to do so *via* Kṛṣṇa. This chapter is an extended argument to the effect that Śaṅkara should not be seen as trying to explain away Kṛṣṇa within the working out of the significance of *ātman-brahman*. Equally, I also point out that a swing to the other extreme of seeing Śaṅkara's position in the light of a wholly devotional theology of Kṛṣṇa is not sustainable, both because it is not possible to defend a personalistic conception of *brahman* (i.e. through taking Kṛṣṇa and *brahman* as just nomenclaturally different) and because Śaṅkara offers an emphatically gnostic reading of the nature and purpose of worship that does not sit easily with pietistic devotion. Instead, we have an account that is distinctive of Śaṅkara, and that too, the Śaṅkara of the *Gītā* commentary: a highly intellectual reading of devotion that nonetheless wholeheartedly endorses devotion to Kṛṣṇa; a sophisticated and balanced account of the nature of Kṛṣṇa as both the subject who is supremely being and as being itself which founds all beings; and circumscribing this theology, an overarching understanding of *brahman* as the ground or fount of being and non-being, that which ontologically permits beings and the ultimately non-being world to be what they are/are not.

We have, therefore, two radical steps in Śaṅkara's reading of the *Gītā*. The first is the non-duality of divine and human being through Kṛṣṇa's proclamation of his universal selfhood; and the second is the location of this non-duality within the overarching non-duality of *brahman* and being/non-being, which is not, as it were, spoken of, but ineluctably reached through inquiry into the conditions for the possibility of gnosis. Let us look at these in turn.

Self and God: Śaṅkara's mapping and Kṛṣṇa's declaration

Since the *Gītā* often has Kṛṣṇa say that he is the self of all beings, Śaṅkara interprets all the other statements of the relationship between God and human beings through this essential declaration. As we have seen, worship is understood as an epistemic quest, the attainment of knowledge of non-duality through systematic thinking of the nature of God (prompted here by Kṛṣṇa's own assurance of that nature). It is also teleologically gnostic; such understanding is meant to dissolve the phenomenology of existence, from the variegated experiences of the individuated and agonistic person into the consciousness of pure presence that is the truth of selfhood, a process that we will look at in detail when examining the nature of self in the *Gītā* commentaries. But it is not just the ontological truth of the non-duality of Kṛṣṇa and selves that prompts worship and permits gnosis, for it is Kṛṣṇa's grace that renders worship successful. Let us look again at the first half of the circle, which is Śaṅkara's mapping of divine and human selfhood, before we turn to the other half, namely, Kṛṣṇa's assurance that the mapping has salvific potency.

At 13.27, Kṛṣṇa says, 'He sees [truly] who sees the supreme god (*parameśvara*) abiding (*tiṣṭhanta*) alike in all beings (*sarveṣu bhūteṣu*), not dying even as they die.' Śaṅkara glosses (p. 209) *parameśvara* as the supreme god with regard to (*apekṣya*) body, senses, mind, intellect, the unmanifest (*avyakta*) and the self, who undyingly abides equally (*samam*) in all beings. This shows, he asserts, the absolute difference (*atyanta vailakṣaṇya*) between beings and the supreme god. How so? The change in the state of being described as 'birth' (*bhāvavikārāṇāṃ janilakṣaṇaḥ*) is the root (*mūla*) of all other modifications; and all changes in states of being end in death/ destruction (*sarve bhāvavikārāḥ vināśāntāḥ*). Beyond death (*vināśāt paraḥ*) there is no change. By saying that this final change in the state of being (*antyabhāvavikāra*) is absent in the supreme god, all modification is denied (*pratiṣiddha*) of him. 'Therefore, it is established that the supreme god is completely other to all beings, is without particularity, is One.'[87] One who sees the supreme god thus (truly) sees. This is contrasted with those who see contrarily (*viparita*). Just as when, compared to those with the eye-defect called *timira* who see many moons, the one who sees the single moon correctly is said to 'see (truly)', so too: 'the one who sees the one undivided self as described is distinguished from those who contrarily see many selves divided, by saying, "he alone sees".'[88] This is another of those tightly crafted passages in Śaṅkara where what appears to be a conventional point about God's otherness – signified by eternality – is quickly reconfigured in terms of non-dual, not-other selfhood. If God is simple, without particularity, free of modifications to the conditions of being, and therefore free of temporality, then obviously the world and worldly beings are other than God. God's otherness is from the states of all beings, their changefulness that ends in the destruction of their particularity. But this otherful God is also not other, abiding alike in all beings. What is common to all beings is their being, which is Kṛṣṇa's presence in and as self in them. As the one self that is the self of all being, God is to be distinguished from the manyness of beings, but is not different from their oneness.

Such an interpretation permits Śaṅkara to read Kṛṣṇa as himself guaranteeing the culmination of non-dual gnosis in *brahman*, for at 13.30, Kṛṣṇa affirms, 'When one sees the diversity of states of being abiding in the one, and their expanding from that alone, one attains *brahman*.'[89] Śaṅkara underlines this affirmation (p. 210) by echoing the Upaniṣadic teaching of non-dual *brahman*: 'one attains *brahman*' simply means 'one becomes *brahman* itself' (*brahmaiva bhavati*), and one does so when one sees, as *Chandogya Upaniṣad* 7.26.1 says, that the self is breath (*prāṇa*), hope (*āśā*), memory (*smara*), space (*ākāśa*), light (*teja*), water (*āpa*), manifestation (*āvirbhāva*) and de-manifestation (*tirobhāva*), and food (*anna*). So, for

Śaṅkara, God is self, and self is *brahman*. (As we will see, Rāmānuja has no difficulty with identifying self and *brahman*, but he interprets the latter quite differently in relation to Kṛṣṇa, an interpretation that will be central to his radical theology.)

Śaṅkara is aware that this non-dualism makes for a curious theodicy, and attempts to provide an answer. Our concern is not really about the effectiveness of this theodicy but the commitment to non-duality evident in it. 13.31 asserts, 'The immutable (*avyaya*) supreme self (*paramātman*) although in the body (*śarīra*), does not act (*na karoti*) and is not stained (*na lipyate*).' The mention of 'stain' leads to an objection (p. 211): Who acts in the body and is stained (affected negatively)? If it is another (*anya*) than the supreme self who, as the embodied one (*dehi*) who acts and is stained, then what becomes of the statement in 13.2, 'Know me as the knower of the field', which shows the oneness of the knower of the field and God (*kṣetrajñeśvaraikatva*)? However, if there is no other embodied being than God (*atha nāstīśvarāt anyaḥ dehī*), then who acts and is stained (for it could then not be God)? Or is it that there is no supreme one (*paro vā nāsti*)? In a few swift steps, Śaṅkara sums up the problem. That something is stained, through moral and existential failures (evil and suffering) is undeniable, and it is the body that is so identified. Kṛṣṇa contrasts this with the supreme self that is not stained thus. A theodicy concerning a God who is completely other to worldly being would seek to answer how such a God permitted the stain. For Śaṅkara, the problem is strikingly different, as can be seen in his honest presentation of it. His answer involves a fundamental Advaitic claim about beings in their limited being. Śaṅkara responds to the objection by saying that Kṛṣṇa himself has already pointed out at 5.14 that what 'sets out' or acts is essential nature (*svabhāvas tu pravartate*); and, Śaṅkara says, that essential nature – the essential nature of beings in the world, who are stained – is unwisdom (*avidyā*). As we will see in his account of the self in human being, unwisdom is the taking of oneself to be an individuated being among other beings, the world as ultimately existent, and God as utterly other. Worldly transaction (*vyavahāra*) is possible only because the human being's essential nature is just unwisdom (*avidyāmātrasvabhāva*); it is this clouded sense of separate beingness within a body that generates action, thereby constructing an individuated entity that becomes stained. The supreme self (*paramātman*) – that is to say, the self as the essential presence of Kṛṣṇa, being itself rather than particular being – is not ultimately the acting, stained entity. So, it is by inscribing all empirical reality to this primal ignorance of being as such that Śaṅkara offers a non-dualist theodicy for Godself.

We should remember that this exploration of the ontology of the non-duality of God and self is only one half of what Śaṅkara says about

Kṛṣṇa; the other half, which completes his theology, is that the attainment of non-duality is guaranteed by God's grace. As Kṛṣṇa promises (9.29): 'Those who adore me with devotion, they are in me and I in them.'[90] Śaṅkara makes clear the relationship involved here. He understands Kṛṣṇa to be saying, 'I exist in them not through the constraint of attachment (*rāganimitta*); but by their own-being (*svabhāva*)' (p. 146). This is the ontological core of the salvific promise. The essential nature or own-being of beings is both characterisable as unwisdom and the locus of Kṛṣṇa's presence. Where we are most chained to the world there Kṛṣṇa is – in us, but more significantly, as us – so that we may be free.

As we have seen before, it is striking that Śaṅkara neither concedes that our *telos* is anything but gnostic non-duality nor asserts that Kṛṣṇa's grace alone takes us to our self-realization. An Advaitic reading of the *Gītā* requires *brahman* to be the final explanation, but Kṛṣṇa is required to provide it. Kṛṣṇa declares himself, whereas *brahman* is anonymous to the world of revelation. Kṛṣṇa, as paradigmatic self that enselves being, offers the right balance to human inquiry for, in the *Gītā* according to Śaṅkara, the gnosis that results from inquiry is guaranteed only after it is acknowledged that God has provided the means to inquiry, by a self-declared presence (that prompts, for Śaṅkara, the only proper devotion, namely, the noetic worship through which gnosis is attained).

But still, it all ends, as it began, with *brahman* – or else there would be no Advaita. Śaṅkara does not shirk from accepting a salvific theology of Kṛṣṇa; but nevertheless, there is something beyond the theology which circumscribes it and makes his Advaita ultimately an inquiry into reality beyond the theology. In the end, Śaṅkara is looking for a sort of transmetaphysics, which seeks to get to the ground that renders being possible.

Kṛṣṇa's signification of *brahman*: the asymmetric mystery of non-duality

At the heart of Śaṅkara's *Gītā* is the elusiveness and mystery of the relationship between Kṛṣṇa and *brahman*, for there is no direct equation in the *Gītā* between the two, and none in Śaṅkara's commentary apart from on one intriguing occasion (on 14.27, to which we will soon turn). Over the course of the commentary, the general impression accumulates of *brahman* encompassing but exceeding God. For example, as we saw in the extended discussion in the first section, especially with regard to 2.16, Śaṅkara points to *brahman* as containing but exceeding being and non-being, the immutable and the mutable. But Kṛṣṇa also undeniably characterises himself as immutable; as we saw in the previous section, on 13.27, modification characterizes beings, while it cannot apply to God. Divine immutability, of course, is the cornerstone of most pre-modern theologies. Compare with Augustine, who says, 'When the words of God reach holy Moses through the angel, to his question concerning his name … the answer was "I am who I am" …, as if, when compared to him who truly is because he is immutable, the things which do change were not; this was vigorously defended and recommended with the greatest possible care by Plato.'[91] Yet, we have seen that Śaṅkara takes reasonable care to say that *brahman* exceeds both the mutable and the immutable, and this despite the fact that he does write loosely and sometimes contradictorily across the length of the commentary.

Śaṅkara's God is not a philosopher's God, but a theologian's – and yet the theology is subjected to a transmetaphysics of *brahman*. Of course, Kṛṣṇa is not to be dis-identified from *brahman*, for *brahman* is all, and we have seen how the realization of *brahman* can be approached only through and in Kṛṣṇa. But non-duality is asymmetric: *brahman* cannot be exhausted by non-duality with Kṛṣṇa or *ātman*. Śaṅkara's Kṛṣṇa speaks of *brahman* but indirectly. As we have seen in the previous section, at 13.30, Kṛṣṇa points to, rather than identifies with, *brahman*: 'When one sees the diversity of states of being abiding in the one, and their expanding from that alone, one attains *brahman*.' Now, if *brahman* were to be understood as the free self, distinct from and subordinate to Kṛṣṇa, as Rāmānuja does, that would be a different matter. But if, as Śaṅkara does, the Upaniṣadic non-duality of *ātman* and *brahman* is preserved even while Kṛṣṇa is repeatedly identified as the *ātman* of all, then either *brahman* is – symmetrically – Kṛṣṇa, or exceeds him. At 13.30, Kṛṣṇa can seem, for Śaṅkara, to be 'sending' (cognitively, as it were) the *ātman* through him to *brahman*, implying the latter option.

But there is one passage in which Śaṅkara struggles to express the very limits of language in the striving towards *brahman*, even when that striving is graced by Kṛṣṇa. At 14.27, Kṛṣṇa says, 'I am the support (*pratiṣṭha*) of *brahman*, the immortal and imperishable, and of the everlasting *dharma*, and of absolute joy.'[92] Śaṅkara's first step (p. 222) is to point out that the 'I' (*aham*) of Kṛṣṇa is the inmost self (*pratyagātman*). The implication is that, while the authority of the claim comes from its being spoken by Kṛṣṇa, it applies as much to each human being as it does to him. This is made clear soon after. Explaining the phrase in the previous verse, 'becomes competent to become *brahman* (*brahma bhūyāya kalpate*)', Śaṅkara says, 'Since the inmost self is the support of the supreme self, which is intrinsically eternal, etc., through complete gnosis, it is ascertained as the supreme self'.[93] But the trickier point here is the notion of 'support' (or 'the underlying place', 'the base'). This becomes acute when Śaṅkara then goes on to explain the relationship between God and *brahman* – the nearest he gets to it – while stressing non-duality. 'The power of God through which, to bless devotees and so on, the *brahman* that is supported, comes forth – I am that power which is *brahman*, the power and the possessor of the power not being separate.'[94] For Śaṅkara, God's supporting *brahman* is not a matter of *brahman* having God as its foundation; on the contrary, God supports *brahman* as an auxiliary might support the principal. In similar manner, the inmost self supports, in the sense of expressing in its being, the supreme self. So Śaṅkara inverts our expectation of the direction in which the asymmetry of 'support' runs. God's being blesses being, and thus the interpersonal relationship at the heart of a theology is secured. But God derives from *brahman*, for God supports *brahman* in the sense of being the personal bridge to beings. God is the power of *brahman* by which being is being and beings have being and are blessed to so realize themselves. But, as the tenet of non-duality affirms, there is no difference between God and *brahman*, for there is nothing other than *brahman*.

This is a radical circumspection of Godliness, for God is not the ultimate point of Advaitic inquiry; but Śaṅkara makes the point quickly and circumspectly. He then rounds off the commentary on this verse with another enigmatic interpretive alternative, because he cannot leave the vanishing point of ultimacy so robustly described as this verse does, as immortal, as absolute joy, and the like. He therefore takes Kṛṣṇa to be saying, 'Or the reference of the word '*brahman*' [in this verse] can mean the *brahman* that is conceptualised. Of that *brahman*, unconceptualised, I myself – and none else – am that which is the support.'[95] Even the *brahman* described as immortal, of everlasting order and absolute joy, while reaching the limits of language remains within those limits, so the role of Kṛṣṇa in being the support for our attainment of such a *brahman* seems somehow to be limited too. If God is the power through which we realize our supreme self, it is that self, which is none other than *brahman*, that must escape our language. God should take us beyond language, bound as language is to the forms of our current being. So Śaṅkara takes Kṛṣṇa to be saying that what can be said is said of *brahman* as we conceptualise it, in our language and our imagination. But that which God supports for our realization is *brahman* beyond understanding, beyond language, beyond concepts. The gnosis by which the inmost self is realized as the supreme self (who is God) is also more than just the realization of reality at maximal understanding – for that takes us only to the conceptualised *brahman*. God – and God alone – takes us beyond our understanding, beyond our becoming, to *brahman* – that which we feebly call the unconceptualised *brahman*.

The great mystery of the God of Advaita's inquiry into *brahman* still remains, although we have tried to draw out what we can from Śaṅkara's ingenious, often breathtakingly unconventional (and to this day, hardly understood and much misinterpreted) reading of the nature of Kṛṣṇa in the *Gītā*. We have to make what we will of the interpretive conundrum in Śaṅkara's description of Kṛṣṇa as the signifier (*abhidheya*) of *brahman*, in the introduction to the commentary: 'This sacred text, the *Gītā*, while particularly revealing the … ritual cosmic order having the highest good as its purpose and the supreme reality called Vāsudeva – being that signifies *brahman* in excess – as its subject matter, is shown to have a special purpose and connection.'[96]

2

Being and the God Other than Being: Rāmānuja on *brahman* and Kṛṣṇa

The *Gītā* is God's self-declaration and, as such, a text ripe for the Vaiṣṇava theology that Rāmānuja is seeking to develop; but nonetheless – or indeed, precisely for that reason – Kṛṣṇa has a great deal to say about *brahman*. So we have to inquire into the nature of *brahman* in Rāmānuja's commentary as well. The hermeneutic challenge in the body of the *Brahmasūtras* for Rāmānuja was always the absence of Kṛṣṇa-Vāsudeva, whose supreme name and form is Viṣṇu/Nārāyaṇa. So there, *brahman* itself had to perform fully the theological function necessary for a faith centred on Nārāyaṇa; and Rāmānuja looked to derive from its statements a reading of *brahman* that leads to Nārāyaṇa. The *Gītā*, of course, is utterly different. It permits a far greater freedom to approach Nārāyaṇa directly (given, of course, the historically complete identification of Kṛṣṇa with Viṣṇu/Nārāyaṇa). A different interpretive task, one focussed on Rāmānuja's overall Viśiṣṭādvaitic position, might well occupy itself with looking at how the *brahman*-oriented commentaries are made to yield a theology that can also cohere with the one available through reading the *Gītā*.[1] But as my intention in this book is to treat the *Gītā* commentary on its own independent terms, as a single source of theological reconstruction, we only need to contrast Rāmānuja's task with Śaṅkara's.

Roughly put, in exact opposition to Śaṅkara, Rāmānuja implicitly asks: what is *brahman* doing here? This is because Rāmānuja explicitly commits himself, from the introduction onwards, to a reading of the *Gītā* as about Kṛṣṇa/Nārāyaṇa (and Nārāyaṇa's consort Śrī), thereby foregrounding Kṛṣṇa's presence as the ultimate significance of the text. We will, of course, have to see what Rāmānuja says about Kṛṣṇa that permits us to call Kṛṣṇa 'God', and thereafter to see what such a God means for him. But we have to explore too what *brahman* means for Rāmānuja, in order to see what 'God' is for him. We have to ensure that, even if Rāmānuja locates an account of *brahman* within a larger theology of Kṛṣṇa, and we have seen Śaṅkara do the opposite, the difference between Rāmānuja and Śaṅkara is more than a mere switching of names such that Śaṅkara's *brahman* is Rāmānuja's God (Kṛṣṇa) and *vice versa*.[2]

I hope to show here that, while Rāmānuja uses '*brahman*' in a way that can exegetically be rooted in the *Gītā* and share some significant conceptual sense with Śaṅkara's use of it – centring around notions of being – he also circumscribes it in a way that significantly opens up his radical vision of Kṛṣṇa/Nārāyaṇa as *bhagavān* (Lord). The upshot is that, while both of them use the word 'God' to describe Kṛṣṇa, they interpret the nature and significance of Kṛṣṇa, and thus the ultimate import of 'God/the Lord' (*īśvara/bhagavān*) very differently. So we must first ask what Rāmānuja means by '*brahman*', just as we did with Śaṅkara.

An inquiry into being/s: The world, the body and the self

In what follows, as with Śaṅkara, I talk of 'beings' when the Sanskrit refers to human individuals, or animals, creatures or 'the world' (*jagat*) in the sense of humanity; the 'being' of beings, that is to say, of their totality, when the Sanskrit uses '*bhūta*', and their 'existence' for '*sattā*'. How 'being as such' ('Being' in Christian or Heideggerian terms, but one I am reluctant to use when translating from Sanskrit) relates to *brahman* for Rāmānuja is the issue I am trying to explore, given that we have seen what it meant for Śaṅkara.

We must first locate Rāmānuja's understanding of *brahman* within a pluralist ontology that decisively rejects Śaṅkara's view that the mutable order and material diversity are ultimately non-being. Precisely in opposition to Śaṅkara, Rāmānuja asserts that there are two distinctions. The first one concerns 'the Lord of all' (*sarveśvara*) who is the supreme self (*paramātma*) and 'the selves that know the field/body' (*kṣetrajñā'tmanaḥ*) (p. 63/33).[3] He draws this out of Kṛṣṇa's saying at 2.12 that, 'There never was a time that I did not exist, nor you…Nor will we cease to exist, all of us…' Whereas Śaṅkara has to say that the use of the plural (*bahuvacanam*) refers to the difference merely between individual bodies[4] and therefore less than real (since all materiality – *prakṛti* – is ultimately non-being), Rāmānuja uses the directness of the verse to assert that the difference (*bheda*) indicated here is ultimate (*pāramārthika*) (p. 63/34). As we will see, this 'ultimate difference' is qualified in interesting ways; for Rāmānuja's position is, after all, called 'Qualified Non-dualism'. But as a first statement, it indicates that his exploration of the question of being is going to differ from Śaṅkara's.

The second distinction concerns self and the body. Rāmānuja does not want to treat the material world as ultimately non-being, but he does have to explain the key contrast at 2.16: 'For that which is non-existent (*asat*), no being (*bhāva*) is found; for that which is existent (*sat*), no non-being (*abhāva*) is found. But the core (*antaḥ*) of both of these has indeed been seen by the seers of reality.'[5] How is 'non-being' to be understood here in a way that does not treat the mutable, material world as of a different order of being in relation to self? Rāmānuja's answer is ingenious: 'For the non-existent, the body, being as an existent is not found, and for the existent, the self, no being as a non-existent [is found].'[6] That is to say, Rāmānuja reads the verse as offering two categories of being (*bhāva*), namely, being as an existent (*sadbhāva*), and what is not found thus. While the *ātman* self-evidently has being through its nature as an existent, the body's being lacks such existence. This can make sense only if 'non-existence' – a term found in the *Gītā* verse, which cannot therefore be avoided – is defined in such a way as to not open the chasm between being and non-being that Śaṅkara discerned. This Rāmānuja proceeds to do. 'Non-existence is that which has destruction as its intrinsic being; and existence is that which has non-destruction as its intrinsic being.'[7] This does not mean that, just because the body is perishable, it is non-being (as Śaṅkara would have it). Rather, it just means that the perishable, or that which undergoes destruction, is called 'non-existent' (by Kṛṣṇa). It is being itself that can be polarised into two orders of being, the indestructible, imperishable selves and destructible, perishable bodies. There are simply two orders of being under being as such. Why then does Kṛṣṇa make this distinction? 'To quell that delusion of his (Arjuna's) – the delusion from ignorance of the intrinsic being of body and self [respectively] – what is to be taught is discrimination between the two: that whose intrinsic being has destructibility as its form and that which has indestructibility [as that form]'.[8] Kṛṣṇa is only using the existence/non-existence binary as proxy for two orders of being, the indestructible and the destructible. In taking the body to be the self (the exact nature of which error we will explore in the next chapter, on the self), Arjuna is taking the one for the other. There is no ontological issue of being and non-being here.

For Rāmānuja then, there is God, there are selves, and there is the material world. The question of the relationship between God and being will concern us soon enough, in the following section of this chapter. For the moment, let us concentrate on Rāmānuja's ingenuity (in the face of *Gītā* 2.16) in preserving a plurality of selves and the material world (including the body) within the realm of being. This permits him to say that both are *brahman*. This does create a tension within his gnostic project of self-realization, which he strives to resolve.

First, we have him declare that the material world, including embodying materiality, is *brahman*. He takes Kṛṣṇa to be saying at 3.15: 'Know sacrificial action to come into being from *brahman*, and *brahman* to come into being from the imperishable.'[9] On this, he says, 'the term "*brahman*" connotes the body, which is of the form of modifications of materiality...[and] in "*brahman* comes into being from the imperishable", the term "imperishable" connotes the individual self (*jīvātma*); the body satisfied by food and drink, which is governed by the imperishable, is the source of sacrificial action; so the body, which is in fact the instrument of sacrificial action, is said to come into being from the imperishable.'[10] By reading origination metaphorically – the phrase that the body 'comes into being' from the self is taken as merely its becoming instrumental due to the self – Rāmānuja preserves the reality of the two orders of being involved, the self and materiality. What is interesting is that, in contexts such as these and elsewhere, e.g. at 5.10 (p. 196/187), Rāmānuja explicitly identifies *brahman* with materiality (*prakṛti*).

Second, of course, is the standard identification of *brahman* with *ātman*, which Rāmānuja uses frequently, although we will see both in this chapter and the next that he interprets this identification very differently from Śaṅkara, especially in relation to God. So, just a few verses after identifying *brahman* with materiality, he takes up this other identification at 5.19, where Kṛṣṇa says, 'when faultless, *brahman* is impartial' (*nirdoṣaṃ hi samaṃ brahma*). Rāmānuja glosses it thus: '*brahman* is automatically impartial when detached from the faults associated with materiality.'[11] The impartiality of *brahman* consists in its being the same everywhere, that is to say, equally present under the condition of freedom from materiality. Here, *brahman* is the being of the individual self, and therefore precisely not materiality. Soon thereafter, at 5.24, Kṛṣṇa calls the *yogin* (the spiritually disciplined individual) the one who, becoming *brahman*, attains *brahman*'s freedom (*sa yogī brahmanirvāṇaṃ brahmabhūto 'dhigacchati*). Rāmānuja says the *yogin* is one who lives solely on the gnosis of the self (*ātmaikajñāno yo vartate*), and defines his attainment as his getting the joy of experiencing the self (*ātmānubhavasukham*) (p. 207/197). The spiritual adept exists as an enselved body, and his phenomenological attainment consists in realizing that the self is not that body. The self purified of identification with the materiality of the body is being itself, *brahman*.

Strangely then, subjective being is being when it attains consciousness of its freedom from material being, although being itself is both the subjective self and the inert material with which it finds itself entangled. Rāmānuja, in wanting to preserve a robustly pluralist sense of being, permits a tension to arise between having different orders of being while also taking our gnostic *telos* to consist in the freedom of one from the other order. Why are the orders of being so entangled and how is subjective being to attain its freedom?

Rāmānuja offers his own interpretation of *māyā*, which can literally mean 'illusion' and which we saw Śaṅkara take to mean the ultimate non-being of the changing phenomenal world. He cannot completely ignore the basic meaning of *māyā* as involving some sort of deception, but he uses it in such a way as to explain the entanglement of two orders of being and indicate that subjective being (selves) may free themselves from material being. When Kṛṣṇa talks (7.14) of 'my *māyā*, consisting of the three qualitative states (*guṇas*)' – purity (*sattva*), urgency (*rajas*) and stolidity (*tamas*) – under which all matter has being, Rāmānuja is quick to point out that *māyā* – in the sense of God's illusory power – does not have the meaning of ontological falsity or unreality (*mithyā*). It can be used figuratively (*aupacārika*), to talk of incantations and potions through which unreal objects give real impressions, but the primary sense of *māyā* does not concern unreal objects but the real mental impression of an object (*buddhiviṣaya*). This immediately indicates that the error of taking what is not the case – which is the fundamental nature of illusion – is not an implication about the non-being of something. Rather, error lies only in not taking what there is as what it really is. Therefore, *māyā* generates only misidentification in experience of the qualities of being, not in the representation of non-being in experience. Rāmānuja neatly quotes from the *Śvetāśvatara Upaniṣad* 4.10 (p. 253/246): 'Know then that *māyā* to be materiality and the *māyin* to be the great God.'[12] The creative power to generate impressions is ultimately real (*pāramārthika*), since it comes out of just the qualitative constituents of material being. What then is the error caused by power – implicitly, the power of illusion, the power to generate misleading impressions – here? 'It conceals the intrinsic form of the Lord and makes the mind naturally enjoy its objects. Thus, through the Lord's creative power of illusion (*māyā*), the whole world is deluded and does not realise that the Lord's intrinsic form is that of limitless, exceeding bliss.'[13] Rāmānuja therefore takes the implication of illusion which is contained in the ordinary meaning of *māyā*, and draws out of it a more general notion of creative force, the divine capacity to wright materiality in experienced forms whose penultimacy we are liable, in our insightless epistemic state, to misidentify as ultimately real.

We are thus beings who erroneously take ourselves to belong to another order of being, namely, materiality. Realizing our being as being free of materiality brings us endless joy – but the very condition of our normal being is unfreedom brought about precisely through God's own illusory power by which materiality is structured. We have to see beyond this to the God who is concealed from us. But we are blessed because God gives us a guarantee: 7.14 finishes with Kṛṣṇa's promise of deliverance, that all those who take refuge in me (*prapadyante*) shall pass beyond *māyā*, that is to say, beyond subjection to epistemic failure in the face of divine creative force. The reality of subjective being's misidentification with material being can only be removed through God's intervention. And in that sense, Kṛṣṇa's teachings in the *Gītā* point to how being can be delivered from being. Understanding the relationship between God and being, then, becomes the next step that we must take.

God, self and God as self: The nature and role of a revelatory ontotheology

We have, then, seen that Rāmānuja uses *brahman* to mean at least two orders of being under which beings come – the subject self in itself (of which there are many), and materiality (which is made up of an infinite number of things). In his commentaries concerning Upaniṣadic teachings, centred as they are on a doctrine of *brahman*, he perhaps has much more to say about a theistic interpretation of the term. In the *Gītā* commentary, on the other hand, given the centrality of Kṛṣṇa himself and Kṛṣṇa's eclectic teachings on *brahman*, it seems that Rāmānuja has the freedom to work out different dimensions to the concept of *brahman*. Inescapably, the conventional Vedāntic identification of Kṛṣṇa and *brahman* must be found in the text (as in 10.12, where Arjuna calls Kṛṣṇa *paraṃ brahma*), but as we saw with Śaṅkara, both the difficulty and the hermeneutic opportunity come from the fact that the *Gītā* is not explicit in what it says about Kṛṣṇa and *brahman*. This permitted Śaṅkara to bring Kṛṣṇa, and thus any theology, under the scope of *brahman*, in an asymmetric non-duality. Rāmānuja, in the introduction itself, addresses Kṛṣṇa as Nārāyaṇa, the *paraṃ brahma* and the *puruṣottama* (p. 41/10). The devotional term for Kṛṣṇa, *puruṣottama*, means the 'foremost person', and its significance – although not always systematically articulated by Rāmānuja himself – will emerge when we consider the theology beyond metaphysics that I argue is found in Rāmānuja.

For now, we find that the standard way in which he links Kṛṣṇa and *brahman* together is through the term '*paraṃ brahma*'; and God is therefore the third way in which Rāmānuja interprets '*brahman*'. Rāmānuja takes God's being to be related asymmetrically to selves and world in both a constitutive and a summative way. God's being makes up and unites within it the being of selves and world; but God's being is also being as such, or culminating being that defines the being of individual and material beings. He does not make the distinction clearly, and treats them as two ways of expressing the same truth: as *brahman*, God is being with sovereignty (*aiśvarya*). The *brahman* who is thus is '*param*', and an interpretation of that semantically generous prefix will help us understand the complex registers of

Rāmānuja's linking of *brahman* with Kṛṣṇa/Nārāyaṇa. But first we must start with the clear evidence that, in linking *brahman* that is the order of selves and the *brahman* that is the material world with the *brahman* that is God, Rāmānuja essays an ontotheology.

Ontotheology: An outline of Christian responses to Heidegger

From the long and complex discussions since Heidegger's reading of the Western past as ontotheology, I want to pick up a few strands that may help structure my reading of Rāmānuja (and in turn bring out the novelty of his method in the context of contemporary postmodern Christian theology). The minimal claim that can be made of what Heidegger said about ontotheology is that he argued that while ontology is metaphysics which thinks of what is common to all entities, theology is metaphysics which thinks of entity as such in totality, i.e., the highest entity which grounds them all.[14] As Prudhomme neatly puts it, 'In such a system, God presents the "not" in virtue of which beings can be represented as a whole. Divine being, as self-caused being, provides the "other" in terms of which all nondivine being may be defined and so be accounted for...God is also a being alongside other beings, albeit the highest or "most beingful" of all beings' (p. 110). Heidegger's analysis is seen as ending in the claim that for the history of Western thought, God is self-caused being, one amongst, albeit other than and superior to, other beings.[15]

Ontotheology, for Heidegger, renders God an entity amongst others, a God who is a being and not Being. Quite apart from Heidegger, there is the widespread notion associated with this line of thought, of a God who must therefore be proven to exist as any other being must, albeit on grounds special to being that particular entity. At least going back to Hume, arguments for the existence of such a being have been eviscerated in the Western tradition, although as John Clayton has astutely argued, the dismissal of proofs for the existence of such a God were made several centuries previously by Rāmānuja himself in the *Śrī Bhāṣya*, which he drew from earlier Indian tradition.[16] Rāmānuja demonstrates in that text that God is not an entity, howsoever endowed with maximal qualities, that can then become the object of epistemic activity aimed at establishing proofs of existence. In the *Gītābhāṣya*, Rāmānuja has no interest in affirming the existence of a being apart from and superior to other beings, as we will see.

The more profound relationship between God and being (or rather, Being) in the Western tradition is especially associated with Aquinas' development of Augustine's argument that Exodus 3.14's Biblical '*Ehyeh 'aser 'ehyeh*, when rendered in Latin as *ego sum qui sum* (which we have seen in turn become in English, 'I am that I am'), is effectively the *esse* or existence of metaphysics. As Paul Ricœur has pointed out in his analysis of the French scholar of medieval philosophy, Etienne Gilson, 'Without the book of Exodus, philosophers would have never reached the idea that Being is the proper name of God and that this name designates God's very essence'.[17] It is not so clear that this alignment of God and Being, the Thomistic understanding of Being as the name of God (without thereby collapsing God to Being, let alone a being) is subject to Heidegger's criticism of ontotheology. This indicates that the debates over ontotheology since Heidegger have led to different positions (not the least of which is what Heidegger himself felt about theology, but that is not a question for this book). Clarifying some of these positions will help me sketch out the relevance of at least one approach to ontotheology for my reading of Rāmānuja.

We have already looked at the view that ontotheology is highly problematic if seen primarily as the treatment of God as a being (albeit the supreme one) amongst beings; and, in any case, it was dismissed by Rāmānuja many centuries before comparable developments in the West. There is also the view that ontotheology is any conjunction of God and Being, and that it must be rejected, because it is the subjection of theology to philosophy. On this view, being is the province of metaphysics and metaphysics the core of philosophy. If God is to be understood in terms of being, then faith is made secondary to reason. It follows that, for a Christian, ontotheology must be overcome by looking at the otherness of God as other than Being. The real import of Heideggerian criticism is then taken to be the subjugation of God to the human exploration of reality that is philosophy.[18] 'Perhaps onto-theology consists in the pride that refuses to accept the limits of human knowledge.'[19] Merold Westphal contrasts this with the life of faith, which he identifies with the one that Heidegger says is lacking, as when the latter complains that nowhere does man encounter himself in his true self, his essence.[20] Westphal claims that Heidegger is here adverting to the rediscovery of God's otherness, an otherness denied in ontotheology's collapsing of the difference between God and us through the commonality of Being. We will return at the end of this chapter to Rāmānuja's conception of God's otherness; but only after we have seen that he nevertheless detects a preliminary role for the metaphysics of being, at odds with Westphal's contrast between faith's exaltation of God's otherness and ontotheology's degradation of God.

Related to this rejection of ontotheology is Jean-Luc Marion's radical response to any equation of God and Being. Whether or not Aquinas made that equation (and Marion is not entirely persuasive that Aquinas did not), ontotheology as criticised by Heidegger is seen as a taint on theology. So God must be understood as somehow without Being, in Marion's phrase,[21] and be taken purely as love, a gift to humanity. The strategy of doing theology without metaphysics is now an established one; it includes Levinas' famous notion of God 'otherwise than being'. But staying with Marion, his tactic of drawing on the Christian apophatic tradition to indicate that God radically transcends reasoning (and thus the metaphysics of Being) has also attracted exegetical criticism – if from the unexpected quarter of Jacques Derrida. Derrida implicitly criticises Marion's position by arguing that even in the apophatic tradition, as in Dionysius, 'God is refused the predicate of existence, only in order to acknowledge his superior, inconceivable, and ineffable mode of being.'[22] So, even if God is above Being, God is spoken of in the apophatic traditions as what God is, as 'some hyperessentiality'.[23] Where Marion says that the God without Being is approached non-predicatively, in prayer, so that the inescapably predicative nature of talking about God and Being is avoided, Derrida responds that Marion mostly deals with praise of God, where something is said about someone.[24] The possibility of an approach to God that is not ontotheological (where ontotheology is the degradation of God) continues to be of great interest today, taking theologians in different directions.[25] We shall turn later to prayer and love in Rāmānuja's account of *bhakti*, as his God who is free of metaphysics comes into view. Meanwhile, let us look again at ontotheology, but in a way that does not problematize it, so that we can approach Rāmānuja's approach to God and being with an appreciation of what he is doing in his commentary.

It has also been argued that the medieval scholastics did not reduce God to a being, even the supreme one. They thought that there was a convergence of Being and God, with Being as a name for God. This left the full mystery of God beyond being, but Being was understood through God. Such an ontology 'does not correspond to the defaming criterion of ontotheology', argues Paul Ricœur.[26] From this reclamation of the link between God and Being, it is but one further step to the conclusion that there can be ontotheology free of Heidegger's defamation. What is required is not a wholesale rejection of any connection between God and Being but a nuanced understanding that God informs our metaphysics although we should not use metaphysics to claim whole understanding of God. Then what becomes important is not the rejection of ontotheology thus construed, but our attitude towards what we do with it. Although he says this in the very different context of offering his own phenomenology, Joeri Schrijvers' comment serves well to introduce what I want to say about Rāmānuja: 'Our comportment towards ontotheology might point to both the unavoidability of ontotheology and a proper comportment towards it.'[27]

What we will see below is that Rāmānuja offers a reading of what Kṛṣṇa says in the *Gītā* about *brahman* that links the *parabrahman* with *ātman brahman* and *prakṛti brahman*, while also placing the former beyond them. Given that the latter two have already clearly been shown to refer to two orders of being within which sentient individual beings and insentient materiality are instantiated, Rāmānuja's identification of the *parabrahman* with the Lord must certainly imply an ontotheology. What *brahman* is it that is God? It is that which is *para*, which indicates that which is supreme, ultimate, beyond. In the light of Derrida's analysis of Dionysius, the conclusion of which I have quoted above, and anticipating how best to read Rāmānuja in the following paragraphs, I want to suggest that the prefix 'hyper-' quite accurately captures the way '*para*' is used. Let us now turn to Rāmānuja's native ontotheology, before we examine its role and how it may be qualified by a fuller study of what Rāmānuja does with it. It is there that I will argue that Rāmānuja's is best understood as a 'revelatory ontotheology', albeit one that still has a parallel with older Christian tradition.

Hyper-being: Rāmānuja on the parabrahman and its relationship with being

Having explored some of the major strands of thinking about ontotheology in the contemporary Western literature, we can approach what seems indubitably to be the ontotheology of *brahman* in Rāmānuja. Let us start with the two ways in which Rāmānuja links God and being, which I have termed the constitutive and the summative.

Rāmānuja deploys several metaphorical linking concepts that indicate the constitutive nature of God's being. Commenting on 13.2, where Kṛṣṇa says, 'And know me as the knower of the field, in all fields',[28] Rāmānuja rejects the Advaitic reading on which this is a statement of the identity (*ekatvam*) of the individual self (*ātman*) and the ultimate self (*paramātman*) (p. 416/414). Rāmānuja will have none of it because he takes this to imply that the ultimate self, who is God (*īśvara*), is also marked by unknowing (*ajñāna*), given that the individual self is ordinarily unknowing of its identity with the former. He follows this criticism with a statement of what is 'real' (*tattvam*): 'Several sacred texts talk of the discrimination between the inherent form of insentient entities, sentient entities and the *brahman* beyond [them] in terms of experiential objects, experiencing subjectivity and sovereignty.'[29] His examples include *Śvetāśvatara Upaniṣad* 4.10: 'Know illusory power (*māyā*) to be materiality (*prakṛti*), and the master of illusory power (*māyin*) to be the great god (*maheśvara*).' Rāmānuja thus takes the *Gītā* to be teaching of God as *brahman* beyond the material *brahman* and the *brahman* of subjective-selves. 'Thus the *brahman* who has the sentient and the insentient, the gross and the subtle, as modes is indeed the effect and the cause, and so *brahman* is the substantial cause of the world.'[30] These modes form his body (*śarīra*).[31] Nevertheless, despite the sameness of being implied by such modality, the formative conditions are a composite (*saṃdhāta*), and so their intrinsic being is unmixed (*svabhāvāsaṃkaraḥ*). Rāmānuja therefore balances out his insistence on the pluralist ontology of a real difference between the being of individual selves, materiality and God with the insistence that God is also being that is beyond selfhood and materiality. Materiality and selves are related to sovereign being through their being modes of its ontological manifestation. Here, we need to understand a mode (*prakāra*), as Julius Lipner puts it, as 'a being, substantival or non-substantival, such that it has no *raison d'être* of its own apart from, or realization independent of, some other entity, namely the "mode-possessor"'.[32] So God as *brahman* is the mode-possessor, of which beings are modes.

Another standard way in which Rāmānuja takes the divine *brahman* to be constitutive of the being of selves and world is through the relational concept of accessory (*śeṣa*) and principal (*śeṣin*). With this concept too, Rāmānuja presents what he takes to be the *Gītā*'s way of explaining *brahman* as divine being differentiated from the rest and yet containing them. At 7.7, Kṛṣṇa says that there is nothing beyond him. Now, whereas *prakṛti* generally means materiality, in the sense of the physical world, at 7.5–6, Kṛṣṇa uses the word in a different way, and talks of his lower *prakṛti*, which applies to not only the physical elements but also the psychophysical constituents of the bodily subject. He contrasts this with his higher *prakṛti*, which is sentient, living being (*jīvabhūta*).[33] Rāmānuja gives under 7.7 a succinct statement of his view of the relationship that Kṛṣṇa is taken to express. 'I am utterly beyond (*para*) everything in two ways. [i] I am the cause of both [higher – sentient, and lower – physical] *prakṛtis* and I am their principal. This principalship over insentient entities is caused through sentient entities, who are the principal of their bodies, which are made up of insentient materiality. [ii] I am also beyond all in the possession of the attributes of knowledge, power, strength, etc. There is no other that has by contrast attributes such as knowledge, power, strength, etc., in excess (*paratararam*) of me.'[34] So, as the individual subject-self is the principal of the (material) body, God is the principal of the self, and thus, indirectly, the causal regulator of materiality. This divine hyperbeing extends also to being the locus of maximal virtues, which are found in limited ways in individual beings. In this way, 'the world abides in its being as the body, with *brahman* as its self'.[35] Lest this be thought to imply that God is tied to sentient beings just as they in turn are to their bodies (which, after all, provide assistance (*upakāra*) to the functioning of sentient beings), Rāmānuja invokes Kṛṣṇa's statement at 7.12, 'I am not in them; they are in me'. He takes Kṛṣṇa to be saying, 'There is, however, no such purpose of any sort served [by their being my body]' (p. 250/243). This asymmetry is at the heart of Rāmānuja's understanding of the relationship between God and self, as taught by Kṛṣṇa himself. Rāmānuja keeps returning to this theme, for example, in 9.4, where Kṛṣṇa repeats his claim that, 'all beings abide in me' (*matsthāni sarvabhūtāni*), and Rāmānuja interprets this in terms of Kṛṣṇa's pervasion (*vyāpti*) of the 'entire universe' (*sarvaṃ jagat*) (p. 296/294). The notion of omnipresence here is not developed by Rāmānuja, but it contributes to the general theme that selves and world are given being by God, even when they have being distinct from each other (and therefore not non-dualistically existent as Śaṅkara would have it).

Kṛṣṇa then goes on to say at 9.5 that, nonetheless, beings do not abide in him, although he is the source of beings (*bhūtabhāvana*) and their supporter. Rāmānuja explains that such abiding is not a physical containment of being, for Kṛṣṇa is not a container (*dhāraka*), like a pot is of water (p. 297/295). But how else does the world abide (if not actually contained within God)? The answer lies in Kṛṣṇa's declaration in the same verse, 'My own self is the source of beings' (*mamātmā bhūtabhāvanaḥ*). Rāmānuja glosses this as Kṛṣṇa saying that he is the source as 'by my will' (*matsaṃkalpena*). This, Kṛṣṇa says, is his 'sovereign discipline' (*aiśvaraṃ yogam*). It is through this will that beings (*bhūtāni*) are produced, supported and regulated.[36] Kṛṣṇa is the God who wills beings into their nature, by pervading them with being. Rāmānuja also expresses this relationship as the one between the substratum (*ādhāra*) and the superstratum (*ādheya*). For example, he states that this is Kṛṣṇa's teaching: 'The self of everything, by being my body, has me as substratum, has being [only] as my accessory, is actuated by me alone.'[37]

These are the main ways in which Rāmānuja expresses the view that God's being constitutes the subjective and insentient orders of being. But, as I mentioned earlier, he also talks of God's being in a summative way, in which the being of beings is God, such that to talk of beings and orders of being is ultimately to end up talking of the God who renders them as they are. Rāmānuja primarily articulates this way of talking of God and being through the grammatical notion of co-ordinate predication (*sāmānādhikaraṇya*). Under 10.20, he explains the notion in a deceptively simple manner: although the significations of words (*śabdāḥ*) commence (*pratipādyanti*) from the body (*śarīra*) of 'deity', 'man', 'bird', 'tree', etc., they culminate (*paryavasyanti*) in the self – which is the Lord (*bhagavān*) (p. 342/343). They are inseparable from (literally, have 'no-being-without', *avinābhāva*) him. This is what makes God the condition of being the self (*ātmatayā'vasthāna*) of all beings (*sarvabhutani*). So, ultimately all that is said of beings and their being is said of God's being. This is reiterated at 10.39, where Kṛṣṇa affirms, 'No being, mobile or immobile, is, without me.'[38] He reiterates that God being the self of all is the reason that he is denoted by everything through co-ordinate predication.[39]

We have seen before that Rāmānuja is realist about orders of being: individual selves and material objects exist separately, and are not, either as non-existents or as sub-reals, collapsible into being, in the way Śaṅkara would have it. What Rāmānuja says here about co-ordinate predication appears to be in tension with that realism. However, as Lipner has insightfully brought out,[40] Rāmānuja uses the concept for two different purposes, although both derive an ontological insight from a linguistic (or as Lipner expresses it, epistemological) concept. Everyone agrees that there is common language usage in which a single substantive is denoted through a differentiated and differentiating set of predicates: Devadatta is young, dark, magnanimous and well-bred, to use Rāmānuja's standard example. Śaṅkara would want this ordinary language implication to be set aside when talking of *brahman* as existence, consciousness and bliss, such that there is no differentiation of *brahman* implied but merely conceptual proliferation of the undifferentiated and undifferentiateable *brahman*. In the normal course (in what Lipner calls the view 'from below'), Rāmānuja disagrees, and says that ordinary language shows precisely the substantival being of the object and the ontological differentiation of the qualities predicated of it in co-ordinate predication. Having thus affirmed pluralist realism, Rāmānuja also offers his view 'from above', in which 'identity' is affirmed. This is what I interpret as Rāmānuja's summative notion of being: all beings and their being culminate in the hyperbeing of God.

This conception of God's being is powerfully expressed in Kṛṣṇa's declaration at 10.39 that he is the 'seed of beings' (*bījabhūtam*). Rāmānuja expatiates: 'All genera, in all states, are unified in my being their self'.[41] The most extended exploration of the relationship between God and the being of beings – conceived as God's selfhood amongst all beings – is in the celebrated commentary on 13.2, which we will remember was also given great importance by Śaṅkara. Kṛṣṇa's words at 13.2 are: 'I am the knower of the field (*kṣetrajña*) in all the fields. That is gnosis (*jñāna*) which is knowledge of the field and of the knower of the field.' Rāmānuja meditates on the meaning of these words (pp. 415–16/412–16) thus. The field – i.e., body – is a qualifying attribute (*viśeṣaṇa*) of the field-knower, and as such does not exist apart from (*pṛthak*) the latter; so, co-ordinate predication describes (*nirdeśya*) them as being of one essential nature ('own-being': *ekasvabhāva*). Kṛṣṇa is taken to be saying in effect, 'In the same way, both the field and the field-knower are qualifying attributes of mine, do not exist apart from me, and through co-ordinate predication, are described as being of one nature with me.' The field of material aggregates and the field-knower that is the individual self together are the body (*śarīra*) of the Lord (*bhagavān*). Co-ordinate predication is possible because their intrinsic form is naturally one (*ekasvabhāvasvarūpa*) with God. He is their self (*ātman*), and their inner controller (*antaryāmin*). Co-ordinate predication therefore harmonises the issue of separateness (*vivekaviṣaya*) and the issue of 'my being the self' (*madātmakatvaviṣaya*) of all.

At this point, Rāmānuja presents the Advaitic view of co-ordinate predication, which we have touched upon already. 'Some say' (*kecid āhuḥ*) that, by coordinate prediction, only the identity (*ekatvam*) of the field-knower and God is to be understood. They maintain that it should be understood that, through primal agnosis (*ajñāna*), God (*īśvara*) becomes the field-knower. The teaching of identity (*ekatvopadeśa*) removes this agnosis. The Lord becomes the authoritative person (*āpta*) to remove the erroneous notion (*bhrama*) that the cogniser of the field is an individuated locus of consciousness, just as the authoritative person removes the erroneous notion of the snake by saying, 'this is a rope, not a snake'. Rāmānuja goes on bitterly that these inquirers (*te praṣṭavyāḥ*) should be questioned about what they say of the teacher (*upadeṣṭā*), Lord Vāsudeva. Has his primal agnosis (*ajñāna*) been removed by 'realisation of the real self' (*ātmayāthātmyasākṣātkāra*) or not? If it has been removed, then there would be only the self 'in reality, the one objectless, pure consciousness' (*nirviśeṣacinmātraikasvarūpa*), allowing of no such differentiation (*bheda*) as Arjuna, the act (*vyāpāra*) of teaching (*upadeśa*), and so on. If it has not been removed, in the absence of such realization, it would not be the case that God could even begin to teach self-gnosis (*ātmajñāna*). (Interestingly, then, Rāmānuja's criticism here is not so much directed at the possibility of an ignorant god as the coherence of teaching by a realized consciousness. God has to be truth-knowing already, and that truth cannot be strict non-duality.)

Rāmānuja offers a tri-partite view in place of Śaṅkara's strict non-duality: the insentient (*acit*) is that which is enjoyed (*bhogyatva*), the sentient (*cit*) is the enjoyer (*bhoktṛtva*), and the hyper-*brahman* (*parasya brahman*) is the sovereign (*īśitṛtva*). The first, which is cosmogonic matter (*pradhāna*) is perishable (*kṣara*), the second, which is the *ātman*, is imperishable and immortal (*amṛta*) and called Hara, while God (*deva*) alone rules over them (he quotes the *Śvetāśvatara Upaniṣad* 1.10 to this effect). Rāmānuja glosses 'Hara' (the seizer) as 'the one who seizes matter as the object of enjoyment' (*pradhānaṃ bhogyatvena haratīti haraḥ*). He then integrates (pp. 417–18/420–1) this tripartite scheme with the leitmotif of the body metaphor: the insentient and the sentient as enjoyed and enjoyer together, in all their states (*sarvāvasthā*) – both gross (*sthūla*) and subtle (*sūkṣma*) – are 'the body of the supreme person' (*paramapuruṣaśarīra*). This makes Him 'the form of the world' (*jagadrūpa*), both in the state of cause (*kāraṇāvasthā*) and the state of effect (*kāryāvasthā*). Since, in Rāmānuja's causal theory, cause and effect are identical (*ananya*), when there is right cognition of the cause (*kāraṇavijñāna*), there is right cognition of the effect (*kāryavijñāna*). When there is correct cognition of the one (the One, i.e. God) (*ekavijñāna*), there is correct cognition of everything (*sarvavijñāna*) else.

The divinity (*devatā*) is the very self (*svātman*) of individual beings (*jīvāḥ*), and they, having entered into (*anupraviśya*) non-sentient matter (*acit*), generate all the 'expressions distinguishing name and form'.[42] This is why 'all expressive terms' (*sarve vācakāḥ śabdāḥ*) actually express something about the 'supreme self qualified by non-sentient matter and individual beings'.[43] In other words, co-ordinate predication of terms for an effect become (*vṛtta*) terms for the supreme self in its state as cause. This presents a version of unity, which is clearly implied in the verse – but Rāmānuja sets it up in such a way that that identity is quite different from the one enunciated by Śaṅkara. He balances this expression of identity with a qualification: the material cause of the world is made up of *brahman* (the controller – *niyantṛtva*), sentient entities (the enjoyers) and insentient matter (that which is enjoyed), and therefore a composite (*saṃghāta*), such that there is no 'mixing' (*saṃkara*) of their essential being (*svabhāva*). The analogy he offers is of a cloth, woven out of red, white and black thread (the composite cause), which are separate, even as they form the single cloth (the effect), without the individual coloured threads losing their individuality. Rāmānuja says that it is important to note here that the hyper-*brahman* is not changed (*avikṛta*) even when entering into the state of being an effect. This is because he enters the state of being an effect only by being the self of both sentient beings and non-sentient things in their named and formed natures. Having argued for this qualified non-difference (although he never uses that term as such), Rāmānuja is free to acknowledge that, of course, while *brahman* is of the form of cognition (*jñānasvarūpa*), this *brahman* is omniscient (*sarvajña*) and omnipotent (*sarvaśakta*).

The opposed (*pratyanīka*) view – that *brahman*'s being the self of the manifold things (*brahmātmakavastunānātva*) is not [ultimately] true (*attatva*) because such things do not ultimately exist – must therefore be rejected. A realism concerning a plurality of beings and things is preserved; but being still has to be understood through God's being. Ontology for Rāmānuja is thus ontotheology – although it should be reiterated that this is only comparable to the Thomistic ontotheology of naming God as Being, and not the vulgar view, with which Rāmānuja has no truck, that God is the supreme Being amongst beings.

Gnosis, divine guidance and revelatory ontotheology

Philosophically, then, Rāmānuja understands our selfhood and the very fabric of the world in terms of God, and God as hyperbeing: both (i) being-as-such beyond the two orders of sentient and insentient being, and (ii) being from which the universal being of beings derives. The double supremacy of divine being – as both the most rigorous abstraction and the most complete encompassing of being – maps all reality through divine presence. But this is not a philosophical undertaking in which Rāmānuja seeks to grasp God through reasoning about being; quite the opposite. We have already noted that elsewhere, in the *Śrī Bhāṣya*, he has been seen to reject any possibility of inferring the existence (and even the being) of God (in this, indeed, he is not like Aquinas, who uses analogical proofs to claim that God exists, even though he admits that we cannot know what God is). In the *Gītā* commentary, certainly, Rāmānuja takes himself only to be seeking to understand what God has revealed. The ontotheology presented to us, while undoubtedly requiring human reasoning – hence the theological work of the devout exegete – is ultimately authoritative only because Kṛṣṇa himself teaches it. For that reason, the charge of philosophical egotism levelled at ontotheology cannot be attached to Rāmānuja. The transition in the history of Christian interest in God and Being illustrates this point nicely. As Paul Ricœur puts it, in the late twelfth and early thirteenth century, 'progress in the affirmation of the intelligibility of Being tended to render superfluous the self-affirmation of the Being of God according to Exodus 3:14. Recourse to this verse tended to become an extrinsic confirmation….'[44] Aquinas, of course, represents a powerful example of this, as he treats the systematic effort to understand God as a divine science.[45] Rāmānuja does not subordinate Kṛṣṇa's words to his (Rāmānuja's) own reasoning, but represents his commentary as only an expatiation on God's promise; he offers, one could say, drawing on Christian terminology, an eschatological reading of the ontology. In sum, the purpose of the ontotheology as revealed by Kṛṣṇa (and not 'constructed' through reasoning by Rāmānuja) is to guide Arjuna, and therefore the rest of humanity, to the salvific horizon. As we go through the commentary with this consideration in mind, we see how the mapping of being onto the hyper-*brahman* is meant to discipline the sentience of the individual self towards gnosis. Even this is not the *telos*, the highest good (*niḥśreyasa*) of sentient beings, but a preparatory step – but that will then take us on to a radically different conception of God as well, a God utterly other than that indicated in (although still encompassing) the ontotheology. For the present, I want to offer this understanding of what Rāmānuja takes Kṛṣṇa to be teaching: a revelatory ontotheology as declaration by God of a relationship of our being with God, a relationship willed by God.

We have seen how Rāmānuja often draws on the notion of selves and the world as God's body, as a way of indicating the infusion of being into the world and us. He also shows how we should understand this as Kṛṣṇa's guidance for spiritual discipline. At 3.30, Kṛṣṇa says: 'Offer up all your actions to me, with thought on your highest self, when you have become without desire, without 'mineness', then fight, with the fever gone.'[46] Rāmānuja expatiates: 'By contemplating on the form of the self as actuated by me through its [i.e., the self] embodying me, offer up all actions to me as done by me alone, the supreme person; and doing everything as purely worship to me, become free of desire and, thus devoid of the 'mineness' of action, with the fever [of our passions] gone, do battle and so on.'[47] The call to act free of desire – as we will see in the next chapter, the key element of the moral psychology taught in the *Gītā* – for Rāmānuja flows from an understanding of the self as imbued with God's being. A similar point is made at 7.19, when Kṛṣṇa talks of the one who has realized that 'Vāsudeva is all (*sarvam*)'. Rāmānuja reads this non-dualistic declaration through the apparatus of his notion of the principal and the accessory. It is the attainment of this realization, at the end of innumerable, blessed births: 'I find deliverance in essentially being an accessory of Vāsudeva, dependent [on him] for my essential form, rest and activity'.[48] The ontotheology is therefore the basis of Kṛṣṇa's substantive teaching about how to think of oneself and act in this world.

The fact that the ontotheology is thus revealed automatically rules out its having been built through the arrogant endeavour of human intelligence; and Rāmānuja emphatically rejects the very need for a philosophical ascent of human understanding to the nature of being (an endeavour he implicitly imputes to Śaṅkara) in comparison with the spiritual vision of the ontotheological relationship. In a resonant verse, Kṛṣṇa takes everything back to *brahman*; and Rāmānuja reads the second half of the verse thus: '...*brahman* alone is attained by one absorbed in *brahman* in his activities'.[49] Rāmānuja says of this verse, 'the meaning is that it [i.e. the self] has to attain its own intrinsic form, which is to be *brahman* by having *brahman* as its self. The actions of one who acts aspiring for liberation are gnostic in their aspect, because they are yoked to contemplation of the hyper*brahman* as self; so, they are a direct means to accomplish the beholding of the self, without the application of [the discipline of] gnosis.'[50] That is, as clear as can be, a repudiation of any project to gain insight into being that is solely through the cognitive disciplining of subjective being. What is offered instead is the divine promise of the vision of the self's being, attained only through proper comportment towards divine teaching about being. Indeed, as Rāmānuja sees it, Kṛṣṇa explicitly and repeatedly locates his ontotheological teachings within the framework of divine promise, as when Kṛṣṇa says at 7.29 that those who resort to me (*mamāśritya*), 'they know this *brahman*' (*te tad brahma viduḥ*) (p. 267/260).

Rāmānuja also takes it that the doctrine of principal and accessory, by which he relates divine being with individuals and materiality in Kṛṣṇa's teachings, works primarily as a prompt to love of God. 'Absorbed in overwhelming love, contemplate on yourself and other factors such as the objects of worship, as determined by me, and therefore having an intrinsic being that finds existential delight (*rasa*) solely in being accessory to me.'[51] The teaching is a prompt in that it offers us an understanding of how it is that we come to relate to God; but it also offers us a modality of love, namely, a devotion which is expressed through awareness of our ontotheological relationship with God. Indeed, Rāmānuja offers an even more radically devotional reading of his own ontotheology: the supreme abode (*paramaṃ dhāma*) that Kṛṣṇa says is his, at 15.6 – the state of union of being, which ends the materiality-fixed (*prakṛtisthāna*) state that Kṛṣṇa mentions in 15.7 – is the supreme effulgence (*paraṃ jyothi*) of the self as a fraction (*aṃśa*) of Kṛṣṇa, a part of his divine power (*vibhūti*). While the being of the self partakes of divine being (and is thus an expression of an ontotheological truth), the capacity to attain that ultimate relationship is itself gifted by God, is itself the munificence of divine power (and thus subordinates the philosophical fact to the salvific act).

While Rāmānuja's primary lesson on revelatory ontotheology is the asymmetric relationship between the salvific God and the devoted individual, he also implies that the relatedness of, through, and in their being makes for the intimacy of ontological resemblance. It has been noted by Frank Clooney that in later Viśiṣṭādvaitins like Vedānta Deśika, we have a developed notion of the likeness of the individual self with God that enables a single fullness of being with God to be realized by liberated selves, a notion that brings to mind a parallel to the Christian understanding of *imago Dei*, especially in the sense of how Aquinas thought the blessed are made dei-form through the light of divine presence.[52] Rāmānuja talks of this too, which suggests that Deśika was working within a tradition outlined by the master himself. At 6.30, Kṛṣṇa says, 'The one who sees me in all things and sees all in me, I am not lost to that one and he is not lost to me.'[53] Rāmānuja uses this to link an ontotheological relationship between human being and God to a divine guarantee of presence. 'He who…has reached homogeneity of nature with me, as declared [in the sacred text, *Muṇḍaka Upaniṣad* 3.1.3], "Stainless, he attains the utmost likeness", sees all subject-selves (*ātmavastuni*) – rid of merit and demerit, stable in their essence ('own-form', *svarūpa*) – as like me; and [therefore] sees "all things", [i.e.] all subject-selves, in me and me in "all", [i.e.,] all subject-selves. That is to say, due to their mutual likeness, in seeing one he sees another to be the same. "I am not lost to one who [thus] sees the essence of the self, because of my likeness [to that self]; I do not become invisible to him. He, seeing his own self in likeness to me, always remains in my view when I see myself, for he is like me.'"[54]

In this intricate passage, Rāmānuja balances the non-duality and otherness of God in relation to our being, while also bringing out the triangular relationality that holds between each individual, others and God. He reads the *Gītā*'s own enigmatic enfolding of reality and God in God's self-declaration of mutuality in the way characteristic of his 'qualified non-dualism', through the notion of 'likeness' (to read '*sama*'/'*sāmya*' as 'identity' here would make his position unsustainable). For the being of the self to have likeness to God is to have a homogeneity of nature (*sādharmya*) – which is, in short, an expression of ontotheology. But this mapping of being is important, not as a philosophical discovery but because it provides the metaphysical basis for what I have called our triangular relationality: because of the nature of being thus, it is possible for the mature (*vipāka*) adept (*yogin*) to see the formal essence of the self (*ātman*) as qualitatively holding between one and another individual person. (The relationship between this formal self and the individual person will be explored in greater detail in the chapter on self.) The subject of such awareness realizes the subject in all other human objects. This can be seen as an ethical stance, in which the otherness of the plurality of individuals is underpinned by the sameness of their being. But crucially, the ethical stance is also a spiritual one, for each subject self, including one's own is also 'like' the self of God, so God is seen in the other, and God is never lost to one who so sees others. Even more significantly, one is never lost to God because God's eternal self-awareness reflects God's awareness of the individual self – God's seeing Godself is also God seeing the individual self. Thus there is a mutual iconicity between God and self. Having been taught the mutuality of being and otherness in this doctrine of likeness, it becomes possible for each of us to become the adept who does not lose God. Once more the revelatory nature of the ontotheology becomes emphatically a guide to our spiritual progress. This teaching is echoed elsewhere, as when Rāmānuja reads Kṛṣṇa's promise that 'one goes to the divine first person, meditating [on that] (8.8),[55] as 'one attains the likeness of my form' (*matsāmānākāro bhavati*; p. 275/269).

Rāmānuja, then, articulates his ontotheology as God's guidance to us about gnostic discipline and realization; but this teaching does not get to our true relationship with God. Whereas what gnosis offers us is the aspect of God's metaphysical encompassing of our being, the true relationship is one built on God's otherness: our devotional love for God and God's gracious love for us, together with the perils of estrangement that come from otherness. The revelatory ontotheology indicates our capacity for realizing being in our wholeness, which is but a part of the divine. We turn, now, from the non-dualism that Rāmānuja accepts in order to map our being on to God's, to his assertion of God's otherness.

Otherness and the meontology of the gracious God: Love, estrangement and eschatology

Rāmānuja is most concerned with our devotional love for God and God's grace. The God who is thus found cannot in any simple manner be identified as the God of his *brahman*-ontology; while God is, of course, *brahman*, God is more and other than *brahman*. For that reason, we may say that Rāmānuja's Kṛṣṇa/Nārāyaṇa lies beyond any ontology and is thought of only through our *bhakti*, our devotional love, requiring, as it were, a meontology which lies beyond the ontotheology we have just explored. In his classic and innovative study, John Carmen speculates ('admittedly guesswork' he says) on how Rāmānuja's generally loose usage of '*svarūpa*' ('own-form') and '*svabhāva*' ('own-being') might be understood in a more systematic way.[56] He argues that *svarūpa* generally tends to refer to what makes clear the distinction between the supreme self and all finite selves and other entities, the former being unique and free of all impurity. In comparison, *svabhāva* is used to indicate God's qualities in relation to and excluding what are modes and parts of his cosmic body (although Rāmānuja does not make this difference consistently).[57] He pertinently refers to the *Vedārthasaṃgraha's* distinction between *svarūpa* as what is 'free of adventitious adjuncts' and 'possessed of essential properties', and *svabhāva* as 'this essential form in the process of being and becoming with and through its essential qualities'.[58] Given that Rāmānuja himself is not consistent, I would not claim that his terminology exactly matches my interpretive distinction; but a useful shorthand would be to think that the ontotheological aspects of *brahman* by which a qualified non-duality with selves and world is established tends to fall under the category of God's *svabhāva* – own-being or essential being – as *brahman*, whereas God's divine otherness as sovereign, inscrutable, generous and compassionate Lordship is indicated as his *svarūpa* – own-form or intrinsic reality, whose exposition is strictly theological.

Rāmānuja usually (if loosely) associates the divine own-form with God's being the First Person, as opposed to the self of hyperbeing. He takes Kṛṣṇa to be both that hyperbeing and the God who is beyond being, expressible, in a paradoxically straightforward way – because of his own care for us – in terms of his concrete presence as Kṛṣṇa. Kṛṣṇa says, 'The insightless think of me as having become manifest; I am unmanifest. They do not know my supreme being, immutable and incomparable' (7.24).[59] Rāmānuja glosses this in a way that teases out the difference he makes between divine being and the God who is other than being. He takes Kṛṣṇa to be saying that while he is unmanifest (*avyaktaṃ*), those without insight think of him as having become manifest (*vyakti*) simply through the workings of *karma* (that is to say, as any being does across lives). But in fact, his supreme beingness (*paraṃ bhāvam*) is immutable (*avyaya*) and incomparable (*anuttatama*). In saying this, Rāmānuja re-states the distinction between hyperbeing and all other orders of being. Then he goes on to speak of the God who, while such being, is also love, and therefore not one who can be understood even in terms of the furthest reaches of our metaphysical understanding. He takes Kṛṣṇa to be saying that, although he is the God of all (*sarveśvara*), the one who has intrinsic nature and being that cannot be defined through language and mind,[60] and who is worshipped in all ritual acts (*sarvaiḥ karmabhir ārādhyaḥ*), because of compassion (*karuṇa*) and parental love (*vātsalya*), he descends amongst us as Vāsudeva (p. 263/257). While containing being, God is more and other than that, concretely present just because of love.

In short, for Rāmānuja, the God who breaks through (even revelatory) ontotheology is a God who comes within our compass out of divine love and compassion for us. Kṛṣṇa talks of his supreme beingness (*paraṃ bhāvam*) as the 'great God of beings' (*bhūtamaheśvara*) at 9.11. Śaṅkara glosses this as being 'the self (*ātman*) of all beings', within space itself (*ākāśātapyantaratama*) (p. 140), thereby characteristically reading the theology back into gnoseology. By contrast, Rāmānuja reads the term as referring to the God who is 'the sole cause of the entire universe' (*nikhilajagadekakāranaṃ*), the one who takes human form 'out of the greatest compassion for the world' (*paramakāruṇikatayā*) so that he can become 'the refuge of all' (*sarvasamāśraya*) (p. 302/300). The metaphysical dimension is retained, but only to be subsumed under what is the most urgent way in which we receive God, which is as the loving habitation of our lives.

The taking of human form – which is God's gifting of divine presence – is, of course, contained in the *avatāra* doctrine that Viṣṇu(-Nārāyaṇa) descends in various forms to save the world. This doctrine grew early on to incorporate the independent figure of Kṛṣṇa; in the *Gītā*, the relationship between the two figures is unclear and it appears more as if it is Kṛṣṇa himself who unambiguously declares his own descent.[61] For Rāmānuja, the doctrine has the settled form of Śrī Vaiṣṇava faith: it is Nārāyaṇa (or strictly speaking, Nārāyaṇa-with-Śrī, the divine consort Lakṣmī who embodies divine grace)[62] who takes the human form of Kṛṣṇa and reveals himself in the *Gītā*. Rāmānuja's reading of Kṛṣṇa's declaration of descent brings out powerfully the point that to take concrete form on earth is God's free choice or wish (*icchā*) and not a metaphysically structured event. At 4.6, Kṛṣṇa prefaces his famous declaration and promise of descent with these words: 'Although birthless, of imperishable self, and the God of all beings, [yet] by governing my own material nature, I come into being through my own creative force.'[63] Rāmānuja says that '*māyā*' here means wisdom (*vayuna*) or right cognition (*jñāna*). The creative force by which materiality is wrought by God into the human being who is Prince Vāsudeva is also divine knowledge, and is expressed as self-will (*ātmasaṃkalpa*) (p. 160/148). Rāmānuja takes Kṛṣṇa to be saying, 'Hence, without losing my quintessence of being the God of all – with uniformly auspicious qualities that belong to me, such as freedom from all sins, and so on – taking a form of the same kind as deities, humans, etc., I come into being through my very own will in the form of deities, etc.'[64] The freedom of God's will is such that the form taken is entirely unconstrained by previous consequential actions (*karma*); also, God does not cease to be God by becoming a being, like a deity or a human. Crucially, this exercise of unconstrained will is for the sake of the world, for in the famous verses that follow (and on which Rāmānuja barely comments, leaving them as self-evident) Kṛṣṇa says: 'Whenever *dharma* declines and the absence of *dharma* increases, O Bhārata, I produce myself. I come into being from age to age, for the establishment of *dharma* – as the refuge of those who do good and as the doom of those who do evil.'[65] Rāmānuja takes this even further than the doctrine of divine descent, and takes Kṛṣṇa to be promising his presence in whichever way people desire him: 'All people who follow me, experience my way, my nature, with their very own eyes, in all places, in every way they wish, even if it be beyond the ken of the speech and thought of yogic adepts.'[66] The gift of tangible presence is multiform.[67]

For this perspective – that of God's graciously gifting presence in the ways people seek it – it is important to note that Rāmānuja sees a God beyond the mappable being of revelatory ontotheology. This God is seen, this God makes himself tangible, this God gifts; this God is other. The very possibility of divine descent is expressed through otherness. As noted above, this descent is different from the cycles of rebirth which beings undergo, for it is utterly determined by divine self-will, unconstrained by the consequences of previous actions. As he paraphrases Kṛṣṇa at 9.9, 'There I sit as one sitting apart (*tatrodāsīnavadāsīnaḥ*).[68] The deeply personal nature of God's otherness presented in the doctrine of divine descent marks a sharp contrast to the revelatory ontotheology that we have looked at before. Indeed, one could say that this latter understanding of Rāmānuja's God is radically meontological; not in the metaphysical sense of God's not-being, but of God's otherness from being itself – which is, in that sense, strictly theological. The distancing of being from God is evident, for example in Rāmānuja's reading of higher/hyper (*paraṃ*) being (*bhāva*) at 8.20 where Kṛṣṇa talks of 'my highest abode' (*mama paramam dhāma*) at 8.21. Characteristically Śaṅkara takes 'my highest abode' to be 'my (Viṣṇu's) ultimate (*prakṛṣṭa*) state (*sthānaṃ*)',[69] thereby establishing complete non-duality. By contrast, Rāmānuja takes 'my highest abode' as 'the highest state under [my] control' (*paramaṃ niyamanasthānam*), which is '[the state of the *ātman*] detached from connection with the inanimate, settled in its own form, of the form of freedom.'[70] So, all elements of a pluralist reality – materiality, selves bound to that materiality, and selves freed of such bondage – are under a 'condition of control' (*niyamanasthānaṃ*) to Kṛṣṇa. And where Śaṅkara takes the 'person beyond' (*paraḥ puruṣaḥ*) 'inwith whom all beings stand' (*antaḥsthāni bhūtāni*) of 8.22 to be the *ātman*, thereby collapsing all difference into non-duality, Rāmānuja takes that person to be he who pervades all, Kṛṣṇa. It is because God is other that God's presence is gifted to us and all orders of being lie within God's power to infuse being.

A crucial element in this narrative of otherness is our relationship to God. At different places in the *Gītā*, Kṛṣṇa notes that people do not recognise him, take him to be simply the princely son of Vāsudeva. We have seen Śaṅkara immediately interpret this as indicative of agnosis. At 7.24, Kṛṣṇa says, 'The unintelligent think of me as having become manifest even thought I am unmanifest, not knowing of my being in the highest, which is immutable and unsurpassable.'[71] As I noted in the previous chapter, Śaṅkara explains this as undiscriminating people (*avivekinaḥ*) not being aware of Kṛṣṇa's being the highest, that is, Kṛṣṇa's being of 'the very form of the highest self' (*paramātmasvarūpaṃ*), instead taking him to be the hidden (*aprakāśa*) that has now become the revealed (*prakāśaṃ gatam idānīṃ*), whereas he is 'the ever-established' (*nityaprasiddha*) God (*īśvara*). Śaṅkara therefore asserts the greatest intimacy possible between us and another – that of identity, albeit one that is forgotten..

For Rāmānuja, by contrast, Kṛṣṇa's complaint about us points, not to agnosis, but estrangement. The foolishness (*mūḍhatva*) of people means that because of Kṛṣṇa's 'human semblance',[72] they do not know him as the God of all (*sarveśvara*), and that 'I have taken up the human condition for all who want to take refuge in me.'[73] Rāmānuja contrasts God's gifted love for us with our alienation from God. Such alienation is not, however, the symptom of a cognitive defect in which we are removed from self-understanding (that is to say, understanding the self that is God); rather, it marks a failure of affect. Here, under 7.25, Rāmānuja traces this failure to an epistemic shortcoming, where we do not recognise God as God. Elsewhere, he glosses Kṛṣṇa's complaint as pointing to a near-fatal moral defect on our part. At 9.11, when Kṛṣṇa again says, 'The foolish disregard me when I dwell in human form,'

Rāmānuja traces the disregard to the sinful actions (*pāpakarmabhiḥ*) of the foolish. That is to say, foolishness results from sinful actions. Much later, in the crucial commentary on 18.66, Rāmānuja takes Kṛṣṇa to explain what sin (*pāpa*) means, which defines precisely the sense of estrangement that we have been discussing: it is, he has Kṛṣṇa say, what is 'antithetical to attaining me' (*matprāptivirodha*).[74] This is sin in 'the form of all acts from beginingless time, constituted by doing what has not to be done and not doing what has to be.'[75]

My contrast here between Śaṅkara's and Rāmānuja's readings of Kṛṣṇa's complaint is fundamentally different from a distinction about the types of religion famously made by Paul Tillich in the mid-twentieth century. However, it is worth looking at it because it suggests an illuminating way of approaching our contrast between Śaṅkara and Rāmānuja. To quote the opening passage from his essay in full, 'One can distinguish two ways of approaching God: the way of overcoming estrangement and the way of meeting a stranger. In the first way, man discovers himself when he discovers God; he discovers something that is identical with *himself* although it transcends him infinitely, something from which he is estranged, but from which he never has been and never can be separated. In the second way man meets a *stranger* when he meets God. The meeting is accidental. Essentially they do not belong to each other. They may become friends on a tentative and conjectural basis. But there is no certainty about the stranger man has met.'[76] He calls the former the ontological and the latter the cosmological view. Setting aside the larger question of God within Śaṅkara's Advaita, we can discern a rough parallel between Tillich's distinction and the two Vedāntins. However, I do not see agnosis (*ajñāna*) – the absence of consciousness of non-duality – as estrangement, for the failure in Advaita is purely about the structural limitation of self-consciousness, whereas estrangement seems to me to be an emotional and relational state. Indeed, the way 'estrangement' semantically enfolds 'the stranger' strikes me as a lexical indication that estrangement is more accurately characterised of the Viśiṣṭādvaitic view of God as the other. There is indeed an element of accident in our meeting God, according to Rāmānuja, because, taking Kṛṣṇa's complaint seriously, we may not recognise him. But whether the strangeness of God calls for uncertainty in the manner Tillich envisages, I am not sure; for without the premise that God's revelation and promise in the *Gītā* is true, there can be no God at all for Rāmānuja. And Kṛṣṇa's (self-)declaration in the *Gītā* and his promise of the descent (*avatāra*) removes all uncertainty.[77]

Rāmānuja therefore conceives of the ordinary relationship between God and us as marred by our distancing ourselves from God through our actions, while God continually and lovingly presents his saving grace to us. We can turn in a moment to the overwhelming self-presentation of God that is the pinnacle in the middle of the *Gītā*, but first let us note that for Rāmānuja, the *Gītā* is not a pessimistic document of a perpetually asymmetric love between God and beings. Rāmānuja offers a lyrical and ecstatic explication of Kṛṣṇa's description of the greatest type of devotee. Kṛṣṇa says, 'I consider, of those yoked to spiritual discipline (the practitioners of *yoga*), the one most yoked to it to be the one who adores me with faith, who goes to me with the inmost self.'[78] Rāmānuja takes Kṛṣṇa to be saying this of the most excellent of all (*sarvebhyaś śreṣṭhatamaḥ*) yogis, that this is one who, "with the inmost self", i.e., with his mind, goes to me, with overflowing love for me, with intrinsic nature supported by none other [than me]; [who does so] "with faith", i.e., who due to loving me exceedingly, cannot bear a moment's separation and strives to attain me quickly; [who] "adores me"...i.e., attends to me, worships me intently.'[79] We are always capable of dissolving our alienation, because we have the capacity to love God with complete commitment, for separate though we are from God's personhood, our realization of our dependence for our very being on God (the lesson of revelatory ontotheology) has the affective consequence of our finding separation unbearable.

We have a threefold context for the eschatology that is offered through the theophany of the eleventh chapter: God gifts his presence out of love for all beings; we are estranged from God by the moral lapses of our agency; and yet we have in us a capacity for returning (to) love, a capacity in which God has faith. The veil that we draw over God's presence is pulled away in Kṛṣṇa's vision of cosmic form (*viśvarūpadarśana*). We will return to its ultimate lesson, about God as beyond metaphysical being, in the concluding part of this chapter. Here, I only want to remark that we must see the cosmic form of the *Gītā* within the context of Rāmānuja's theology; for, like Śaṅkara, he says very little directly on this chapter, letting the *Gītā* speak for itself, through the words of the charioteer God and the very human prince, about what is beyond speech. Kṛṣṇa's vision of cosmic form is the purest giving, what could be called a super-donation, for as the *Gītā* has it (e.g. 11.11) in this chapter, it indicates the eternal/infinite (*ananta*); when Kṛṣṇa says, 'I am world-destroying time, time grown old' (*kālo'smi lokakṣayakṛtpravṛddhaḥ*; 11.32), Rāmānuja notes of 'time' (*kāla*), 'time is calculative timing',[80] indicating that God is fulfilled time, within which are beings entangled materially in time. It is this infinitely other God who is revealed to us, after he has given Arjuna the divine eye (*divyaṃ cakṣuḥ*), which Rāmānuja glosses as extra-natural (*aprākṛta*) vision (11.8). With this visionary capacity, Arjuna sees all reality encompassed in the cosmic form.[81]

At once, then, all being is contained in God and God is wholly other than beings – nowise does the theophany offer God as supreme being or the most being of beings or even being-as-such; and certainly all that Rāmānuja says in the commentary on the chapters around the eleventh indicates nothing else. Instead, through the density of the mythic-poetic representation of reality – of sages and creatures, language and music, birth and gender and fame and fraudulence – Kṛṣṇa offers a vision to Arjuna through which the God beyond is indicated. It is hard not to think that this speaks of an iconicity that fits Merold Westphal's Christological description of a vision that 'transpierces it [the visible] towards the invisible of which it is a trace'.[82]

The theophany's potency lies in the vividness of the phenomenal givenness of God, both in self-declaration and in Arjuna's awe-filled and halting description. The promise of this eschatology is developed by Rāmānuja in the major commentary on 18.66, the significance of which will concern us in the chapter on self. The saturation indicated in chapter 11 is given, of course, by the personal presence of Kṛṣṇa, reinforced by his return to normal form; and Rāmānuja's view of divine personhood is an essential element of his meontological, supra-ontotheological theology.

Otherness and the divine person

We have now seen that Rāmānuja's non-dualist ontotheology is particularised – even subverted – through the meontology of a God of otherness. This otherness is deepened through his radical restriction of true personhood to God, even while it is presented as in fact leading to a deep attachment between God and us. In other words, while God's attachment links God and creature in the bonds of unconditional love, this bespeaks of God's otherness rather than non-duality.

The divine person as the only true person

We have already seen, albeit briefly, that human and other beings (gods, animals) are constituted by the entanglement of two orders of being, the sentient and the material, the self and body. It is a topic to which we will return in much greater detail in the chapter on self. But two points from previous discussions need to be reiterated here. First, a sentient being (the self) is under error, i.e. in agnosis, if it takes its true being to consist in the personhood given by identification with the material being of its body. Second, gnosis consists in the realization of the self's likeness to God. This likeness, we have seen, comes from the mapping of sentient being on to the being of God. But – and now we have Rāmānuja's undercutting of ontotheology – this does not imply that the freeing of self from the materially conditioned state of personhood topologises a God free of personhood. We are truly selves, not persons; but God, while the highest self, is also – and uniquely – the first person. God's personhood is not an erroneous construct of agnosis; and here we see a sharp contrast with Śaṅkara's view that the distinct personhood of God is primal error on the part of individuated consciousness (namely, human and other persons). The first person is the only true person for Rāmānuja, for the meontological God is the God who transcends ontotheology precisely by being the divine person. The material world is indeed the body of God, but God is not entangled with materiality: the true mystery of the divine person is that we cannot give an ontotheological account of that personhood, which for Rāmānuja is the duplexity of Nārāyaṇa-with-Śrī (Śrīman-Nārāyaṇa). As we have seen in the previous section, the loving grace with which God renders us aware of divine presence is expressed in the intense density of Kṛṣṇa's person. For example, when, at 9.26, Kṛṣṇa says 'I accept (*aśnāmi*)' whatever is offered by the devotee, Rāmānuja expatiates on who the 'I' is in the form of a self-declaration by Kṛṣṇa: 'I [am] the all-god, whose sport is the production, evolution and dissolution of the entire world, whose desires are wholly attained, whose will is true, whose auspicious qualities are limitless and pre-eminent, who enjoys the limitless and pre-eminent bliss that is intrinsic to me ...'[83]

The true and irreducible personhood of Kṛṣṇa is brought out at some length in a discussion of 15.12–17. In verses 12–15, Kṛṣṇa talks of himself as the light in the sun, the moon and fire, of entering the earth and sustaining all beings (*bhūtāni*), and as the personification of digestive fire (*Vaiśvānara*), residing in the bodies (*deha*) of all creatures (*prāṇinām*); and as seated in the heart of all, from whom comes memory, knowledge and their loss (*apohana*), from whom comes the Vedānta and who knows the Vedas.

This richly personal cosmology of Kṛṣṇa is then followed by the *Gītā*'s taxonomisation of persons. At 15.16, Kṛṣṇa says: 'There are two kinds of persons (*dvāv imau puruṣau*) in the world, called the perishable (*kṣara*) and the imperishable (*akṣara*). The perishable is all beings (*sarvāṇi bhūtāni*), the unchanged (*kūṭaṣtha*) is the imperishable.' Rāmānuja points out that this is the difference between the materiality-entangled self, which is the human person, and the free self: 'There [in the verse saying there are two kinds of persons], persons called perishable, and also called *jīvas* (individual selves), are all the beings, from Brahma [i.e. even the senior-most of the deities of the celestial realm] to a blade of grass, associated with insentient matter that is intrinsically perishable. Here, the term 'person' is treated as a singular to indicate the single (common) contingency of being formed through conjunction with insentient matter. That which is defined through the term 'imperishable', as immutable, separate from any conjunction with insentient matter, and settled in its own intrinsic form, is the free self. It is called 'immutable' since it lacks any conjunction with insentient matter and is without any specific connection to the causal transformations of such matter as the bodies of Brahma, etc. Here too the designation is singular, because of the single [common but generic] contingency of being without conjunction with insentient matter. But this does not mean that in beginningless time there was always just one free self.'[84] Apart from resisting the Advaitic reading of the singular as implying the non-duality of all free selves, Rāmānuja simply re-articulates the relationship between ordinary personhood and free selfhood, although, inconveniently, the *Gītā* talks of both of these states as belonging to persons. (It may be remembered that Śaṅkara has an even greater task, since he has to read this robust statement of two orders of existence within a non-realist metaphysics.) Personal identity is given by conjunction with materiality, and the immutable self is immutable precisely because it has no such identity dependent on causal transformation. In any case, the importance of this verse lies in its contrast with the next one, which takes us to the personhood of God.

Kṛṣṇa teaches at 15.17: 'But beyond this is the foremost person (*uttama puruṣa*), who is called the supreme self (*paramātma*)/and entering the three worlds, upholds them, as the unchanging (*avyaya*) God (*īśvara*).'

Rāmānuja is characteristically keen to emphasise the otherness of God discernable in this verse. 'Since all the sacred texts use the designation, "supreme self", it can be understood that the foremost person is an element with an entirely different meaning from the bound and free persons. How?'[85] Rāmānuja offers a response to his own question (p. 500/491): there are three worlds that God supports – that of the insentient (*acetana*), the sentient (*cetana*) that is associated with it, and that of freed selves (*muktāḥ*). From the fact that the *Gītā* talks of the supreme self 'entering and upholding' (*āviśya bibharti*) them, he concludes that it is an element or entity with an entirely different meaning (*arthāntarabhūta*). He also equates 'entering' with 'pervasion' (*vyāpti*), the completely spread presence of God. The foremost person is the God of the three worlds (*lokatrayasyeśvara*). By sharply distinguishing the foremost person from all the possible orders of being – matter, life, liberation – Rāmānuja re-emphasises the otherness of God.

Whereas Śaṅkara uses the *Gītā*'s interchangeable talk of 'foremost personhood' and 'supreme self' to dissolve divine personhood into the non-dual self, Rāmānuja does the opposite. He de-emphasizes the gnostically significant ontotheology – where the supremacy of divine selfhood consists in its being the self of all – that he himself has constructed, and focuses instead on the metaphoric sense of God's selfhood, as the pervasion of the three worlds of being. The selfhood of God, in this indirect sense, is not about the being of God, but only an indication of God's will to pervade the world. The density of God's personhood is not merely left intact but placed at the centre of our fumbling understanding of God's pervasive presence.

Interdependence and otherness

But Rāmānuja's theology always modulates itself, and just as the revelatory ontotheology gives way to God's otherness, so too the otherness implies a radical interdependence. Rāmānuja's expression of intense love of God in all of God's sheer personal transcendence takes him too to a deeply surprising[86] inversion of that transcendence. Already in the introduction to the commentary, he talks of Kṛṣṇa as 'helpless with tender affection for those who have taken refuge [in him]' (*āśritavātsalyavivaśaḥ*).[87] For Rāmānuja, this weakness of God's is not an alternative to a theology of ontic/ontological might, as has eloquently been espoused in the context of the Christian event by John Caputo.[88] Nevertheless, it is an important aspect of Rāmānuja's vision of the divine, and on the surface, at odds with both the revelatory ontotheology and the sheer otherness and sole personhood of Nārāyaṇa-with-Śrī.

Without doubt, it is clear that Rāmānuja does juxtapose the strength and the weakness of God, but he does so at unexpected points in the text. At 7.18, Kṛṣṇa says, 'I think the wise one (*jñāni*) to be my very self (*tv ātmaiva*)'. Where Śaṅkara sees this as simply the assertion of non-duality (God as the self and *vice versa*), Rāmānuja reads it as God's dependence (*ātmadhāraṇaṃ*) on the devotee. 'I too find that, without him, I cannot support Myself'.[89] The expectation of divine supremacy is subverted here through divine dependency, so that being each other becomes a mode of intense intimacy, with power exchanged, and cosmic order turned inside out. Yet this weakness of God does not, strangely enough, make God other than God, for it is not that God ceases to be God by being supported by the devotee; rather, God is God by deliberately being so supported. That is the power of spiritual intimacy.[90] Where Kṛṣṇa says, 'I am easily gained' (*ahaṃ sulabhaḥ*; 8.14), Rāmānuja has it, 'I am easily gained because, being unable to bear that separation from him, I myself choose him.'[91] Where before we have seen Kṛṣṇa offer unconditional love, as gift and as theophany, here we see him condition himself: the gift is given through a love that is unbearable for God to withhold. So, the gift of God's love is not seen here as something we desire to have (although it is that too), but something that God desires to give. In so giving love helplessly, Kṛṣṇa also receives our offering, not as sovereign accepting tribute (although he does that too) but as grateful donee. Kṛṣṇa says that devotees are generous (*udāraḥ*; 7.18), and Rāmānuja glosses these generous ones as donors (*vadānyāḥ*; p. 258/251). Thus we have 9.26's eager 'I accept' (*aśnāmi*), of whatever is given by the devotee – leaf, flower, fruit, some water: for Rāmānuja, Kṛṣṇa is saying that it is 'as if I had obtained something dear far beyond the reach of my heart's desire'.[92] God's declared incapacity to conceive of the power of our devotion says, of course, not so much about the greatness of our love as the way our love is made great by God's ultimate (and deliberate failure to) measure.

This is unsettling, and Carmen is probably right in drawing on a reading of Rāmānuja here than might sit more easily with the subsequent tradition itself.[93] He sees Rāmānuja here as offering a 'paradoxical reversal of values', which can be understood only as God's generosity (*audārya*). There is, as in 7.18, indeed a reversal, as the donor becomes the donee. To preserve the transcendence of God, Carmen has to say that it is God's generosity that leads to his calling his devotees generous, and quotes Vedānta Deśika to this effect.

But perhaps the tradition itself is too anxious to right Rāmānuja's radicalism here. He is willing to up the stakes even more. When, at 9.29 Kṛṣṇa says of devotees that, 'They are in Me and I in them' (*mayi te teṣu cāpy aham*), Rāmānuja goes further (p. 318/316), taking Kṛṣṇa to be saying that 'they dwell (*vartante*) in me' – 'as if their qualities are like mine' (*matsamānaguṇavat*) and 'I too dwell in them as if they were my superiors' (*aham api teṣu madutkṛṣṭeṣv iva varte*). So, the likeness we have seen before is not enough; Kṛṣṇa abnegates himself, fulfilling our humanity with his own humility. Perhaps we should not read God's personal eminence and deliberate self-abnegation as being in tension, and look to resolve it in favour of the former for fear that it may otherwise seem as if Rāmānuja was subverting the theology of divine pre-eminence. Instead, we could consider reading the whole theology presented in his commentary as a rhizomatic account of divine accessibility. As Gilles Deleuze and Félix Guattari developed the idea, which has become very influential,[94] a rhizome is a dynamic network system of multiple entryways (like underground roots, contrasted to an arborescent system that is vertical and linear). Instead of trying to impose some hierarchical order on Rāmānuja's gladly stated spiritual paradoxes, I suggest that we take God's sovereign grace and God's unbearable humility towards and longing for our love as simultaneously available and equally accessible. In his house are many mansions and they all have many doors …

The transition from revelatory ontotheology to the loving God who is other is clearly hierarchical – the former is merely the gnostic discipline that feeds into the pure devotion that is the proper response to the latter. However, the relationship between God's foremost personhood and self-abnegating dependence is rhizomatic. They are always and together the characteristics of the divine person, who is the only person. This is because their simultaneity is constituted by what God is for us, and we can see of God only what God is for us, no more. In that sense, the rhizomatic accessibility of God is the only meaningful way in which we can understand what God means, that is to say, means to us. So, even and precisely in being accessible, God's otherness – the sheer challenge presented by accessibility – is made clearer still. Being does not seek to access itself, for it is the condition of being that it is what it is. The accessibility (what subsequent commentators on Rāmānuja developed as the technical term '*saulabhya*' – well-gained) of God is not in tension with or subordinate to God's transcendence (what the tradition likewise termed '*paratva*' – otherness). Rather, access itself is a spatially coloured term that implies movement towards that which is other. This otherness, as we are beginning to see, is other than the being that ontotheology offers as the goal of gnostic discipline. We will conclude this theological reading with some consideration of Rāmānuja's God as the answer of otherness to the question of being.

The abode of being: Other than ontotheology

Rāmānuja strives, through the length of the commentary, to indicate the otherness of God and the love that comes with it (both from God and from us). Indeed, it is because of this difference that Rāmānuja takes love – divine grace and human devotion – as the defining feature of the *Gītā* itself; previously, Śaṅkara had subordinated love to knowledge as the defining feature of the *Gītā*, and argued that knowledge was the overcoming of an imagined difference. In the remaining length of this chapter, I will explore the way Rāmānuja presents us with this God, as both the God other than being and as the God of our love.

We saw that Tillich's notion of the 'ontological' approach to God, where the human being 'discovers something that is identical with *himself* although it transcends him infinitely' bears some resemblance to Śaṅkara's theology, provided we always remember that Śaṅkara subsumes that theology within a larger exploration of the *brahman* that is the ground of all being and non-being. This Tillichian ontology can also be compared to Rāmānuja's ontotheology in a modified way, in that while Rāmānuja's pluralist realism does not identify our being with God as such ('[T]he certainty of God is identical with the certainty of Being itself'[95]), nonetheless, he does permit the mapping of our being on to God. In that sense, Rāmānuja includes a complex ontotheology, in which exploring being as such is at the same time realizing the order of our own being, because God has revealed being and its (self-) attainment. However, Rāmānuja places this ontotheology (comparable to a qualified Tillichian ontology) at the service of a cosmology of otherness. Merold Westphal effectively charges Tillich with failing to be Christian.[96] His reasoning is that Tillich's ontology is 'pantheistic', whereas the real Christian narrative involves precisely a contingent reconciliation across otherness, only when 'the grace and generosity that give forgiveness are met by the humility and contrition that are willing to receive it.'[97] In short, a theology that truly expresses the relationship between God and us (and Westphal, of course, means by this a Christian theology) through our sinfulness and redemption has to be a theology of otherness.

Rāmānuja does, as we have seen, recognize both our estrangement and our sinfulness (albeit within an entirely different cosmo-moral economy from that of Christianity – through the accretion of beginingless consequential action (*karma*) rather than the fall from Eden). The otherness of God that this picture of the human condition requires is presented by him primarily through the intense and lyrical love of God, the emotional yoking together that is called *bhakti*. The response of *bhakti* is the only one left in the face of the divine person, who is other than being and all that it brings in its ontological wake; but as we have seen, Rāmānuja never denies that being too is God. Indeed, the supreme gnostic attainment is of the end of ontotheology.

Gnostic discernment (*vijñāna*) is, he takes Kṛṣṇa to be saying, that 'I am other than the universals of sentience and insentience, completely removed from all that is hateful, and endowed with an endless host of great manifestations of limitless, pre-eminent, auspicious qualities.'[98] Once having attained awareness of being itself, a being (human or divine) is at the stage of going on to receiving God as godly. There is, as it were, an ascent from the philosophical achievement of phenomenological reflection on being to the devotional state of response to God's personhood. Rāmānuja always takes care to present being as encompassed by God. When, at 11.37 (in the midst of the theophany) Arjuna says of Kṛṣṇa, 'You are the imperishable, existent, non-existent and in excess of them' (*tvam akṣaraṃ sad asad paraṃ yat*), Rāmānuja steps in to repeat his standard clarification of the terms: The imperishable is the principle of the individual self (*jīvātmatattva*), which is the intelligent consciousness (*vipaścit*) mentioned in *Katha Upaniṣad* 1.2.18. The term 'non-existent' (*asat*) indicates (*asacchabdanirdiṣṭaṃ*) the principle (*tattva*) of materiality (*prakṛti*) as effect (*kārya*), which is diversified by name and form (*nāmarūpavibhāgavat*). The 'existent' (*sat*) indicates the same materiality as cause (*kāraṇa*), which does not have such diversification. Kṛṣṇa is both; but also in excess of both (i) the imperishable (the individual self) which is the free self (*muktātma*) and (ii) materiality (*prakṛti*), i.e., the material order of being as well as the individual self (*jīvātma*) which is bound with materiality (*prakṛtisambandhinaḥ*).[99]

As always, the '*param*' carries with it the uncertainty of *hyperousios ousia* – hyperbeing to being in apophatic theology – that is, the uncertainty over whether what is indicated is God as the being beyond being, or whether it is the God who exceeds being and thus is other to it.[100] Rāmānuja has both uses, but the ontotheological use, as we have seen, is subordinate to his views of a God other than being. The important point to remember is that this particular declaration comes in response to the event of the theophany, when Kṛṣṇa is seen by Rāmānuja as decisively breaking through the revelatory teaching of the gnostic path (*jñāna mārga*) to his irreducible and foremost personhood. So we should be inclined to think that here, Rāmānuja means that what is left is the God of love.

Crucially, the excession of God over being is indicated by Rāmānuja through Kṛṣṇa's relationship with *brahman*. We have seen that God is also being as such, as *param brahman*, but at critical points in the text, Rāmānuja indicates the radicalism of his theology. Famously, at 13.12, he differs sharply from Śaṅkara and embraces the very interpretation the earlier thinker had rejected. Śaṅkara had read part of Kṛṣṇa's statement there, as we saw, as '*anādimat param brahma*': 'the *brahman* beyond is without beginning' (or 'the hyper*brahman* is without beginning'). It is this *brahman* of which it cannot be said that it is or is not, i.e., that it is being or non-being. Despite the fact that the '*mat-*' suffix is then rendered redundant, he takes it that this is used to complete the verse. He rejects, while acknowledging it, an alternative analysis, namely, '*anādi matparam brahma*': 'the beginingless *brahman* has me beyond it' ('I am the hyper of *brahman*'). This is precisely how Rāmānuja reads it; for then, it is the speaking God, Kṛṣṇa, who is not being or non-being, for he is in excess of *brahman*.[101]

This is brought home in another famous passage, the commentary on 14.26–27. Verse 14.26 talks about the qualified adept becoming *brahman* (*brahmabhūya*). While Śaṅkara merely notes that this is the state (*bhavana*) of *brahman*, Rāmānuja clarifies that this state of being (*bhāva*) is the self as it ultimately is (*yathāvasthitam*), immortal (*amṛtam*) and immutable (*avyayam*). This leads into his understanding of the next verse. For how is the attainment of the being of *brahman* possible? Kṛṣṇa says then, 'For I am the support of *brahman*, the immortal and imperishable, and of the everlasting *dharma*, and of absolute joy.[102] Having identified *brahman* with being, Rāmānuja is able to say that the 'I', i.e. Kṛṣṇa, is the support (*pratiṣṭhā*) of *brahman*. The attainment of that state consists in the understanding of 'Vāsudeva is all' (7.19), through refuge (*prapatti*) in the Lord (*bhagavān*). We have seen Śaṅkara striving to interpret 'support' here as indicating that God supports *brahman* to express the power of being (since God is the supreme being for Śaṅkara while *brahman* is the ground of both being and non-being). In that case, 'support' indicates an auxiliary (as when the subordinate supports a superior). Rāmānuja takes 'support' in the opposite (and possibly more straightforward) way. God is the support of *brahman* in that being requires God, and is dependent on God, who is otherwise than being. Such is the God towards whom nothing more or else is called for than taking refuge in him (which the subsequent tradition interprets at great length as loving surrender, an act of faith).[103]

Rāmānuja's lyricism frequently indicates how the careful ontotheologian ultimately finds his most fulfilling self-expression as the theologian of God's love and the love of God. But as he explains in the introduction to chapter 10, loving devotion requires gnosis of ontotheological truths. It is 'in order to induce *bhakti* and develop it' (*bhaktyutpattaye tadvivṛddhaye*; pp. 325/324) that it is explained fully (*prapañcyate*) in the following chapters that 'the host of the Lord's auspicious qualities are infinite, that he has unrestrained sovereignty over the entire universe, that it is his body, with he its self, and [that it is] brought to activity [by him]'.[104] One searches through being to what is other than it, and then love becomes the only possible medium of expression for the promise that one encounters there. Given this, his commentary at the end of chapter 9 expresses the peak of this love of the God who is other than being. Here Rāmānuja offers an intensely personal description of Kṛṣṇa, given as what Kṛṣṇa is actually saying at 9.34, a verse of much poetic and emotional resonance in the Śrī Vaiṣṇava tradition: 'With your mind on me, be devoted to me, sacrifice to me, bow to me in reverence. Disciplined in this way, with me as the final end – you will come to me alone.'[105] Rāmānuja clarifies that 'what is called 'sacrifice' is the conduct of one who knows he is wholly an accessory [of God]' (*yajanaṃ nāma paripūrṇaśeṣavṛttiḥ*; p. 322/322), thereby relating the revelatory ontotheology to come in the next chapter – the doctrine of accessory and principal by which being and beings are mapped on to God as being as such – to his lyrical devotionalism. In the commentary here, he talks of this very same hyperbeing (*paraṃ brahma*) and foremost person (*puruṣottama*) as he 'with the long eyes like a lotus petal' (*puṇḍarīkadalāmalāyatākṣe*), with 'the appearance of pellucid blue clouds' (*svacchanīlajīmūtasaṃkāśe*), 'whose splendour resembles a thousand suns simultaneously dawning' (*yugapaduditadinakarasahasrasadṛśatejasi*), 'the great ocean of nectarine beauty' (*lāvaṇyāmṛtamahodadhau*), 'with blazing yellow raiment' (*utyujjvalapītāmbare*), who is 'adorned with a crystal crown, capricornian earrings, garlands, bracelets and bangles' (*amalakirīṭa makarakuṇḍalahārakeyūrakaṭakabhūṣite*). Being is left behind in the face of the charioteer God.

We must acknowledge here that we are not any longer trying to explain philosophically where Rāmānuja's faith has taken him. As we saw earlier, Derrida has argued that there is a difference between prayer, as an absolute, supplicating address of the other that implies no determination of being, and praise, which is predicative affirmation that says something of someone (namely, a being, howsoever it 'is' exceedingly).[106] Any negative or apophatic theology, that sought to both arrive at the notion of the hyperessential and sought to say so non-predicatively, would be hard-pressed to show how there could be prayer without praise, unless prayer be non-discursively meditative. It is not my task here to determine whether the position of Jean-Luc Marion, who is the target of Derrida's critique, is so vulnerable. Certainly, Rāmānuja's prayer, while including such non-predicative address as the act of sacrifice, the waving of lights, and the offering of flower and water, also expresses itself in the lyrical praise we saw, especially and pointedly put here as God's self-declaration. But Rāmānuja does not offer us a negative theology that must avoid censure through praise, as it were. The positive ontotheology itself having been presented only as gracious divine guidance and not doubtful human achievement, Rāmānuja draws its limits, not through mystical silence but through a robust and exalted expression of love. The mystery lies, for Rāmānuja, not in how prayer may reach the divine but in how the divine permits praise to express love on both sides.

Śaṅkara circumscribes a theology that might be called, in Tillich's terminology, ontological, in that God is found as the self. This circumspection is done in order dramatically and utterly to transcend all exploration of being, in the outermost limits of understanding, as the ground of both being and non-being, realized in the liberation of consciousness. Rāmānuja circumscribes all ontology, including an ontotheology of being, in order that we may encounter an authentically other God, in a theology that Tillich would have called cosmological. If a theology that cannot be circumscribed requires the otherness of God, then it requires no fear of that otherness.[107] Rāmānuja's final and complete reliance on devotional love makes sense only in a context where God is not oneself and therefore might be missed or misunderstood in our estrangement; but it also makes sense only in a context of having no fear that God is other. It is a deeply illuminating and fascinating aspect of the classical commentarial tradition that Śaṅkara and Rāmānuja could have arrived at these positions from reading the same sacred text.

3

A Comparative Study of Śaṅkara and Rāmānuja on Self and Person, Gnosis and Loving Devotion

Introduction to the metaphysics of self, setting aside moral psychology

A disorienting feature of the contemporary scholar's encounter with these commentaries is that the issues of moral psychology – what are Kṛṣṇa's arguments to get Arjuna to fight (and more generally to get us to act in a moral framework), and whether his arguments work philosophically – play hardly any role at all in what Śaṅkara and Rāmānuja take to be the great lessons of the *Gītā*. For them, the *Gītā* is about the deepest principles of human existence and an insight into ultimate reality. We can see this, for telling example, in how they treat the disquisition on the *sthitaprajña*, the one with equanimity or, literally, stable insight (2.54ff.). Kṛṣṇa talks of the one who renounces (*prajahati*) all desires (*kāmā*) passing in the mind (*manogata*), who is 'free from anxiety' (*anudvigna*), who 'abstains from coveting pleasures' (*sukheṣu vigataspṛhaḥ*), who has 'no fondness anywhere' (*sarvatrānabhisnehaḥ*), who 'neither loves nor hates' (*nābhinandati na dveṣṭi*); a rich psychological description calling for deeper analysis of the content of such attitudinal stances and emotional states, and their moral worth. Yet neither commentator has much to say on these verses, providing merely a quick gloss of the terms. Śaṅkara's concern is only to state that equanimity belongs to the formal renouncer (the *saṃnyāsin*) and Rāmānuja's is to state that such discipline amounts to focussing on Kṛṣṇa, the God of all (*sarveśvara*). In other words, this complex passage in the *Gītā* is simply noted in the context of their respective projects. There is nothing at this point on the immediate and practical concern within which this disquisition is set in the original text: how is the attainment of such equanimity supposed actually to get Arjuna to fight?

The *Gītā* offers a series of interlocking suggestions in its second chapter: that the self is not the embodied being as such, since it is not the body, and therefore the killing and being killed affect the body alone; that one has to perform one's duty (*dharma* as both the content and the performance of duty), and Arjuna's is that of the *kṣatriya*, which is to fight righteously; that the cultivation of the faculty of discrimination (*buddhi*) permits one to see that the ritual worldview and its rigid adherence to consequentiality (*karma*) can be transcended, such that detached action devoid of consequentiality can be undertaken by one who is indifferent to its fruit; and that the detachment required for this is found in the one who has equanimity.

All these are framed in the *Gītā* as Kṛṣṇa's reasoning for why Arjuna ought to fight. But for the commentators, only the first reason, the metaphysical one about the nature of self, is adduced as the primary reason that should inform Arjuna's (and our) moral psychology. Even there, they do not attend to the issue of undertaking unpleasant yet necessary actions. Instead, they are concerned with how the metaphysical teaching and its consequent attitudinal choice of equanimity can help us orient ourselves to the highest good (on the nature and content of which, of course, the two disagree). The *Gītā*'s complex combination of endorsing the need for ritual/action and denying its ultimate value is read by the commentators, not as what should get Arjuna to fight, but as saying something schematic about the connection between the action-transcending *ātman* and the action-encoded bodily life. (Although a vast and complex topic in its own right, by 'action' I mean here volitional and intentional action, and therefore that wide and nebulous range of things we conventionally consider 'doings', dependent on and manifesting agency (*kartṛtva*). The commentators' concern is broadly with the ultimate implications of the relationship between awareness of the world and our directed actions in it; it would be a different task altogether to explore the sophisticated classical and medieval Indian debates on action.) The appeal to the duty of the warrior, again, is seen only incidentally as being about Arjuna and the battle; it is seen much more as about the limits of agency and the action-transcending nature of the *ātman*. Finally, discriminative equanimity is turned entirely into competing interpretations of how the highest good is sought and attained. In short, Śaṅkara and Rāmānuja treat the *Gītā*'s teachings about *ātman* as metaphysics and theology, rather than as moral psychology.

Not only in keeping with the theme of this book, then, but of the intrinsic concerns of the two commentators, this chapter on self seeks primarily to see a cluster of questions – on being, the relationship between divine and human, and the modes of relationality – from 'our' side, the previous chapters having been about the 'other' side. The one philosophical interest common to contemporary scholars – what Arjuna should do about the battle

– and the classical commentators – what Kṛṣṇa is teaching about reality – is the psychological consequence of Arjuna's understanding of the relationship between himself and his *ātman*. Looking at this allows us to enter into a deeper study of the *ātman* in the two commentaries.

Śaṅkara and Rāmānuja broadly agree on the *Gītā*'s diagnosis that the distinction between the unchanging being of self and the changing being of bodily materiality should make both grief at death and fear of killing – which are only altered state of materiality – unwarranted. This is the case even though they interpret the metaphysical status of materiality very differently, as we have seen in the previous chapters, especially in their respective commentaries on 2.16 (on *sat*, *bhāva*, *asat* and *abhāva*). Śaṅkara takes materiality as non-being because it is changeful, while Rāmānuja takes materiality to be changeful being; but in common, they draw a contrast between it and the changeless self. At 2.18, Kṛṣṇa takes the call to join battle (*yuddha*) as directly a consequence of seeing that the corporeal (*deha*) has a limit or ending (*anta*), while it is possessed by the limitless or eternal (*nitya*) bodied one (*śarīriṇ*). It is the realization of this distinction that is held to motivate Arjuna to fight. Śaṅkara and Rāmānuja give short but arrestingly different explanations for how the realization of the distinction is connected to motivation; and while those explanations are interesting in themselves, they point towards the larger question with which we are concerned here, which is the meaning of 'self' in these commentaries.

For Śaṅkara, Kṛṣṇa's call at 2.18 is to be understood in terms of a gnostic transformation. '"Since the self is thus eternal and unchanging, therefore do fight, do not desist from fighting" that is the meaning. Here, there is no injunction to fight. Although set on fighting, he [Arjuna] is silent because obstructed by grief and delusion. So, the Lord is only taking away the obstruction to his task. "Fight" is, then, an explanatory repetition [of Kṛṣṇa's teaching on the nature of *ātman*] and not an injunction [to act]'.[1]

What Kṛṣṇa does here, according to Śaṅkara, is to remove Arjuna's ignorance of the reality that, when he kills or his familial opponents are killed, the materially constituted persons involved do not alter the eternal and singular consciousness, the *ātman*, that renders them such persons. The consciousness or *ātman* that renders the material entity Arjuna is intrinsically aware of its being as not the non-being of the material entity; however, the clarity of its reflexivity is clouded by the deluded condition of its location in that material entity (which is to say, as an individual person). Kṛṣṇa's teaching removes that obstruction to the reflexivity of consciousness located in Arjuna. But here things get tricky. Śaṅkara can explain that what is happening with Kṛṣṇa's teaching is that the *ātman*/consciousness is brought back to its intrinsic reflexive state by the removal of obstruction.

But strangely, the purpose of this realization by the *ātman* that it is constitutively free from the material complex (i.e., the person, Arjuna) is to assist that person to carry out tasks premised on his being that very person! The duty to fight and the capacity to do are Arjuna's, for only that material entity, the person called Arjuna, has a duty and the means to carry it out; these do not pertain to the *ātman*, which is what is held to realize its freedom from materiality upon hearing Kṛṣṇa's teaching. Śaṅkara is therefore implicitly working with a distinction between *ātman* and the person (the latter being that as whom the *ātman* finds itself). Furthermore, this distinction is meant both (i) to express the metaphysical difference between being and non-being, and (ii) to explain the moral psychology that prompts Arjuna to carry out his duty. Śaṅkara's interest in exploring the former makes him quite prepared to brush off the latter issue, although he cannot completely ignore the nature and status of the person and his duty.

Rāmānuja has a different approach to Kṛṣṇa's words at 2.18. He analyses the differences between self and body, explains how this should lead to an attitude fit for battle, and then suggests that such an attitude prompts the necessary psychological stance (and virtue) for fighting. 'The self is eternal, as it is uniform, not of composite nature, is the epistemic subject, and is pervasive. The body is perishable because it is of composite nature, its purpose is for the corporeal being to experience the fruit of consequential action, it is pluriform, and pervaded [by its self]. Thus, the body being naturally perishable and the self naturally being eternal, neither is a fit object of grief. Hence, bearing with courage the inevitable stroke of sharp or hard weapons, likely to be received by you or by others, start this action called war, without being attached to the fruits, but only for the sake of attaining immortality.'[2]

Rāmānuja seeks to explain why the realization of the distinction between self and the materially constituted person should lead to equanimity: and for this, he offers an implicit diagnosis of grief, namely, the inevitably failed expectation of stability (unchangingness) in what always changes. From such a perspective, when reality is seen as being constituted by two wholly different orders – the always unchanging self and always changing materiality – then grief should not occur at all, for the distinction between what changes and what does not is always stable. (Of course this is a dauntingly simple reading of grief; we would tend to think that grief occurs because of the timing of change and not because of an expectation that there will be no change at all.) The self never changes and therefore need never be the object of the anxiety that it may be unstable and change; the materially constituted body-world always changes and ought never to be the object of any expectation that it will be stable. Rāmānuja then suggests that the equanimous attitude that ought to result from seeing the pointlessness of grief should prompt fortitude or courage (*dhairya*) – a psychological leap from the metaphysical teaching, but a plausible one. The transformation in consciousness that he calls for is not as fundamental or radical as Śaṅkara's, but it does keep the eternal self and the material person more intimately connected when it comes to the action at hand, namely, the duty of war. Nevertheless, he too does work with a distinction between the uniform *ātman* (even if he means something different by it than Śaṅkara) and pluriform persons, of whom Arjuna is the case in point.

We must, then, first turn to this distinction that both of them make between Arjuna and his *ātman*, before we proceed to their contrasting accounts of the nature of that distinction. Then we can look at the implications that their respective accounts have for the existential truth that we – who, like Arjuna, are enselved material entities – face, and the response that we must offer to it.

Situating the *ātman*

We should make a broad distinction between *ātman*, which we have translated conventionally throughout as 'self', and more concrete senses of individual being, which I propose more narrowly to call 'person' and which pertains to Arjuna (and therefore others, human, demoniac or divine). The exegetical task would be simpler if this concept were precisely associated in the *Gītā* with a term like '*puruṣa*', and distinguished thereby. But while this is usually the case with a great deal of classical Indian philosophical material, like in Nyāya and later Advaita (indeed, to some extent with Śaṅkara himself in his other commentaries), the *Gītā*, with its deep reliance on the terminology of early Sāṃkhya thought, often uses the two terms interchangeably. Its characteristic polyvalence is typified by the fact that '*puruṣa*' at base refers in the *Gītā* to the entity that is principally defined as conscious (as opposed to being inert, *jaḍa*).[3] As such, it usually means a spirit, that which is not material but reflexive, the subject of phenomena or experience, albeit requiring the co-presence of *prakṛti*, or materiality. Śaṅkara and Rāmānuja are constrained by the *Gītā*'s usage, but also exploit it. Śaṅkara does not use '*puruṣa*' to mean *ātman* unless it is used in just that way in the verse itself, because for him *ātman*, as the general principle of consciousness, is never an individual non-material entity amongst many. Rāmānuja is more concerned with *puruṣa* as it applies to Kṛṣṇa/Nārāyaṇa, who we saw in the previous chapter to be ultimately the only true person; but because, for him, *ātman* is one of a plurality of abstract selves, he helps himself to the equation of *puruṣa* and *ātman* in that sense, while being careful to gloss '*puruṣa*' in a different way when it appears to pertain to an individuated entity with personal identity (and therefore not *ātman*). Setting aside, then, the loose terminology of the *Gītā* itself, we must look more closely at how both commentators make a conceptual distinction between what we may call 'self' and 'person', for it is crucial to their narrative about our highest end. This distinction has its roots at the very origins of ancient Indian thought, and a quick historical note will help situate my reading in what follows.

The key point to consider is that in the time of the interaction between the ideas found in the *Upaniṣads* and those articulated by the Buddha (and Mahāvīra) in their challenge to the *brahman*ical worldview, a two-fold development in the understanding of *ātman* occurred. First, a strictly abstract and conceptually narrow understanding of it became widely accepted. Second, this understanding became the focus of a critical metaphysical disagreement between those who considered it central to their gnoseology and those who considered it an incoherent idea. The *ātman* in classical Indian debates combined two ideas: first, there is a principle of being which subsists in and somehow provides the condition for the embodied life of an individual (human or other); second, it is conscious, with an idiosyncratic, subjective access to the fact of its own being. Together, this means that there is a temporally persistent (indeed, sempiternal) subject of experience. In many ways, the *ātman* concept resembles that of the psyche and the soul in pre-modern Western thought, by referring very generally to the essence of a human being (at the very least). But generally, and especially in the *Upaniṣads* and the tradition based on them, the *ātman* does not provide personal identity, i.e., the set of criteria by which the individual being is distinguished from another through a complex combination of qualities that gives each a distinct(ive), potentially nameable, narrative existence. The *ātman* does not pertain to personhood in such a manner. The eager seekers of the *Upaniṣads* who pester the sages about what and how they should know of *ātman* are not asking about precisely what it is that makes them Uṣata, Indra, Janaka or Gārgī. And the elliptical answer that they receive from their teachers, which formally identifies their *ātman* (whether it be one or many amongst them) with *brahman*, makes it clear that whatever the principle that identifies the essence of their being, it is not something which adverts to their substantive individuality as those particular human (or divine) beings. Instead, the essence is a principle of existence that renders possible the conditions of individually different beings, but is not itself individuated by psychological and somatic features. Presumably, this detaching of essence from personhood went hand in hand with the presupposition of a cycle of lives and rebirths: a distance was created between the person inquiring into reality and the existence they might have in other lives, as other persons.[4]

The Advaitins will later interpret the *Upaniṣads* to mean that one principle – of consciousness – is the essence of all individuated beings, so that ultimately, the individuation of consciousness within the structural locus of a psychosomatic – material – entity turns out to be erroneous. By contrast, the Viśiṣṭādvaitins will follow what they take to be the more intuitive view that there is a plurality of *ātman*s, and that there is no error in consciousness' presence to itself in individuated loci. But despite there being a plurality of selves, for the Viśiṣṭādvaitins too, the separateness of selves is not based on individually variable personal characteristics, but on the purely formal fact of there being infinitely many persistent entities with the common feature of possessing the quality of consciousness.

There is, then, a double comparison here in relation to dominant ideas in the pre-modern Western philosophical traditions. On the one hand is the de-linking of selfhood from personhood. In general, Western philosophy is marked by the thought that the essence of the self is also that which, being distinctive of that self, is substantively differentiating about it – namely, its personal identity. This is how, in Christian thought, the soul becomes the essence of a person. The other concerns the degree of abstraction. In a great deal of Western thought (and in Christian theology) there is a sort of dialectic between richer, somatic, psychological and sociological conceptions of the self and more austere ones that seek to pin selfhood down to a strict principle – of rationality, intellect, reflexivity, agency or something else: the former going back broadly to Aristotle and the latter to Plato, and in Christian thought, going back to Augustine's combining of the Greek with the Biblical tradition.[5] I am suggesting that the *ātman* is always about the more austere conception. But – bringing together these two comparisons – even austere conceptions of selfhood often still relate in the West to personal identity. Locke's response to Descartes' attempt to anchor the self in the incorrigibility of the *cogito* brings this out clearly. Locke articulates the problem of a consciousness which incorrigibly represents the self in terms of the determination of personal identity over time through psychological continuity.[6] It is not surprising that so much modern analytic Western philosophy of self has been about the conditions for personal identity.

Kant is a major exception on at least some interpretations of his distinction between transcendental and empirical identity, as when he points out that the diachronicity of the 'I' does not point to an enduring personal entity but a single logical subject of unified consciousness.[7] The phenomenological tradition from Husserl onwards has much that is congenial to the distinction I am drawing attention to in the classical Indian material, and has attracted attention recently.[8] Whatever personhood is, Indian debates do not focus as such on its continuity (although debates over the ethical life have a great deal to say about the consequential demands of personhood). It must, of course, be emphasised that there is no lack of richer and more extended notions pertaining to personhood amongst a range of classical thinkers. But both our commentators problematise this extended sense of self, which is built out of a range of psychological, ethical, and sociological features and constitutes the materials of personhood.

It would therefore be in order to get a sense of both the similarities – formality, impersonality, conscious beingness – as well as the differences – over singularity and plurality, but also virtual and ontological shifts in the self-consciousness of being – in our commentators' notions of *ātman*. This will inform us, too, of the ways in which they distinguish between *ātman* and the personal identity provided by material conditions. We can then see how, while they agree that it is erroneous for *ātman* to take itself to be the person under conditions of embodiment, they differ radically in their analysis of the error and the way in which freedom from that error is attained.

The formal, abstract and impersonal *ātman* and its distinction from the individual and individuated person

For our commentators, the *locus classicus* of the *Gītā*'s teachings on *ātman* comes in 2.17–25. At 2.17, Kṛṣṇa talks of the *ātman* as the indestructible (*avināśin*), which is immutable (*avyaya*). Rāmānuja expands on this through recourse to his notion of two distinct (*vyatirikta*) orders of being, the sentient (*cetana*) *ātman* and the insentient (which is implicitly taken to be synonymous with materiality). Their ontological status is not reciprocal: the *ātman* pervades (*vyāptam*) all that is insentient but not *vice versa*. Rāmānuja holds that *x* can pervade *y* only if *x* is more subtle (*sūkṣma*) than *y*. The *ātman* pervades all non-sentient entities because it is unsurpassedly (*niratiśaya*) subtle. Changes to entities occur through their being pervaded by other entities; 'destructive instruments, like water, fire, wind, etc., pervade the destructible, and disintegrate them'.[9] (He interprets the breaking apart of a thing by being struck with a hammer as the rousing of wind through violent contact, and therefore a sort of pervasion by the subtle wind of the less subtle object.) The *ātman* is subtler than any material entity, and destruction requires pervasion of the less subtle by the more subtle; the *ātman* cannot be pervaded, and hence cannot be destroyed.

When, in 2.18, Kṛṣṇa says that the body (*deha*) by contrast does come to an end (*anta*), Rāmānuja adds another layer to his analysis: anything being less subtle consists in its being complex (*upacaya*), that is to say, composed of elements (*bhūtasaṃghāta*). So the bodily being is complex, not simplex as the *ātman* is; also, it is pervaded by the conscious self. The being of the self is uniform (*ekarūpatva*) and pervasive (*vyāpakatva*) (p. 72/48–9). 2.20 underscores the fact that personal identity is confined to the body and the eternal self is impersonal. Rāmānuja says that the *ātman* is untouched by birth and death, unlike the body; this is so even if the body is born at the beginning and dies at the end of an aeon (*kalpa*), as happens to the divinity who presides over life, Prajāpati or Brahma (p. 74/54). The personhood of gods too is subject to impermanence, and not identical with the eternal and impersonal self. Finally (p. 76/55), Rāmānuja takes there to be a plurality of selves (*ātmānāṃ*), having already argued (2.12; p. 62/34) that the plurality of people mentioned by Kṛṣṇa indicates an ultimate (*pāramārthika*) difference (*bheda*) between the selves that they embody.

In his reading, Rāmānuja disagrees with much of how Śaṅkara had earlier presented his theory of *ātman*, although some basic features are similar. Śaṅkara is committed to a much more radical reading of the nature of *ātman*: on Kṛṣṇa's mention of a plurality of people at 2.12, he argues (p. 15) that the plural termination ('we') (*bahuvacana*) pertains to the distinction between bodies (*dehabheda*) and not to selves. What is eternal (*nitya*) is the intrinsic ('own-form', *svarūpa*) self of all. On 2.17, where Rāmānuja presents a general principle of pervasive and pervaded entities of which selves are the most pervasive (and unpervadable) of all, and therefore indestructible, Śaṅkara offers a single, global candidate: 'that which this, the whole universe with [its] space, is diffused with, is pervaded by, is *brahman*, called "existent", as pots and other things are by space.'[10] The uniformity implied by the spatial metaphor is used to point to how only *brahman* is all-pervasive; and *ātman* is *brahman*. So the plurality of pervasive beings is ruled out, while the singularity of conscious being – and thence, the ground of being and non-being – is asserted. (Śaṅkara equivocates between the Upaniṣadic terming of *brahman* as 'existent' (*sat*) and his own, often implicit and more radical notion, which we explored in the first chapter, of *brahman* as the ground of both the existent and the non-existent.)

The other step is also an integral part of Śaṅkara's non-dualism. When Kṛṣṇa says (2.17), 'But know that to be imperishable' (*avināśi tu tad viddhi*), Śaṅkara quickly explains, 'the "but" word is meant to distinguish [it from] the non-existent' (*tu śabdo 'sataḥ viśeṣaṇārthaḥ*)'. All else than consciousness is non-being. The error of taking conscious being as the individual person is not the error of conflating two orders of being, as Rāmānuja later would have it; instead, for Śaṅkara, the error consists in taking being to be non-being. Bodily beings (*dehāḥ*) belong to the *ātman* but, just as 'the idea of the reality' (*sadbuddhiḥ*) of mirages is removed (*avacchinna*) through the use of the means of knowledge, so too in true discrimination (*viveka*), bodies come to an end like bodies in dreams and magical illusions (*svapnamāyā*) (p. 18). The realization is not a withdrawal from entanglement with another ontological order of being, but the separation of purported being from being itself. To be a person is to take being to be non-being, and consciousness' coming to itself is the self's seeing through to its being as such.

Śaṅkara's radical non-duality holds that all that we take ourselves to be, as acting and knowing beings, is seen to be mistaken in the intrinsically reflexive light of the self's selfness, freed from primal unwisdom (*avidyā*) about being. This makes for a very fine distinction between self and person. Śaṅkara has already stated that 'the specific ground for the impossibility of all action' (*sarvakarmāsaṃbhavakāraṇaviśeṣaḥ*) lies in the unchangeability (*avikriyatva*) of the *ātman*. At 2.21, Kṛṣṇa asks rhetorically, 'For one who ultimately knows the indestructible, the eternal, the birthless, the imperishable, how does that person cause to die and whom, Pārtha, how does he kill and whom?'[11] In the commentary, reading killing as action, Śaṅkara puts to himself (p. 21) the reasonable question as to what bearing this can have on even the ultimately knowing one (*viduṣa*): action cannot become impossible for someone just by apprehension of unchangeability; then an unchanging stump of a tree would do it!

His answer densely states his entire reading of the nature of *ātman*: 'The ultimately knowing one is essentially self. Ultimate knowledge does not belong to the bodily aggregate. What is left is the ultimately knowing one who is the unchangeable self without aggregation. Thus, action being impossible for the ultimately knowing one, the denial [of action] in "How can that person…" is appropriate. Just as, because of the non-cognition of the difference between self and mental states, the self – although unchangeable – is conceived through primal unknowing to [itself] apprehend objects like the spoken word; so too, the self, although transcendentally unchangeable, is said to [itself] be the "ultimately knowing one" because of its association with the gnostic discrimination between self and what is not self, this [gnosis] itself being a mental state and non-existent by nature.'[12] So it is both the case that personhood conceals and contains impersonal, reflexive consciousness and the case that such consciousness is the only true being while personhood is not. This is due to the necessary structures of the metaphysical illusion that is primal unwisdom: what we call and mean by 'knowledge' derives from and requires what is ultimately non-existent, namely, the apprehending apparatus of mental states (and the bodily capacities for perception). The self itself is only the condition for the possibility for knowledge; but it is taken by its cognitive apparatus, the mind/intellect[13] to be the knower. All epistemic states, in the course of life, are ascribed to the consciousness that renders such states possible, but in fact such states are those of the bodily complex called the person; consciousness itself – the reflexive presence that alone is 'self' for Śaṅkara – is not, strictly speaking, the knower. Epistemic states come and go, by definition being transient, whereas *ātman* is unchanging. What is unchanging is only the presence that makes the states possible, and that cannot itself be those states themselves (let alone their content). The startling conclusion to this train of reasoning is that even the insight into the non-self of the bodily person and their mental life is an epistemic state, and therefore an occurent in the realm of the ultimately non-existent. The liberating, non-dualising gnosis that makes a person an ultimate knower is paradoxical: what is to be known is the distinction between self and non-self, and yet, to know that requires the functioning of the non-self. At that point, the knower is essentially the self, and as ultimately there is only self (which is to say, consciousness as such), the consciousness of the knower is on the verge of going beyond the appurtenances of knowledge that made that person a knower. Gnosis liberates even as it ends. The knowing person is truly knowing, just on the verge of being a person no longer. The self is the condition for both unknowing and knowing, even while it is itself neither; thereby does freedom become possible, for the self realizes itself through what it is not.

We have, then, two accounts of the impersonal self and its relationship to personhood; as, also, different ontological valuations of personhood. These differences and their purposes will concern us for the rest of the chapter, but it may be useful to think a little more about the distinction between the two subjectivities that we have seen above. Both commentators talk of the human person in terms of the bodily-determined material entity which, in order to be such, requires as its ground condition that which will render it the human person (and not merely an agglomeration of material). There is, then, a fundamental distinction between the subject seen as the human being (exemplarily, the person called Prince Arjuna) who has an identity constituted from material features, and the formal and impersonal subject, *ātman*, which is required to unite those features so that there is a person called Arjuna. The intimacy of this relationship is indicated by the *Gītā*'s own repeated naming of the *ātman* as the *dehin*, the bodied one. (Through this strange translation, I try to mediate between two other concepts: to call the *dehin* the 'embodied one' suggests too sharp a dualism of self and body, while to call it 'the bodily one' collapses all difference.)

There are rich comparative possibilities here with at least some interpretations of Kant and Husserl. Kant's notion of a principle of identity that gives unity and coherence to experience but is itself not an object of experience can be compared to the Vedāntic *ātman*. Again, the phenomenological distinction, going back to Husserl, between the transcendental subject that is pure consciousness, and the empirical ego with its own acts, habitualities and capacities, also resonates with the contrast we have been exploring here.[14] Although structurally *ātman* ultimately means something very different to the two commentators (as we will see), in common they treat it somewhat like a transcendental subjectivity; this is the subjectivity that results from the phenomenological reduction away of the objective contents (including reflexive ones) of consciousness, to what is required for there to be objects in consciousness at all. At the same time, the concept of *ātman* is more radical, in that it is neither activity nor phenomena but merely and only the consciousness (in Śaṅkara) or the possessor of consciousness (in Rāmānuja) that metaphysically precedes the presentation of the world. (It should be remembered from previous chapters that Śaṅkara then offers the world as non-real, dependent upon consciousness, and ultimately non-existent; by contrast, Rāmānuja is a realist, in that he maintains that while consciousness presents objects to its owner, objects themselves have an equally independent status as members of the existent order of materiality.)

On this Husserlian theme of two subjectivities, it has been pointed out by Lewis and Staehler that, 'The empirical ego with its own character and name is thus substantially different from the transcendental ego, and when we usually speak of the "I", we mean the empirical ego.'[15] I make this comparison, not to explore the ways in which phenomenology may (or may not) parallel Vedāntic concepts in any depth,[16] but to note that there is something compelling about the distinction between the formal and abstract self on the one hand and the richly charactered, experientially and materially constituted person on the other. A study of the tensions between these two conceptions of the subject, and of the different ways in which Śaṅkara and Rāmānuja seek to dissolve them, will enable us to understand more about the relationship between being, divinity and self that each commentator offers us.

So far, we have only looked at the distinction between a formal and abstract *ātman*-self (whatever it may mean), and the richly charactered materially composite person. But, as we would expect, the significant aspect of our study comes from looking at the differences in the two accounts. In a verse that, as Laurie Patton remarks, is often taken to be the best definition of *ātman*, Kṛṣṇa says, albeit referring to *puruṣa*, in the sense of the spirit or conscious spirit: 'The highest spirit in this body is also called highest self, the great lord, the one who enjoys (*bhoktā*), who supports (*bhartā*), who assents (*anumantā*) and who observes (*upadraṣṭā*).'[17] The commentators have to come to interpretive grips with the *Gītā*'s enigmatic teaching on how the self comes to be the empirical agent, and their responses take us in very different directions.

Śaṅkara reads this verse to be asserting an existential chasm between the self and the agentive being of which it is the ground. He says of the proximate observer (*upadraṣṭā*), 'while stood nearby, the seer itself does not function'.[18] He compares this observer with the peculiar priest (the *brahmā*) who beholds the virtues and blemishes of the activities of the priests and patron of a ritual, and is well-versed in the science of the rituals, but who does not himself function within the ritual. There is a presence within the parameters of the ritual for this individual, and yet he is not to be counted as a performative element of the ritual itself, unlike the participants. The self is the presence in the material body, but while consciousness gives bodily life, it does not itself provide agency to that living entity. The self is most intimate (*pratyak samīpe*) with the living body (*deha*), in being the observer of it. This fundamental separation, simply by virtue of emphasising an intimacy between self and body, is re-emphasised with the *Gītā*'s description of the self as the one who assents (*anumantā*). Śaṅkara struggles to gain the balance between denying agentive function (and thus change) for the self and acknowledging its transcendental involvement in bodily life. He glosses assent as 'delighting' (*paritoṣaḥ*), but then weakens this implication of agency; 'even though itself inactive in the activities of the working body and its organs, it presents itself as if (*iva*) favourable towards and functioning with them.'[19] This locution permits him to indicate that the agentive aspect of the *ātman* is only apparent, a point reiterated by resorting to another standard formulation: the self is the witnessing being (*sākṣibhūta*); its not functioning as agent is clear in that it 'never impedes' (*kadācid api na nivārayati*) the activities of the body and its organs.[20] The entire burden of activity is therefore laid on the apparatus of the material living body.

Śaṅkara then glosses two more terms from 13.22. The self is 'one who supports' (*bhartā*). The self is called 'the one who supports' because: '"support" means retention of the essential nature of body, organs, mind and intellect, which are agglomerated so as to become the means to serve the purpose of the other, [i.e.,] the consciousness that is self, and have the appearance of consciousness; and that [retention of nature] is only due to the consciousness that is self. Thus the self is called "the one who supports".'[21] Although 'support' sounds like an action, Śaṅkara reads it structurally as the ontological fact of the dependence of the living body on self. This agglomerated entity is active for the purpose of the self (which purpose is the ultimate gnosis of non-duality), since the states of cultivated cognition (as well as devotional activity and even ritual) require the dynamism of bodily functions. Of course, it remains puzzling as to how the phenomenal changes in the body actually have any causal link to the rigorously noumenal self; but that is a question that will takes us beyond Śaṅkara's text.

Then there is the description, 'the one who enjoys' or who partakes (*bhoktā*); and here too, Śaṅkara mysteriously maintains the double aspect of the self's transcendental relationship with the body, separate and present. 'Like heat with fire, the intellect's experiential states, of the nature of happiness, sorrow and delusion pertaining to all objects, although born as though grasped by the consciousness that is self, are distinguished by the self – that is of the nature of eternal consciousness – as distinct [from it].'[22] Here Śaṅkara is striving to get at a transcendental notion of consciousness: it is what is distinct from (because independent of and presupposed by) all intentional states (i.e., experiential states pertaining to all objects). At the same time, the phenomenal is the phenomenal only by virtue of being intentional content. However, phenomenological states are, strictly speaking, given content by material states: their changefulness is the change of the states of the body (specifically here, the intellect as ratiocinative faculty). Empirical consciousness is not, then, (observer or witness) consciousness at all; and this latter, transcendental consciousness – consciousness-that-is-self – is fundamentally capable (in anticipation of the Husserlian epochē, one is tempted to add) of distinguishing its pure presence from what clutters up and animates the empirical life of the body. Śaṅkara goes on to add that it is primal unwisdom (*avidyā*) that leads to the invention (*parikalpana*) of the self as bodily being, when in truth the self is only the observer; that is why Kṛṣṇa calls the self the 'highest' self. The implication is that what is normally taken to be the self – the bodily-extended individual, the subject of experience – is 'lower'. Finally, in a relatively trivial sense – Śaṅkara makes nothing of this – the self is called the 'great god' because it is the self of all, and independent (*svatantra*) of everything else. We have seen in a previous chapter how the self is the self of all for Śaṅkara, God being supremely the self of all.

When we turn to Rāmānuja, we find a very different emphasis on the relationship between the non-agentive *ātman* and the bodily being who is the locus of agency, activity and change. 'This *puruṣa*-self that is established in this body becomes the "observer" and the "assenter" in this body by means of volition in accordance with the functioning of the body. Likewise it becomes the "supporter" of the body. Likewise too, it becomes the "partaker of the happiness and sorrow born of the functioning of the body."'[23] Rāmānuja concludes that all these factors render the body the accessory (*śeṣa*) of the self, and therefore the latter is called the 'great lord' and 'supreme self' of the body. Rāmānuja therefore does not see any difficulty in treating the self as agent (in apparent contravention of the teaching that *ātman* is non-agentive (*akartāraṃ*) in 13.29), so long as the expression of will accords with the functioning of bodily being. In that sense, the self undergoes a substantive change when it is entangled with materiality: the formal self is actually the core of the person, the bodily being. The self has to cease its entanglement with bodily being in order to become free. The willed mastery of the body that the self exhibits in fact closes the ontological gap between two orders of being; in becoming master of material being, but having to do so only in conformity with the causal structures of materiality, the formal self engages in the life of the individual person. (The life of the individual person is vital for Rāmānuja, since it is the personal being who can and does love God; so it is not surprising that Rāmānuja is ambivalent about the freeing of self from the conditions of personhood.)

From these two different approaches to the relationship, or lack thereof, between *ātman*-self and person, the commentators have to grapple with the *Gītā*'s teaching that 'the self is non-agent' (*ātmānam akartāraṃ*; 13.29), for it is incomprehensible that individual human persons are non-agents. (Indeed, it is precisely because Arjuna cannot simply be non-agentive – since not fighting is itself doing something significant – that Kṛṣṇa teaches the *Gītā*.) Śaṅkara and Rāmānuja agree that the *ātman* is non-agentive because it is conscious being: agency is held to be incompatible with seer consciousness. As the former puts it, the *ātman* is the cogniser of the field (*kṣetrajña*) and devoid of all contingency (*sarvopādhivivarjitaṃ*; p. 210), and therefore unchanging; agency requires and manifests change. Rāmānuja says much the same thing, taking the *ātman* to be of the form of cognition (*jñānākāra*; p. 455). As the same verse clarifies, all activity (*karmāṇi*) is due to materiality (*prakṛti*). Śaṅkara explains that actions are those 'initiated by language, mind and body' (*vāṅmanaḥ kāyārabhyāni*), which complex is material, while Rāmānuja clarifies that it is in materiality that 'the undergoing of happiness and sorrow' (*sukhaduḥkhānubhavaḥ*) – the cause and consequence of agency – occurs.

Of course, because of its different compositional layers, the *Gītā* is hardly systematic in its usage of key terms. At 13.20, Kṛṣṇa makes the distinction between materiality (*prakṛti*) and the conscious being (*puruṣa*) in order to make the point that the former is the cause (*hetu*) of activity (*kārya*) and the modes of activity (*karaṇa*), while the latter is the cause of the experiencing (*bhoktṛtva*) of happiness and sorrow. Given the rigorous stricture against an agentive self, the *puruṣa* here, which undergoes the experiences resulting from the generation of agency through its bodily apparatus, cannot consistently mean the *ātman*. Śaṅkara reads the *puruṣa* as the individuated being (*jīva*), which is consciousness epistemically limited to a locus determined by materiality, and thereby rendered capable of phenomenology. He therefore takes 'activity' and 'modes of activity' to be the body (*śarīra*) and the so-called thirteen organs (*trayodaśa*): the five senses, the five corresponding motor organs, the mind (*manas*, which structures the internal states as the 'inner sense'), the intellect (*buddhi*, the faculty of discrimination or higher-order rational functioning upon mental states), and the ego (*ahaṃkāra*, the 'I'-maker that associates all states with a sense of belonging to one idiosyncratic bearer). In short, we have here the constituents of personhood: the psychophysical complex and the consciousness that it erroneously individuates.

As we have seen, Śaṅkara is careful to detach talk of the *ātman*, which for him is consciousness or being as such, from talk of the individuated entity, which is the *puruṣa*. Under 13.20, he identifies the *Gītā*'s use of '*puruṣa*' with '*jīva*', his favoured term for consciousness as it is materially individuated – that is, erroneously limited in its local access to the psychophysical range of a body. It is consciousness as *jīva* that is the *bhoktṛtva* or experiencer (p. 203). The 'I'-form or egoity (*ahaṃkāra*) is an expression of the material limitations of the body, and individuates consciousness' access to itself; individuated and limited thus, consciousness occurs to itself as if it were a particular being amongst beings. That is when Śaṅkara calls consciousness the *jīva*. It is in this way that he glosses the *Gītā*'s '*puruṣa*' as '*jīva*'. By contrast, he uses '*ātman*' only as the general name for conscious being as such; and it is that which is asymmetrically non-different from *brahman* (in that *ātman* is *brahman* but *brahman* is not exhausted by *ātman*, as we saw in chapter 1). Ultimately, there is only the one consciousness under different conditions of manifestation; but consciousness associates itself with agency only when taking itself to be found individuated through the material of the body; for it is then that it gains an erroneous and reducible personal identity through the features of that body.

Rāmānuja, too, has to reconcile 13.20's talk of the *puruṣa*'s agency with 13.29's talk of the non-agency of *ātman*. But unlike Śaṅkara, he is not committed to two levels of explanation, the first for how a uniform and universal consciousness becomes individuated, and the second for how individuation conditions generate both agentive factors and the erroneous sense that the individuated consciousness is an agent. (Furthermore, as we noted in the commentary on 13.22, individuation is a strictly cognitive limitation for Śaṅkara; recall that materiality is non-being for him, and therefore cannot really bind and limit consciousness. The individuation of consciousness to generate personhood is itself, strictly, a cognitive error.) By contrast, Rāmānuja only has to give an acount of how the same impersonal individual conscious being (*ātman*), while ultimately free of agency, functions as an agent when entangled materially under the condition of personhood. Also, he does not need to deny that the impersonal self is ontologically transformed into a person when located materially.[24] (It is true, too, that there is a cognitive error in the impersonal, non-agentive and formal self representing itself as the agentive person given identity through the body; but, as we saw under 13.22, that error is based on the ontologically substantive role of materiality in its interaction with the *ātman*.) Consequently, where the *Gītā* describes the *puruṣa* as the cause of experience, Rāmānuja explains that this is because experience is generated through the *puruṣa*'s intimate association (*saṃsṛṣṭa*) with materiality, as the seat (*āśraya*) of experience. Its agency comes through its being the cause of the volitional effort (*prayatna*) to support the body (*śarīrādhiṣṭhāna*) (p. 448/443). In this way, Rāmānuja delineates the nature of personhood, while artfully leaving aside the *Gītā*'s requirement that the *ātman*-self be non-agentive and devoid of the individuating conditions of personhood. It should be remembered that although Rāmānuja offers a metaphysically robust relationship between self and person, he does not fail to distinguish the two. 15.10 says that confused people do not see the self truly, since it enjoys or partakes of life through the material qualities that define a person and therefore appears only as that person to itself. Commenting on this, Rāmānuja reiterates (p. 492/485) that the self has to be distinguished from the assemblage of human and other fleshly formations (*manuṣyatvādi saṃsthānapiṇḍasaṃsṛṣṭaṃ*) that make a person.

The question that will concern us over the next two sections is what bearing the metaphysical distinction between self and person has on the respective systems of the commentators. Their main challenge is to integrate the undeniable agentive and perspectival nature of our experience as persons into their account of the *ātman*.

The qualitative constitution of persons

Both commentators adhere to a fairly conventional ancient brahmanical view of how the personality of persons is broadly revealed through the three-fold quality types or *guṇas* – purity (*sattva*), urgency (*rajas*) and stolidity (*tamas*).[25] They also associate this typology with the issue of how to be and act appropriately in this world, that is to say, with the fluid notion called '*dharma*' and its attendant dhārmic agency. However, while the *Gītā* itself seems most directly concerned with what this implies for how Arjuna should act, the commentators are interested only in what it says about the metaphysical constitution of the individual and the implications that constitution has for the role and limits of agency.

Chapter 14 of the *Gītā* offers the typology of qualities, to which the commentators add little; but it is interesting to note how they gloss its somewhat surprising teaching that even purity of personality is bondage. Kṛṣṇa says of the *guṇas*, arising from material nature, that 'they bind' (*nibadhnanti*) the immutable (*avyaya*) bodied being (*dehin*) to the living body (*deha*). Śaṅkara is mainly concerned to qualify binding as binding 'as it were' (*iva*) (p. 215), since materiality cannot really bind, being ultimately non-being. Rāmānuja has a more realist notion of the bond, saying the *guṇas* bind the *dehin* by being the contingent conditions (*upādhi-s*) that are constitutive of the body (p. 464; 461). The *Gītā*'s strict account of why the quality-types of urgency and stolidity bind (14.7–8) are to be expected, and the commentators add nothing: urgency ties through action (*karma*), bringing a connection of the embodied one to passion and thirst, while stolidity ties through distraction (*pramāda*), bringing a connection through delusion and ignorance. On the binding by the quality-type of purity (*sattva*), however, they have interestingly different points of emphases. How can purity bind the self to flesh? By attachment to happiness (*sukha*) and knowledge (*jñāna*), the *Gītā* says (14.6). Śaṅkara is, as ever, anxious to point out the ontological unreality of the attachment; for him, this attachment is only a cognitive error. '"Through attachment to happiness" [the *Gītā* says, meaning]: [The thought] "I am happy", produces a conjunction between happiness that is an object and the self that is subject, which is indeed a false association [of the self] with happiness.'[26] Since the property (*dharma*) of an object (*viṣaya*) cannot be that of the subject, the association is simply a manifestation of primal unwisdom (*avidyā*), the incapacity of consciousness to discriminate itself from the unreal. In the same way, when the *Gītā* speaks of attachment to right cognition or knowledge of the world (*jñāna*), this is not a confluence of an objective state with the *ātman*; epistemic states are properties of the mind, called the internal organ (*antaḥkaraṇa*), and as such, a part of the body (and the ultimately less-than-real world). Even purity binds for Śaṅkara, because all qualities are objective, objects are part of the order of non-being, and if the self takes its being to be associated with non-being, it is bound by it even if it is ontologically distinct from objects. Bondage and limitation occur through the cognitive trope of unwisdom (*avidyā*), which is the incapacity of consciousness to become free of the changing states of the internal organ of the body. The result of freedom even from purity is what Kṛṣṇa promises at 14.26: one then becomes ready to become *brahman* (*brahmabhūyāya kalpate*). Śaṅkara reads that as 'to be fit' (*samartha*) 'for becoming *brahman*' (*brahmabhavanāya*), that is to say, for liberation (*mokṣāya*). That means, of course, to be free of all individuation conditions.

Rāmānuja has a simpler reading of how even purity binds. 'When attachment to happiness and knowledge is born, in order to secure them, one engages in worldly and Vedic activity. Then, one is born to a womb as such a being as will secure the experience of those fruits.'[27] The self is ontologically transformed by even purity, because it then performs acts appropriate to all virtuous standards; but that generates the fruits of consequential action, which is rebirth in a body apt for enjoyment of good works. Even such embodiment is, after all, bondage for the self. For Rāmānuja, Kṛṣṇa's statement at 14.26 that a person qualified by freedom from purity is ready to become *brahman* indicates that *brahman* is the true being of the self: 'he becomes disciplined to be *brahman*: the meaning is that he attains the self as it is, immortal, immutable.'[28] Freedom from even purified personhood is attainment of the self's formal nature. However, while technically adhering to the teaching of bondage, we notice that Rāmānuja gives a minimal account of it, offering the dis-evaluation of the virtuously acting person strictly in ontological terms, with no further moral or epistemic charge. This is important, because I will argue later than he is ambivalent about the role of body. The virtuously acting embodied being alone is capable of the fullness of devotion, not the essential self that is freed (that is to say, stripped) of the very psychophysical apparatus through which love can be offered to God and received as gift.

The *Gītā* applies the three-fold qualitative typology to all the elements of personhood; this is especially clear in chapter 17's treatment of the type of trust or faith (*śraddha*) that individuals place on the ritual orderliness of the world and, consequently, the type of people they become. It is also clear in 18.19–35, when cognition, action and the nature of the agent are all similarly typologized. Although the commentators add very little to what the *Gītā* says, it is worthwhile to note what is said in the text, before we turn to their theorisation of the significance and explanatory limits of the *guṇa*-typic modelling of the person. To start with, both commentators reject the premise of Arjuna's question at the beginning of chapter 17, where he asks, 'What is the standing of those who perform action filled with trust, while letting go of the injunctions of sacred text? Is it of purity, urgency or stolidity?'[29] Śaṅkara argues that these people cannot be those who literally ignore sacred injunctions. 'For it cannot be imagined that, even after seeing some sacred authoritative injunction on the worship of gods and others, they let that go out of a lack of trust, but set out to worship the gods and others through being endowed with trust!'[30] And Rāmānuja says, 'To affirm the fruitlessness of trust and sacrifice not enjoined by sacred text, and to show that the threefold division of qualities is only about sacrifices, etc., enjoined by sacred text, the Lord expounds the threefold nature of trust enjoined in the sacred texts.'[31] So, all directions towards the attainment of a virtuous life, or directions towards the cultivation of pure intention and action, have to be consistent with the injunctions of the sacred texts (*śāstras*). The quality of purity is, by definition, found only in living according to those injunctions.

The ontological significance of faith or trust (*śraddha*) is explained at 17.3: 'Everyone's trust follows the form of their essence …;[32] a human is made of trust; as his faith, even so is he'.[33] Śaṅkara and Rāmānuja agree that the 'essence' here is the 'internal organ' (*antaḥkaraṇa*) or mind, the former adding that it is the internal organ 'possessing particular trace-tendencies' (*viśiṣṭasaṃskāropeta*). One's stance towards the world – what to aim for in it, how to deal with what it throws at you – is both what is given in one's dispositions, and also one's intention or resolve to act for particular ends. This mentality is the very core of personhood. Set up in this way, the commentators can simply follow, without much detail, subsequent verses (17.4–22) in this chapter on various *guṇa*-typic manifestations in the world. Pure sacrificial worship is to the gods, urgent such worship is for demi-gods and demons, while stolidity is directed towards the spirits of the dead and to ghostly hosts. Flavourful and smooth foods, salty and sour foods, and stale and spoilt foods, are also classified respectively under the three quality-types, thereby marking those who prefer one or the other type. Sacrificial worship that desires no fruit is pure; that which seeks its fruit is urgent; while that in which *mantras* are neglected and which is undertaken without confidence is stolid. Discipline that produces true, agreeable and beneficial speech is pure; wavering discipline undertaken to earn honour, respect and favour is urgent; while discipline that is self-deluded and with the purpose of destroying others is stolid. The gift given without expectation of reciprocity, at the right time and place, is pure; the gift given in expectation of reciprocity, and given grudgingly, is urgent; while that given disrespectfully, at the wrong time and place, without decorum, is stolid. The individuality of a person is expressed through the interactive connection between actions and mental processes.

This process is developed in the next chapter too, where a section (18.19–40) typologizes people according to the *guṇas*, under the categories of cognition (*jñāna*), action (*karma*) and agent (*kartā*). Again, since the commentators adhere closely to the *Gītā*'s words, we need only get a general view of what is taught there. As we will soon see, what is relevant here is the outline of the intentions and actions (and therefore the temperamental constitution) of the pure individual, which the commentators endorse. Angelika Malinar sums up the whole of this section succinctly, and the outline of the *sattva* person is worth quoting *in extenso*. 'He knows that only one being is present in all creatures; he performs his duties without showing any desire for reward; he acts without egotism and is indifferent to failure and success; and he understands the difference between activity and non-activity, right and wrong, bondage and release. He remains steadfast and self-controlled …, his happiness resulting from constant self-purification, which results ultimately in liberation from karmic bondage.'[34] The contrast of this ideal-typical character is with *rajas* and *tamas* persons; the former individualistic, greedy, pleasure-seeking, the latter, ruthless, violent, crooked and lazy. We have, then, a materially grounded account of the constitution of persons, that is at once descriptive and prescriptive: descriptive because the latter two types speak of ordinary human vices and the first type has a list of traits we do see partially in virtuous people, and prescriptive because the entire typification is instructive of a way of being and a form of behaviour that the *Gītā* considers fully ethical. The main point is that action, trust, mind and other aspects of individual being have to be *sāttvika*, and the virtues listed under that type indicate all that a person can be and ought to seek to become.

The concern of the commentators is not about ethics as such (the content of what is pure) but the state of being (what purity means in relation to the metaphysics of selfhood). In other words, the point about the *Gītā*'s teaching on the quality-type of purity (*sattva guṇa*) is not about its value as guidance for particular actions. The presence and cultivation of purity are important because they prepare the person for the realization of selfhood, as precisely what is free of even purity itself. The other quality-types are sharp descriptions of how persons respond to the world they find themselves in; implicitly, Kṛṣṇa is pointing to Arjuna's state on the eve of battle (and the eve of the revelation of the *Gītā*) as being characterised by these other quality-types. One could say, following Heidegger's startlingly apposite terminology, that in the world into which Arjuna has been 'thrown' – i.e. one in which he already finds himself and with regard to whose features (the teachers and elders he faces, the causes for which he battles, etc.) – he is unfree. To continue Heideggerian terminology, Arjuna is also, in the negative sense, in the condition of 'falling', which is to misunderstand himself or lose himself in everydayness,[35] to understand himself only in terms of the world in which he finds himself. Generally, it is this condition of falling that is thought by Heidegger to be the inauthentic state, 'in which we are immersed in the world, which is to say our experience is a purely common experience that limits entities to their function and is not concerned with the singularity of the entity that is actually performing that function.'[36] Heidegger's idea that to be authentic is to be resolved to find out how to determine one's actions[37] – for all that he means something very different by it – serves well to explain the purpose of the cultivation of *sattva guṇa*. Arjuna will be most himself in a determination to be sāttvic, pure in his way of being, and to look for the course of action that he must take. Seen that way, it would seem that Kṛṣṇa's aim is to teach Arjuna to be authentic, which is to discover what is unique about himself, and become properly and correctly himself. As we are in no sense comparing the content of Heidegger's different articulations of the concept of authenticity with what the *Gītā* says about Arjuna – instead, merely drawing on the notion of the authentic as a formal concept of self-discovery against the fact of being functionally tied to the world – I am not going to suggest that there is any particular similarity to their views of appropriateness. But clearly, the commentators note that the *Gītā*'s descriptive/prescriptive account of the person with *sattva guṇa* is meant to take someone who is tied to exigent circumstance and make him attain a state of appropriate engagement with the world.

Illuminating though it is to think through Arjuna's situation in the Heideggerian terms of authenticity and resolution, the commentators could not possibly be seen as endorsing the central precept of Heidegger, where he takes it that resolution means that 'it is uniquely *up to me* to take my world up in a meaningful way'.[38] From what we have seen thus far in this book, we can take this to be the Śaṅkarite attitude: yes, the task is indeed up to me, for I have to attain gnosis; but the meaningful response in that case is precisely to see beyond the world and its ultimate non-existence, to *brahman*. Rāmānuja's point of view would be: yes, my world has to be seen in a meaningful way, but ultimately, it is not up to me but God to bring me to it. What this indicates is that both want to go beyond the ethical dimension of being that is indicated by the *guṇa*-typification of personal being. They are seeking the ground of being itself. For Śaṅkara, that is *brahman*, which is asymmetrically identical with conscious being (*ātman*); and to re-attain that, *ātman* must see through its erroneous limitation of itself to personhood. For Rāmānuja, of course, that ground is God, who is the source of being and yet other than being. For these different reasons, then, while adhering largely to the contours of the *Gītā*'s description of how personhood is constituted, and its prescription for how a person – Prince Arjuna – should live in relation to the situation into which he is thrown, the commentators circumscribe the ultimate significance of personhood, by denying the ultimate significance of agency.

Personhood, body and the limits of agency

Agency is central to the authenticity of the pure or sāttvika person – marking the resolve to be appropriate in dealing with the world and then deal with it accordingly. But in different ways, the two commentators limit that agency. Śaṅkara does this in a radical and thoroughgoing way that ties agency to an ultimately non-existent locus, the individuated subject. Rāmānuja is more ambiguous. First, he too limits agency to a materially constituted personhood, since the bodying *ātman* (the *dehin*) has to be non-agentive according to the *Gītā*; second, he also limits it theologically, taking agency to lie finally with God alone. But he returns to it because, as we can already discern, to love God (to be a *bhakta*) is to exercise personal agency after all.[39]

Our commentators frame the in/significance of agency in two steps. First, both are agreed that what counts as appropriate action has to be circumscribed by authoritative text; the ethical is text-normative. At the end of Chapter 16 Kṛṣṇa enjoins Arjuna to let sacred teaching (*śāstra*) be epistemic authority (*pramāṇa*) for what is to be done and not done; and, he goes on, after understanding this, 'you ought to do what has to be done here' (*karma kartumihārhasi*) (16.24). Śaṅkara understands this to draw the boundaries within which action is to occur: '"here" is meant to point out the sphere of entitlement to [ritual] action'.[40] He thereby limits the scope of action, indicating one should go beyond it to gnosis. Rāmānuja treats this injunction differently, but equally to circumscribe action. He says one should accept the teachings as being directed towards attaining (*prāptnoti*) God, and those alone (*tadeva*) should be accepted (p. 521/514). We have already seen that, at the start of chapter 17, whereas Arjuna asks about those who act with trust but ignore sacred teaching, both commentators read against the text to conclude that trust, by definition, requires commitment to sacred teaching, and that therefore Kṛṣṇa's answer can only be about those working within sacred injunctions.

Second, and more profoundly, they use the twin notions of *saṃnyāsa* (renunciation) and *tyāga* (letting go).[41] At 18.2, Kṛṣṇa says, 'The wise know the laying aside of actions done out of desire to be renunciation; the discerning call "letting go" that letting go of the fruit of all action.'[42] Despite the apparent distinction readily available here, Śaṅkara and Rāmānuja agree that there is no difference, that across the *Gītā* Kṛṣṇa uses the terms interchangeably, and that the underlying concept is in any case *tyāga*, because it is the detachment from the fruit – even of obligatory ritual action (*nitya karma*) – which accrue in the afterlife. The significant point comes in their subsequent interpretation of this renunciatory letting go. For them, what is important is not primarily the ethical demands of the intentional detachment from the world apparently called for in the *Gītā*, but the implication it has for the ultimate goal of human existence. The sacrifice of agency is a critical step in the attainment of the truest state of self. They offer rather different implications for the sacrifice of agency that comes in the letting go of the fruit of obligatory action; but this is to be expected because they have very different conceptions of the truest state of the self.

Śaṅkara is unwaveringly committed to the dismissal of any ultimate significance for agency. The agency required even for the performance of obligatory actions can be located only in the bodily apparatus of a person; and personhood, of course, is an error about the nature of the non-agentive self. Śaṅkara concedes, however, a penultimate role for agency in self-realization, in the very particular and rigorous form of obligatory ritual action.[43] At 18.9, Kṛṣṇa calls that letting go pure (*sattva*) which lets go of attachment and of fruit, while carrying out obligatory action because it is to be done. In his commentary on 18.10 Śaṅkara says that a person who acts only in this manner, his mind or internal organ untainted by passion for fruit, becomes clean and refined by the obligatory actions (p. 253). For the mind of such a person, 'When it is completely purified and perspicuous, it becomes capable of reflecting on the self.'[44]

This is the bridge between personal agency and the non-agentive self: purified action leads to the realization of non-agency, by preparing the mind of the person to contemplate its self. Śaṅkara is not willing to grant anything more than that penultimate role to agency. 18.10 describes the *tyāgi*'s dispassion towards all activity; he neither hates inauspicious activity nor clings to auspicious ones. This appears to suggest that Kṛṣṇa is talking only about the intentional stance towards the objects of agency, and not about agency as such. However, Śaṅkara limits the application of this teaching to only someone who, while having the authority (*adhikāra*) to perform proper rites, holds the conceit that the body is self (*dehātmābhimāna*) and therefore still thinks, 'I am the agent' (*ahaṃ kartā*). Such a one is incapable of letting go of action entirely.[45] So he is really qualified only to act and let go of the fruit. But Śaṅkara sees a more far-reaching state of letting go for the authoritative person (*adhikāri*), who has understood (*saṃbuddhaḥ*) the non-agency (*niṣkriya*) of the changeless (*vikriya*) *ātman*. Such a one is steadfast in gnosis (*jñānaniṣṭhā*), which is characterised by absence of action (*naiṣkarmyalakṣaṇa*) altogether. Then, when 18.11 talks of how the one who bears a body (*dehabhṛta*) cannot let go of actions entirely, and can only let go of the fruit of such actions, Śaṅkara takes this to mean that complete renunciation of action (*aśeṣakarmasaṃnyāsa*) is possible only for the one who has, further, forsaken the notion of body as self (*dehātmabhāvarahita*) and may therefore (metaphorically) be called, 'one who does not bear a body' (*adehabhṛtā*) (pp. 254–5). It might seem that the *Gītā*'s teaching here is that bodilessness is impossible and agency therefore inescapable; consequently, one can only cultivate detachment from the fruit of even the purest of actions for which one becomes qualified. But Śaṅkara takes bodilessness to be a cognitive state, not a physical one: the seer of transcendence (*paramārthadarśi*) is one who has forsaken the disposition to take body as self (*dehātmabhāvarahita*) (18.11; p. 255). The state of transcendental seeing is one in which the mind has grasped that it is not itself the consciousness that is the necessary condition for its functioning, but only the internal organ of the material bodily complex; this permits witness consciousness alone to be present to itself. It must be remembered that Śaṅkara consistently takes only consciousness – the self (*ātman*) in his special sense – as being, contrasting it with materiality, which is non-being. The self's freedom from body is thus never an ontological change, only a cognitive one, as consciousness already and always is ontologically unentangled with body. Consciousness' presence permits the mind, as a functional element of the material body, to think its way to its own non-being, thereby freeing consciousness from the illusion of bodily individuation. Freedom is when consciousness' presence is no longer taken by its material superstrate (the bodily complex) as itself (its self). Freedom from agency is thus a gnostic switch, and can be attained by the self; this is the ultimate letting go of action, and it goes much further than merely the mind's attainment of the intentional stance of detachment towards the fruits of the body's action. Śaṅkara has a comprehensive view of non-being: action, agency, the physical body, the mind and its states are all non-being.

The entire psychological drama of the *Gītā* is penultimate in meaning for Śaṅkara. 'Regardless of whether the qualifying adjuncts [constituting the psychophysical body] have ontic being or whether they are conceived through agnosis, action is their attribute. It is because it [action] is mistakenly superimposed out of agnosis on the self that it has been said that the unwise person "never, not even for an moment" (5.3) is capable of completely letting go [of action]. But the wise person is able completely to let go of action when agnosis has been dispelled by gnosis; for then it is not possible for there to be any remnant of what had been mistakenly superimposed through agnosis.'[46]

When we turn to Rāmānuja, we find a rather more complicated attitude to the body and agency, metaphysically more conservative yet theologically daring. In brief, Rāmānuja has to finesse the role of body and agency: on the one hand, there is the Vedāntic commitment to the *Gītā* doctrine that the *ātman* is non-agentive, while on the other, loving devotion to God is inescapably agentive and person-centric. Whereas Śaṅkara's tactic for limiting the efficacy of agentive action is to argue that it merely purifies the mind in preparation for the ultimate attainment of gnosis, Rāmānuja asserts that 'action is not the cause of mental grace in a direct way; but rather [indirectly], by way of divine grace.'[47] This is not so much a stricter restriction on the efficacy of action than Śaṅkara's as an alternative to it: characteristically, where Śaṅkara subsumes action to gnosis, Rāmānuja subsumes it under divine grace. Ritual action is completely re-configured to the teleology of worship, so that the Vedic injunctions become theologised. It leaves intact the actual performative content of rituals but wraps them in the Śrīvaiṣṇava cosmotheology of God as the recipient of all ritual intention and the bestower of grace upon the performer.[48] This is the first half of Rāmānuja's argument for the restricted role of agency: it drives authoritatively sanctioned action, but action whose fruit is to be given up; and such action renders the agent fit for divine grace.[49]

Rāmānuja then flatly disagrees with Śaṅkara's claim about the possibility of complete freedom from action under 18.11. The living flesh (*dhriyamāṇaśarīra*) cannot let go of action entirely. The mention of the one who lets go of fruit (*phalatyāgīti*) is for illustrative purposes (*pradarśanārtha*), in that it implies something more: it is about the 'one who lets go of fruit, agency, and attachment to action' (*phalakartṛtvakarmasaṅgānāṃ tyāgī*) (p. 553/547). In saying this, Rāmānuja sharply pulls back from the radical theory propounded by Śaṅkara; letting go is only letting go of the fruit of action and attachment to action, not action itself. However, he does acknowledge that there is letting go of agency. Does this not amount to the same position as Śaṅkara's? In one sense, Rāmānuja has no choice; the *Gītā* is clear in asserting that *ātman* is non-agentive, so letting go of agency has to occur at some point on the spiritual path. But, as we would expect, his analysis of this letting go is profoundly theological.

At 18.12, Kṛṣṇa gives the assurance that no consequential fruit accrues to a renouncer. Rāmānuja does show that he accepts renunciation to be the letting go of agency. He goes on, 'Now he [Kṛṣṇa] explains the manner in which one realises that the self is non-agent: by understanding that agency is God's, who is the supreme person and inner ruler. Thusly, one is able to utterly let go of the "mineness" of fruit and action.'[50] The organs (*karaṇa*), the corporeal body [the körper] (*kalevara*) and vitality (*prāṇa*) of individual selves (*jīvātmanā*) are God's own belonging (*svakīya*), and their actions are for the purpose of divine play (*līlāprayojana*). While we cannot go into the concept of *līlā* here, for our purposes, it is sufficient to note that Rāmānuja means here to indicate that the sacrifice of agency is the indication that the person recognises that the unconstrained will of God subsumes human activity.[51] He then goes on to say more about the nature of this letting go of instinctive possessiveness.

In giving up the conceit (*abhimāna*) that 'I do' (*ahaṃ karomi*), the one who contemplates the 'agency of the supreme person' (*paramapuruṣakartṛtva*) is freed from the fruit of his actions. The intentions of such a person towards actions are structured by this stance: 'My agency does not exist in this action, its fruit is not connected with me'[52] (18.17; pp. 560/559–60). In keeping with his Vedāntic commitment, Rāmānuja therefore does think there is a crucial gnostic element to letting go. There has to be a fundamental restructuring of one's natural understanding of the ownership of action, something that can happen only through the disciplining of mental functions. Only then is the performance of ritual action unaccompanied by the conceit of 'mineness'; only then is agency – inescapable because of the very form of bodily existence – let go.

On the content of renunciatory gnosis, Rāmānuja's view is that it consists in realizing the ultimate agency of God. In that realization, the person sacrifices the assumption that their essential being, the self, is the agent. He says under 18.14–15: 'By means of the sense organs and the corporeal body, that are granted by the supreme self – and having him [the supreme self] as the foundation, through his beneficent power and therefore deriving power from him – the individual self sets forth of its own will in the effort to direct the sense organs, etc., to actions formally based on the senses and so on. With the supreme self abiding in it [and] imparting its will to act, the individual self, through its own discernment, is the cause of its actions.'[53] Bodily being cannot be without agency, and Rāmānuja's realist metaphysics cannot tolerate Śaṅkara's complete rejection of body and agency through the restriction of being to non-agentive consciousness. But by locating renunciation in the sacrifice of agency to God – the sacrifice consisting in the recognition of the all-pervasiveness of divine will – Rāmānuja elegantly preserves the *Gītā*'s teaching that *ātman* is non-agentive, within a rich psychological account of the individual person-as-devotee, who acts for the love of God and is therefore agentive.

Looking back at the last two sections, we can see how little both commentators have to say about ethics.[54] Neither of them denies that the moral locus of responsibility is the person, the materially constituted individual. It is not that they do not understand or seek to solve the moral dilemma that attaches to the person of Arjuna. Rather, each has an overarching account of reality – Śaṅkara's transcendental metaphysics of *brahman*, Rāmānuja's metaphysics-transcending theology of Kṛṣṇa/Nārāyaṇa – that they see as offering a supreme end within which moral issues are subsumed. This is clear in their response to the *Gītā*'s teaching that the self is not-agent, which teaching has the apparent implication that understanding its true meaning will inform and transform Arjuna's attitude to what has to be done.

As we have seen, Śaṅkara offers a completely revisionary metaphysics in which the non-agency of the *ātman* is read in a radical way. At 2.21, Kṛṣṇa talks about the transcendental nature of *ātman*, as eternal, indestructible, unborn, and imperishable, before asking the transformative questions: how can a person who knows the self thus kill, whom does he kill or cause to kill? This is meant to free Arjuna from the paralysis that had come with his metaphysical guilt, since he is now to see that *ātman* transcends change. But Śaṅkara focuses instead on how such insight frees one from action, even dutiful action, altogether. He takes Kṛṣṇa to be saying that the idea that the self is 'an agent, the object of agency or the [indirect] cause of [another's] agency' (*kartṛtvaṃ karmatvaṃ hetukartṛtvaṃ ca*) is due to agnosis (p. 23). 'Also, agency being caused by agnosis is common to all actions equally, since the self is changeless. Only that agentive self who is changeful instigates another who is within the remit of action, by saying "do [this]". So, it is to show the absence of any requirement to do rituals in the case of the wise person, thus negating [direct] agency and [the indirect] causing of agency [in another] with regard to all actions without exception, that the Lord says, "He who knows the eternal…", "how can that person", and so on.'[55] Śaṅkara therefore draws a very different conclusion from that which we might have thought: not a psychological prompt to action but a gnostic switch to freedom from action.

Rāmānuja does acknowledge the moral challenge facing Arjuna, and recognizes that Kṛṣṇa's teaching prompts action to meet that challenge. Nevertheless, the ultimate point of the teaching is still taken to be insight into the nature of the self, rather than ethical guidance. 'In you the contradiction is recognisable: [there is] the grief at the thought, "Shall I slay them?", but also talk of right (*dharma*) and wrong (*adharma*) as if it were caused by knowledge of the distinction of self from body. So you do not know of the essential nature of the body, nor of the eternal self that is distinct from it; nor, too, the duty (*dharma*) of war by which to obtain it [the self]. Nor too that this war, [fought] casting aside any hankering for fruit, is the means to the attainment of the truth of the self.'[56] Here we see again Rāmānuja's delicate balancing of the scope and limitation of agency. The doctrine of the eternal self cannot allow any role for agency, and the metaphysical lesson on the difference between body and self can only point to the limitation of agency to bodily being. And yet there cannot be a total rejection of agency: Kṛṣṇa is concerned to get Arjuna to act, and Rāmānuja is not willing to read completely against the text on this. So he takes the removal of agnosis to come through the sacrifice of the sense of agency – in the manner he will discuss later in the commentary and which we have already examined – that leaves intact the imperative to act. But the circle is closed, because it is through dutiful action, freed of desire of the fruit, that one eventually gains understanding of the non-agentive nature of *ātman*. We know already that Rāmānuja will say later on in his commentary exactly how this happens, namely, through gaining divine grace.

Despite their profound differences, we can see that the two commentators are committed to a basic tenet in the *Gītā*, which is perhaps a tenet common to practically all classical Indian systems committed to a theory of ultimate freedom: our ordinary notion of who we are is an erroneous one. To take the self (howsoever it is construed) to be the person who experiences his or her selfhood, is to be in error. Let us look at the two accounts of this error and the realization of self, before we conclude with a general comparison of the two animating principles of their exegesis, gnosis and devotion.

The error of personhood

Śaṅkara and Rāmānuja agree in their reading of the *Gītā*'s lesson on Arjuna's confusion of the formal self with the bodily being of the person: the agreement is that the confusion is due to 'I'-ness (or literally, the 'I'-maker), conventionally, if misleadingly, translated as 'ego' (*ahaṃkāra*). But they disagree over the error involved in that confusion. We have seen repeatedly that letting go of 'mineness', i.e., the possessiveness towards action and its fruit, is a leitmotif of the *Gītā* and the commentaries. By 'mineness', the commentators mean the psychological bond a person has to agency and consequence. It is the forensic sense of perspectival continuity that informs personhood, and makes the person who acts responsible for the consequences of their action. We have seen them offer different accounts of how this letting go happens. For both of them, 'I'-ness indicates the individuality of personhood.

Under 16.18, Śaṅkara says: 'That is "I"-ness which thinks the self – on which have been imposed qualities, both found and not found – as "I", is called agnosis, and is pernicious.'[57] Śaṅkara takes the mental functions of the person to construct their personhood, by systematic ascription of qualities, whether they be empirically correct or imagined. The qualitative ascriptions are idiosyncratic to the mental locus of experience, and it is such ascription that generates the sense of an 'I'.[58] But, Śaṅkara says, this is the fundamental cognitive error (*ajñāna*), a failure on the part of the mind – the internal organ (*antaḥkaraṇa*) of the bodily entity – to grasp that it has only constructed an apparently unified locus for first-personal usage, when ultimately there is no such individual entity.[59]

Rāmānuja's construal of 'I'-ness, in contrast, is explicitly psychological. Indeed, he applies this to all the other vices Kṛṣṇa mentions at 16.18, force, arrogance, desire, and anger. 'They follow "I"-ness in this form, "Without depending on any other, I do all"; in the same way, with "force", in doing everything, "my power is sufficient"; then, arrogance is [of the form], "there is none like me". Desire is [in the form of], "As I am thus, by my mere desiring, everything is fulfilled"; while anger is, "Anyone who does me harm, I shall kill".'[60] What concerns Rāmānuja about 'I'-ness is its indication of a person's disregard for God. The error in 'I'-ness consists, not in unawareness of the cognitive auto-construction of an illusory self but of existential subsidiarity to God. Egoity is the general condition of taking oneself to be volitionally and ontologically independent of the divine. From the same terminology of 'I'-ness, then, the commentators devise utterly different views of the ailment of the human condition.

As we would expect, each commentator's analysis of the error of personhood is based on his metaphysics. We have seen that personhood is understood in terms of materiality (*prakṛti*), with individuality generated by the qualitative characteristics of the psychophysical apparatus of the body. As we know, for Śaṅkara, materiality is less-than-real (*mithyā*), as it is of the order of non-being. The error of personhood consists in agnosis, a failure to grasp that individuation is altogether illusory. For Rāmānuja, materiality is real, an order of being that is dependent on God, and indeed, part of the body of God-as-being. The error of personhood consists in the phenomenological entanglement of two orders of being, the sentient and the insentient, within being itself.

In his extended commentary on 13.2, Śaṅkara makes a series of points clarifying his view that the error of personhood is a cognitive failure of the psychophysical apparatus, while the *ātman*-self is attributeless consciousness. For one thing, Śaṅkara argues that *ātman* is being as such, and not some immortal entity with a set of virtuous attributes. 'If cognitive objects such as happiness, sorrow, delusion and desire, which are the attributes of the field that is the body, belong to the subject-self, then the reason has to be given as to why some attributes of the field of cognitive objects imposed by primal unwisdom belong to the self, while others like decriptitude and death do not.' (commentary on 13.3) [61] So, he argues, none of these qualities pertain to the self, since obviously a putative opponent who takes *ātman* to be a category of plural, qualified entities would not want to deny its immortality. Secondly, he is always anxious to point out that primal unwisdom (*avidyā*) (Śaṅkara uses this interchangeably with agnosis (*ajñāna*)) – while central to his revisionist view of human existence – is not a state of *ātman*, because *ātman* is consciousness only in a rigorously unqualified, or 'witness' (*sākṣi*) state. He compares the error of conflating *ātman* with any attributive object, i.e., the body or its states – with a perceptual defect (*doṣa*). When there is a visual false apprehension (*viparītagrahaṇa*), the failure to see correctly is due to a defect of the organ (*karaṇa*), like an eye disease; it is not a problem with the subject of perception (*grahītṛ*). This, he says, is demonstrated by the fact that if the disease is cured, there is correct perception again. This is a rough analogy with the failure of a person to see the body for what it is – not a failure on the part of consciousness but of the relevant organ, in this case, the mind (p. 188). Once the defect is removed, consciousness is left in its true state, of unconstrained being. Thirdly, Śaṅkara repeats a classic Advaitic assertion: the self is always the subject, never the object. As he asks of his opponent, 'If primal unwisdom, sorrowfulness, and the rest are attributes of the *ātman*, then please do say, how are they directly apprehended? How can they be attributes of the cogniser of the field? If it is maintained that all cognitive objects are the field and the cognitive subject is the cogniser of the field, then it is a contradiction, based only on primal unwisdom, to say that cognitively objective attributes like unwisdom, sorrow, etc., qualify the cogniser of the field, and that they are directly apprehended.'[62] Anything at all that can be said of oneself can only be said of the object that one takes oneself to be (the psychophysical person), because all attributes are objective. But the self as such, the *ātman*, is always that which enables the mind to take it to be something; it is not what it takes itself to be. He goes on to say a little later, 'Surely, it is not possible for you, the cogniser, to apprehend at the time [of cognising your unwisdom] the relationship [of the self] with unwisdom, because the cogniser is then engaged with unwisdom as an object of cognition.'[63] In these considerations, Śaṅkara's fundamental insight is that whatever is considered, it is an object of cognition, and not that which considers (or more carefully, that which enables the mind to consider), which is the subject-self. The subject always escapes its own attention, for it is that which attends, through the mental apparatus. Every thought is capable of being attended to, every reason and every state, for they are cognitive objects; that is why there is the illusion that one can have any specific grasp of oneself: but the self is the source of grasping, not the content of what is grasped.[64] Even the insightful apprehension of the primal error (that of misidentifying the self with the bodily entity) is an apprehension of an object, namely the error itself, the unwisdom. When engaged in that, the self with which the unwisdom is associated is not itself also apprehended, since it is that which is apprehending the unwisdom. So the non-objectivity of the self is absolute. It altogether escapes objectivity and, therefore, attribution. By contrast, the persons we take ourselves to be are objective, with attributes – and ultimately non-existent. Our normal condition is to be in error. Realization is to rid the mind of the error of unwisdom, leaving the consciousness on which the mind and the rest are superimposed (by unwisdom itself) to be free in its being.

Rāmānuja takes the materiality from which our personhood is composed to be ontologically real; indeed, we have seen in the previous chapter that, for him, it is an order of being, *prakṛti* as *brahman*. So personhood is not ultimately an illusion. At the same time, there is indeed an error involved, namely, our taking the *ātman* to be the person each of us normally take ourselves to be. The ambivalence he feels towards this error – an error according to the *Gītā*'s enigmatic exposition, and as such to be acknowledged by the exegete – is clear in his interpretation.

Conceptually, metaphysical realists are generally uncomfortable with any error theory that holds that any domain of discourse may be directed towards objects that do not exist as they are taken to be.[65] This is because, of course, error theory raises questions about subjects' access to subject-independent states of affairs. Rāmānuja is fundamentally opposed to Śaṅkara's radical revisionism about the nature and content of reality; therefore, he cannot possibly countenance the possibility that our being erroneous about who we are consists in the ultimate non-existence of who we take ourselves to be. But the *Gītā* is clear that Kṛṣṇa teaches us that we are in error about our personhood. Rāmānuja's response to this situation is to locate the error in the confusion between two orders of being, both existent. The error is fundamental, and requires divine teaching to correct; but it is structurally only a common type of epistemic fault, taking two separate things to be one and the same, a mere conflation of two reals. In no way is it an ontological mistake, a confusion between the real and the unreal. As we have seen in the previous chapter, he ingeniously reads the *Gītā* as teaching about being in three ways: there is *brahman* that is made up of insentient materiality (*prakṛti*), there is *brahman* that is the non-material being of conscious selves, and there is God as *brahman*, being as such, the source of being, or being from which material and sentient beings derive their own being. So selves form a plurality of individual nodes of being that constitute one order of *brahman*, an order auxiliary to God as *brahman*. Each such self (*ātman*) is eternal, impersonal and formal when it is in a state free of entanglement with the material order of *brahman*. We have seen how ordinary personhood, constituted through the qualitative typology of the *guṇas*, is formed out of materiality when animated by *ātman*.

Rāmānuja rejects the rigorous non-duality that underlies Śaṅkara's error theory of self and person. Under 2.12 (p. 62–3/31–9), where Kṛṣṇa says, 'There never was a time when I did not exist, nor you nor any of these kings, nor will there be a time when we shall all cease to be', he argues that the divine mention of 'I', 'you', 'any', 'all' and 'we' shows that difference (*bheda*) is ultimate (*pāramārthika*). Kṛṣṇa could not possibly carry out such activities as teaching (*upadeśa*) if his perception arose from agnosis. The implication is that non-dualists, who claim that activity is based on the agnosis of dualities, must either concede that Kṛṣṇa is ignorant or that they are wrong.

The *Gītā* also talks, famously at 2.16, of the non-existent or unreal (*asat*) never coming into being (*bhāva*) and the existent or real (*sat*) never ceasing to be. We saw in the first chapter how this permitted Śaṅkara to map this utter divide onto the difference between conscious self (as being) and materiality (as non-being). Rāmānuja has to grant that, in this context, materiality, including the living body (*deha*) is taught by Kṛṣṇa to be non-existent (*asat*). Again, with ingenuity, he assumes the standard metaphysical identification of the real with the imperishable (that Śaṅkara accepts), and turns it around to say, 'the nature of the non-existent/unreal is perishability' (*vināśasvabhāve hy asatvam*) (p. 69/43). So the unreality of body simply indicates its perishability. And he has always granted that material objects are perishable, even if the material order of beings, as *brahman*, is not. In this way, Rāmānuja leaves intact the ontological status of the basis of personhood. This permits him to then offer his reading of the self-body confusion: 'Given the delusion [Arjuna has] due to agnosis of the essential being of body and self, what has to be taught [to him by Kṛṣṇa], in order to extinguish that delusion, is the discrimination between the two – their intrinsic forms of being perishable and imperishable respectively.'[66]

We may recall from the first chapter that at 13.12, the two commentators have a celebrated disagreement about how to read Kṛṣṇa's phrase '*anādimatparam brahma*'. There, we looked in detail at Śaṅkara's reading: '*anādimatparam brahma*' – 'the *brahman* beyond is without beginning', thereby making it squarely a statement about *brahman* as Śaṅkara understands it. But Rāmānuja reads the phrase as: *anādi matparam brahma* – 'beginingless *brahman* having me as the supreme'. Rāmānuja makes this teaching into one about the individual self (*pratyagātman*) ontologically under the divine. Having said of *brahman* that it is 'attached to great qualities' (*bṛhatvaguṇayogin*), Rāmānuja argues that the term '*brahman*' is surely applicable to the *ātman* (*ātmany api brahmaśabdaḥ prayujyate*). He refers forward to 14.27, where Kṛṣṇa declares, 'I am the ground (*pratiṣṭha*) of *brahman*, who is immortal (*amṛta*) and immutable (*avyaya)*', to substantiate his claim that the *brahman* that is so dependent on God is *ātman*. (By contrast, we know that when he refers to the divine in terms of *brahman* – being as such – he uses the qualifying term '*para brahman*', which is to say, hyper *brahman*.)

Then Rāmānuja explains (p. 438/434–5) why 13.2 teaches that *brahman* is neither just existent (*sat*) nor non-existent (*asat*), now that he has identified it with *ātman*: the intrinsic form (*svarūpa*) of the *ātman* is thus, because it is neither cause (*kāraṇa*) nor effect (*kārya*). It may be called existent or non-existent purely in terms of its entanglement with materiality. Then, in the condition of effect (*kāraṇāvasthā*), it is existent (*sat*) because it has name and form (*nāmarūpa*), that is, it is manifested through its presence with material qualities, as a person. It is called non-existent (*asat*) in its causal condition (*kāryāvasthā*) in a purely empirical sense, because then it does not have name and form and does not manifest itself, between lives. But the *ātman* gets into its causal and effect conditions only when beset by primal unwisdom in the form of consequential action (*karmarūpāvidyāveṣṭana*). Rāmānuja offers an entirely different gloss on agnosis from Śaṅkara, interpreting it in terms of unsacrificed agency and the attendant accretion of the fruit of action. Bondage to *karma* only occurs when the self is still entangled with the dynamics of materiality. Such a state is not the *ātman*'s intrinsic form (*svarūpa*), which, although Rāmānuja does not say so here, is a state of freedom from both causal and effectual conditions, and therefore from reflexive connection with material reality. The purified intrinsic form (*pariśuddhisvarūpa*) of the *ātman* cannot be called either existent or non-existent in this sense of whether or not it is manifest in the material world. Rāmānuja offers here an implicit ontology of the in/apparent, asserting a continuity between what becomes phenomenologically available to and as persons and what remains veiled in between the lives of persons. Both are bound states of being, within which a restricted distinction between the existent and the non-existent can be made; restricted, because it is one that holds only within the condition of entanglement between the conscious and material orders of being. The greater distinction is between these restricted realms and the condition of freedom itself. What is plain is that at no point does Rāmānuja want to concede that the error of personhood can be a matter of fundamental non-being. Any talk of the non-existence of the materially constituted person has to be re-read as two states of worldly being, namely, manifested and unmanifested entanglement.

What happens when the error is corrected? At 13.18, Kṛṣṇa says that the one who has insightful comprehension (*vijñāna*) of his teachings that correct the error of conflation, 'accomplishes my state of being' (*madbhāvopapadyate*). Śaṅkara glosses 'accomplishes' (*upapadyate*) as 'utterly entered into' (*ghaṭate*), which is his 'going to liberation' (*mokṣaṃ gacchati*). 'My state of being' is the 'being of the supreme self' (*paramātmabhāva*) (p. 202). Ultimately, there can only be non-duality when duality itself is the error. Once the gnostic switch occurs in the mental apparatus of the consciousness that appears to itself to be located in the body, then consciousness witnesses its own being as that which is always, and supremely, not non-being. We have already seen, in the first chapter, the nature of the asymmetric identity between *brahman* and *ātman*.

The cognitive non-dualism suggested by the *Gītā* verse sits naturally with Śaṅkara's reading, whereas Rāmānuja has to extract a theological difference from it. 'What is called "my being" is my natural being, which is being without transmigration. The meaning is that one [in that state] accomplishes the attainment of being without transmigration.'[67] An ontotheological reading of Kṛṣṇa's 'my state' being called for here, Rāmānuja restricts the apparent identification of the being of the divine and that of the free self to just one – if significant – feature: never having births, which is to say, never being entangled with material being. God's being as such is ever to be the source of material being, whereas a self's being is constantly and repeatedly to interact with and become instantiated in material being. Freedom means to become as God in this particular sense, which is to attain that freedom from materiality that is eternally God's. As ever, Rāmānuja helps himself to an ontotheology, while also restricting it in such a way as not to confound God's Otherness.

There is, then, an intimate connection between the essential non-agency of the *ātman*, the agentive nature of the person constituted through the *ātman*'s relationship (apparent or real) with (apparent or real) materiality, the consequent requirement to sacrifice agency in order to attain freedom for the *ātman*, and the ultimate state of such freedom. From the material in the *Gītā*, we have seen the two commentators extract two completely different accounts of the very same conjunction of ideas. Towards the culmination of the *Gītā*, Kṛṣṇa talks of how the 'conqueror of the self' (*jītātma*) 'goes to the highest fulfilment, beyond action' (*naiṣkarmyasiddhiṃ paramāṃ gacchati*; 18.49). The commentators agree that 'conquering the self' means to subdue the mind (*manas*) or internal organ (*antaḥkaraṇa*), although we know that they interpret that conquest differently. For Śaṅkara, 'his being is beyond action who is without action because of the realisation of the self as the actionless *brahman*'.[68] He also parses this state without mention of *brahman*: 'the fulfilment of the state marked by the intrinsic form of the self as actionless is the attainment of being beyond action; it is the highest, of the form of being in the state of immediate liberation, superior to the fulfilment born of action.'[69] By contrast, Rāmānuja's understanding of the fulfilment that transcends action goes back to God: the one who goes to the highest fulfilment is the one 'who, by contemplating the agency of the supreme person is free of the desire for agency for the self'.[70] Even while acting (*karma kurvan*), he goes to the highest fulfilment, beyond action, says Rāmānuja. In this difference of interpretation is summed up the complex rival accounts that we have studied in this chapter.

On *jñāna* and *bhakti*: The signification of *ātman*

The competing theories of the self that we have just examined function to indicate in the case of each commentator a (different) view of the fundamental animating principle of the human endeavour for ultimate meaning. In other words, to conceive of who we truly are is also to locate ourselves in reality and to posit how we reach our larger purpose. The *Gītā* has a persistent concern for ritually structured action, and we have seen how both Śaṅkara and Rāmānuja hasten to demonstrate that they do not deny its role altogether. But equally, they are clear on what each considers to be the culminating teaching of the *Gītā* about the *telos* of the self (as each conceives the self). For Śaṅkara, it is gnosis (*jñāna*), the insight into what the *ātman* truly is. Rāmānuja agrees that gnosis concerns self (*adhyātmajñāna*). But for him, everything ends in loving devotion (*bhakti*), the outpouring of human emotion towards the divine presence, a presence that is to be received by us as gracious gift.

As we have seen several times, this leads Śaṅkara and Rāmānuja to see Kṛṣṇa's guidance in different terms. At 2.61, for example, Kṛṣṇa says, 'Having brought all of them [the senses] under control, he should remain concentrated on me as the supreme.'[71] Śaṅkara takes the cognitive discipline exhorted here to point to a realization of non-duality. 'He for whom I, Vāsudeva – the inmost self of all – is supreme, is the one who has me as the supreme; the meaning is he should remain [concentrated, thinking], "I am not other than that".'[72] Kṛṣṇa is the self-aware source of guidance on how we are to gain self-awareness, an intensified locus of wisdom and the teacher through whom we orient our inquiry. Consequently, the disciplining of the senses is the redirection of attention away from the non-being of the world-manifold, towards the one presence that is truly being-not-other-than-our-being, namely, the consciousness we conceive of as Kṛṣṇa. For Śaṅkara, devotion itself is a gnostic discipline. The intensity of love for God that *bhakti* implies seems to be read by Śaṅkara as a mystical search for oneness; but far from being an ecstatic union with the Other, it is an enstatic focusing on the continuity of being between self and God. For example, in 10.10, as elsewhere, he glosses the 'supreme God' (*parameśvara*) as 'the being of the self' (*ātmabhūta*) (p. 151). Given the way we saw him locate theology within his transmetaphysics of *brahman*, it is entirely consistent of Śaṅkara to read devotion as the rigorous search for non-duality of self and God within *brahman*.

Rāmānuja does exactly the opposite: he sees Kṛṣṇa's instruction on cognitive discipline as a theological directive. 'When the mind is on me as its object, such a mind, purified by the burning away of impurities without remnant, rid of attachment to objects, is able to control the senses. Such a mind that has control of the senses excels in the vision of the self.'[73] While Rāmānuja acknowledges that gnosis is the goal of Kṛṣṇa's instruction here, it is the otherness of Kṛṣṇa that is the critical element of ontological self-discovery. For Śaṅkara, Kṛṣṇa prompts the self's self-clarification; for Rāmānuja, it is Kṛṣṇa who clarifies the self to itself. All this points to the fundamentally different role for cognitive discipline (*jñāna yoga*) in the two commentaries. While agreeing on what it is, one makes it the vehicle for the ultimate goal of self-realization, whereas the other makes it a vehicle for a penultimate goal about whose status and value he is ambivalent. Under 15.5, Rāmānuja offers his reading of the true state 'as it is' (*yathāvasthitam*) of the self as 'the aspect of unlimited awareness' (*anavacchinnajñākāram*). We know that this means something rather different from Śaṅkara's conception of the self's ultimate state as the realization of non-duality. But furthermore, while, technically – because the Vedāntic dimension of the *Gītā*'s teachings requires it – this gnostic attainment is the ultimate ontological state, Rāmānuja does not take it to be the end of the story; he goes on, 'Consequently, for those who take refuge in me, by my blessing (*prasāda*), all undertakings are easily performed, until perfect fulfilment is attained.'[74] It seems that the act of seeking refuge in God, and the reception of God's grace follow from – and are therefore of greater significance than – self-realization.

The Vedāntic traditions, especially Viśiṣṭādvaita, attach great importance to Kṛṣṇa's promise at 18.66: 'Forsaking all *dharma*, take refuge in me alone; I shall free you from all sins, have no fear.'[75] Śaṅkara uses his commentary mostly to argue for his radical claim that Kṛṣṇa is calling for the giving up of all structured action. But he also has things to say about the intimate connection between this radical eventuality and the significance and content of *jñāna*. While Rāmānuja too talks about what is meant by the *dharma* that has to be forsaken, he wants to point to the true purpose of this divine promise – the call to *bhakti*. As such, we can see here, in the exegesis of this celebrated verse, the two competing visions of the self and its signification, with which I propose to end this study.

Under verse 18.66, Śaṅkara frames the sacred text (*śāstra*) of the *Gītā* as teaching about the supreme means (*paraṃ sādhanaṃ*) to the highest good (*niḥśreyasa*) being gnosis, and not either action or a combination of the two (p. 280). This is because, he argues, 'gnosis of *ātman* alone is the cause of the highest good; through the removal of the idea of difference, it delivers the fruit of singularity (*kaivalya*)'.[76] The highest good is the return of individuated consciousness to the singularity – the non-duality, the sole ground – of *brahman*, and it occurs through the onset of the freeing realization in the material mind, regarding its very own self: 'I am singular, non-agentive, actionless, without fruit, there is none other than myself'.[77] The egoity of the linguistic formulation is inescapable, but the content of the realization is that consciousness is free from the individuating mark of egoity. The self is that which realizes that its being is not other than the ground of being; and the pedagogic purpose of the *Gītā* is to bring self/consciousness to that realization, through the very apparatus of the superimposed bodily non-being.

To this end are bent the *Gītā*'s teachings of (i) the letting go of action and agency (which two are taken to constitute the duty of ritual virtue (*dharma*)), (ii) the central narrative presence of the personal God, Kṛṣṇa, and (iii) Kṛṣṇa's own invitation to us to take refuge in him. The letting go of all action alone liberates, says Śaṅkara, because binding consequentiality does not accrue to a person who has taken 'refuge' (*śaraṇam*) in the truth of 'the unity of the intrinsic form of God and self' (*bhagavatsvarūpātmaikatva*) (p. 285). Taking refuge for Śaṅkara is a strictly cognitive change from ordinary intentionality to a concentration of mental acuity on the unified beingness of God and self. It does not at all carry the emotional charge of surrendering to God's love. For Śaṅkara, worshippers – 'they who perform works for the Lord' (*bhagavatkarmakāriṇaḥ*) – even if they are the most devoted (*yuktatamāḥ*) to such works, are still caught in agnosis (p. 285). The fundamental mental and physical acts of devotion, because they are actions, cannot be integral to the supreme means to liberation. Devotion – inescapably taught in the *Gītā* – can only be a particular aspect of gnosis, namely, the attentive contemplation to the content of the thought, 'I am not different from God'. As we have seen all along, the theological liveliness of the *Gītā* must, for Śaṅkara, give way to the self's inquiry into, search for, and attainment of the non-dual ground of its being.

Rāmānuja maintains here, as elsewhere, that letting go is only of agency and fruit, and not of devotional ritual action altogether. Moreover, 'sins' are theologically relevant for him in a way they are not for Śaṅkara. Śaṅkara glosses (p. 280) freedom 'from all sins' (*sarva pāpebhyaḥ*) as freedom 'from all bindings in the form of virtuous and non-virtuous ritual orderliness'.[78] Rāmānuja does see 'from all sins' in a similar manner, as 'from all sins in the form of the endless not doing of what should be done and the doing of what should not be done, accumulated from beginningless time'.[79] The real danger of sin, however, does not lie in the violation of a ritual ethic; 'from all sins' most fundamentally means, he has Kṛṣṇa say, 'from what is opposed to attaining me' (*matprāptivirodhibhyaḥ*). It is the estrangement from God that strikes at the heart of human fulfilment, and what Kṛṣṇa is teaching here is the way in which we can overcome that, through the letting go of agency and fruit of worshipful action.

Finally, Rāmānuja considers too the true extent of our distance from God, and offers *bhakti* as our only possible response; and in doing so, he leaves behind all the ontotheological concerns that he has had to examine previously. He frankly states it is very unlikely that ritual action – in particular, expiatory rites (*prāyaścitta*) for the removal of sin – can actually fulfil its purifying purpose for many people; a lifespan would not suffice to do enough of them (p. 598/600). On the other hand, it might be thought that 'the discipline of devotion is attainable only for those people who are liberated from all sins and to whom the Lord is beloved.'[80] Realizing this, it may be that Arjuna was in despair thinking himself unfit for it. It was to reassure him, says Rāmānuja, that Kṛṣṇa said what he did in this verse. Taking refuge in Kṛṣṇa will render expiatory rites beside the point; they can be forsaken.

Rāmānuja therefore offers two readings of the verse: one is the theological point that sins are potent, not for the mere reason of personal suffering or even ethical failure, but because they obstruct the relationship with God. The other is psychological: when we are in despair due to the enormity of our task and the limitations under which we labour, there is the divine promise that just our love of God will do to save us. Here, at the end, after all the careful Vedāntic exploration of the formal *ātman*-self, Rāmānuja reveals his truest and deepest concern, which is for the human person. For the persons we are, there is nothing more, nothing greater and nothing more reassuring, than God's guarantee of receiving our love.

Endnotes

Introduction

1 The situation is different, and more complicated in Indian universities, where 'theology' itself is deemed problematic under the secular Indian state, and where the study of different religious traditions is a fraught negotiation between political balance and intellectual freedom. The depth of scholarship regarding the Hindu traditions still remains despite formidable economic challenges, but English-language writing in a recognisably 'theological' form has not been a major area of activity; perhaps understandably so in a context where the first requirement is to preserve the continuity of traditional learning through a time of radical post-modern globalisation.
2 Zaehner 1969.
3 Sharma 1986.
4 Chari 2005.
5 Brockington 1998.
6 van Buitenen 1981; p. *xi*.
7 For a crisp and comprehensive survey of this development, see Malinar 2007; chapter 1.
8 Malinar, p. 17.
9 The classic collection of papers dealing with such figures as Vivekananda, Tilak and Gandhi is in Minor 1986.
10 For a clear and comprehensive introductory presentation on the biography, dating and works of Śaṅkara, see Isayeva 1993; Chapter III.
11 The tradition remembers that there were ancient commentaries on the *sūtras*; and famously, Rāmānuja refers to several, of whom especially Bodhāyana is seen as the author of the first commentary, the now-lost *Vṛtti*; van Buitenen 1956; pp 18–30.
12 Mayeda 1965.
13 Lester 1966.
14 It is a matter of interpretation whether Rāmānuja was primarily a Vedāntin who assimilated popular Vaiṣṇava devotionalism into the brahmin community (van Buitenen 1966) or whether he was a Vaiṣṇava who took the Vedānta purely as 'the general framework' within which to present his sectarian religion (Kumarrapa 1934; 185). The community itself finds these mono-directional aetiologies baffling, taking him to have synthesised harmoniously the philosophical and devotional aspects of his tradition within his theology. The Western scholarly understanding of this integrated view is first and best articulated in the classic work Carmen 1974.

15 Paul Hacker is the most famous exponent of the theory that Śaṅkara was a Vaiṣṇava; see Hacker 1995.
16 van Buitenen 1956; p. 59.
17 Grant 2000; pp. 160–3. For the developed treatment of her position, see Grant 1991.
18 Ram-Prasad 2001, p. 166; *passim* for a fuller treatment of the relationship between *ātman*, *jīva* and *brahman* in Śaṅkara.
19 For an exploration of this Śrīvaiṣṇava theology, especially as the later tradition understands Rāmānuja, see Clooney 1996, 2008c.
20 The classic formulation in modern Western scholarship on access and transcendence in Rāmānuja is Carmen 1974, pp. 77–87.

Chapter 1

1 *nāsate vidyate bhāvo nābhāvo vidyate sataḥ/ ubhayorapi dṛṣṭo'ntastvanayosta ttvadarśibhiḥ //.*
2 *na, sarvatra buddhidvayopalabdheḥ – sadbuddhirasadbuddhiriti. yadviṣayā buddhiḥ na vyabhicarati tat sat, yadviṣayā vyabhicarati tadasatiti. sadasadvibhāge buddhitantre sthite, sarvatra dve buddhī sarverupalabhyate*; Śaṅkara 1950. All references to the commentary are to this edition, although the 1935 edition of multiple commentaries has also been consulted.
3 This is an early articulation of the Advaitic point that 'existence' is not some quality or property of things; an argument developed in detail several centuries later by Śrī Harṣa, it bears an uncanny resemblance to and anticipation of twentieth century Western debates about the predicative nature of 'exists' and its Kantian roots. See Ram-Prasad 2002: III.2.
4 *tasmāt dehādeḥ dvandvasya ca sakāraṇasyāsataḥ na vidyate bhāva iti. tathā sataḥ cā'tmano'bhāo'vidyamānatā na vidyate sarvatrāvyabhicārādityavocāma*; p. 17.
5 *taditi sarvanāma, sarvaṃ ca brahma; tasya nāma taditi. tadbhāvaḥ tattvaṃ, brahmaṇaḥ yāthātmyam*; pp. 17–8.
6 John Grimes has patiently explored the parallels between Śaṅkara's *brahman* and Heidegger's Being, as also, inevitably, the fundamental differences between them (Grimes: 2007, orig. 1989). Apart from my reluctance to see *brahman* as Being (and therefore comparable), I also take my task here to be different, in that it is not comparative in any straightforward way. Rather, it is to present a philosophical and theological project that is cross-culturally accessible, perhaps even intercultural in conceptual content, seeking to interpret Śaṅkara and Rāmānuja through categories intrinsic to their thought but utilising language and ideas from the developed contemporary traditions of Western philosophy and Christian theology.

7 *kūṭasthaḥ kūṭaḥ rāśiḥ rāśiriva sthitaḥ. athavā kūṭaḥ māyā vañcanā jihmatā kuṭilateti paryāyaḥ ... saṃsārabījānantyāt na kṣaratīty akṣara ucyate*; p. 230.
8 'If we examine the emergence of beings into phenomenological visibility, there is an implicit difference between the dynamic *showing* and the more passive *lasting* of those beings – a difference Heidegger will later formalize as that between 'presencing' (*anwesen*) and 'presence' (*Anwesenheit*). In other words, in the process whereby beings come into being, linger, and pass away, we can distinguish between their dynamic emerging and disappearing, on the one hand, and the more static aspect of that which lasts, on the other;' Thomson 2000: p. 317.
9 *parastasmāttu bhāvo'nyo'nyo'vyakto'vyaktātasanātanaḥ/ yaḥ sa bhūteṣu naśyastu na vinaśyati*; 8.19, p. 133.
10 *tvamakṣaraṃ sadasattatparaṃ yat.*
11 *na me pārthāsti kartavyaṃ triṣu lokeṣu kiṃcana/ nānavāptamavāptavyaṃ karta eva ca karmaṇi//.*
12 For a study of the exemplary Christian use of *via eminentiae*, in Aquinas, see Elders 1990: chapter 6.
13 *ahameva bhagavān vāsudevaḥ nā anyo'smi*; p. 122.
14 *sarvātmānaṃ māṃ pratipadyate*; ibid.
15 *ahamātmā guḍākeśa sarvabhūtāśayasthitaḥ.*
16 Śaṅkara is more concerned with the ontology of other deities elsewhere, primarily in the *Brahmasūtrabhāṣya*. For an insightful analysis of the mediatory role of such entities, invoking too a striking comparison with angels in Aquinas, see Clooney 2000.
17 *avyaktaṃ vyaktimāpannaṃ manyante māmabuddhayaḥ/ paraṃ bhāvamajānanto mamāvyayamanuttamam//*; p. 124.
18 This is explored through other commentaries of Śaṅkara in Ram-Prasad 2010: 226–32.
19 *kathaṃ tu punarucyate'sau mamātmaiti? vibhajya dehādisaṃdhātaṃ tasminahaṃkāramadhyāropya lokabuddhimanusaran vyapadiśati mamātmaiti na punarātmano"tmā'nya iti lokavadajānan*; p. 138.
20 Cp. Meister Eckhart (1979–81: Sermon 28), who says, 'The world 'I' is proper to none, but to God in his oneness'.
21 *paraṃ brahma vāsudevākhyaṃ*; p. 250.
22 Generally and correctly, *prakṛti* is translated as 'material nature', especially in the Sāṃkhya school whose early ideas heavily influence the *Gītā*, but at 7.5, the *Gītā* itself – quite apart from Śaṅkara – talks of the higher (*parā*) *prakṛti* being of individual beings (*jīvabhūtāṃ*) who bear up (*dhāryate*) the world (*jagat*); therefore, *prakṛti* is not materiality alone, but all limitation.
23 *māyāvinaṃ svātmabhūtaṃ sarvātmanā*; p. 121.
24 *na hīśvaradvayaṃ saṃbhavatyanekeśvaratve vyavahārānupapateḥ*; p. 172.
25 Gilson 1936: p. 47.
26 *bhagavata īśvarasya nārāyaṇākhyasya vibhūtisaṃkṣepa uktaḥ viśiṣṭopādhikṛtaḥ* '*yadādityagataṃ tejaḥ*' (15.12) *ityādinā. athādhunā*

tasyaiva kṣarākṣropādhipravibhaktatayā nirupādhikasya kevalasya tattva nirdidhārayiṣayottare ślokā ārabhyante; p. 229.
27 *paramaścāsau dehādyavidyākṛtātmabhyaḥ*; p. 230.
28 *ātmā ca sarvabhūtānāṃ pratyakcetanaḥ*.
29 *īśvaraḥ sarvajñaḥ nārāyaṇākhya īśanaśīlaḥ*; ibid.
30 Heidegger 1975 p. 86.
31 Rāmānuja, p. 300/299.
32 *phalasaṅgarahitamabhimānavarjitamahaṃ karomīti*; p. 139.
33 Quoted by Paul Tillich, in Tillich 1959: p. 15.
34 *na kaścidātmānaṃ vināśayituṃ śaknotīśvaro'pi. ātmā hi brahma*; p. 18.
35 Kerr 2002: p. 94.
36 Kerr *ibid.*; Kearney 2001: 155.
37 *brahmaśabdavācyatvāt savikalpakaṃ brahma*; p. 222.
38 *tasya brahmaṇaḥ nirvikalpako'hameva nānyaḥ pratiṣṭā'śrayaḥ*; *ibid.*
39 Kearney 2001: 157.
40 Fiorenza and Kaufman 1998: 145.
41 Hacker 1995(4) pp. 57–100.
42 *ibid.*; p. 96.
43 *mayā'pakṛṣṭaṃ parityaktaṃ nirātmakaṃ śūnyaṃ hi tat syāt*; p. 157.
44 For this definition of pantheism, see Owen 1971: 74.
45 *mayā tatamidaṃ sarvaṃ jagadavyaktamūrtinā/ matasthāni sarvabhūtāni na cāhaṃ teṣvavasthitaḥ//* He uses the same phrase elsewhere too, as at 7.12, but he says little interesting about it there.
46 *samyakekenā'tmanā vyāpnoṣi*; p. 171.
47 *tvayā vinābhūtaṃ na kiñcidasti*; ibid.
48 Otto 1970.
49 Isayeva 1993: 117–18.
50 For his analysis of this proposition, see Latin Works I in Maurer 1974: pp. 93–104.
51 Colledge and McGinn 1981: 32–3.
52 *ibid.* The following discussion is largely based on this analysis by Colledge and McGinn.
53 Colledge and McGinn 1981: 33.
54 *ibid.*; p. 34.
55 Kearney uses this term, and then refers to Eckhart: Kearney 2001: fn. 11, p. 174, drawing attention to the in/famous, 'God's isness (*Istigkeit*) is my isness'.
56 Gresich quotes Sermon 77 of Eckhart's German works, Greisch 2001: 254.
57 Kearney 2001: 157.
58 In Śaṅkara's thinking, while the notion of being clearly plays an important role, and is articulated through his understanding of Kṛṣṇa, the key term that brings them together is self, the essence of what it is to be. He does not particularly focus on identifying Kṛṣṇa as being itself ('Being'), although such a claim would not be inconsistent with his position. Contrast this

topography of defining divine being with the rather different one in the history of thought pointed out by Paul Ricœur, where the encounter of Greek metaphysics and biblical religious thought led medieval philosophers to reach 'the idea that Being is the proper name of God and this name designates God's very essence' (Ricœur 1988: 353).

59 *bhūtānāṃ parameśvarasya cātyanta vailakṣaṇya pradarśanārthaṃ*; p. 209.

60 *tasmāt sarvabhūtaiḥ vailakṣaṇyamatyantameva parameśvarasya siddhaṃ nirviśeṣatvamekatvaṃ ca*; ibid.

61 *na tadasti yat vastu 'asti' śabdena nocyate*; p. 198.

62 *astibuddhyanugatapratyayaviṣayaṃ syāt*; *ibid.*

63 *viditāviditānyatvaśruteravaśyavijñeyārthapratipādanaparatvāt*; *ibid.*

64 *na kenacit śabdenocyate'tyuktaṃ*; *ibid.*

65 For Śaṅkara's non-realism, see Ram-Prasad 2001: chapters 1–3.

66 For a succinct outline of Aquinas on divine simplicity, see Kerr 2002: pp. 76–7. He illustrates Aquinas' position by reference to sections of the *Summa Theologiae*.

67 *ibid.*

68 De Smet 2010, 133.

69 Mojsisch 1998: 69.

70 As quoted in Mojsisch 1998: 70.

71 *ibid.*; p. 71.

72 *ibid.*; p. 72.

73 I am not making the claim that the only interpretation of creation *ex nihilo* should be in the form that Śaṅkara dismisses, only that this is the reason he does. A comparison of medieval Christian and classical Hindu conceptions of creation is a task for another time.

74 Summerell 1998; p129, describing Heidegger's position.

75 *ibid.*; p. 132.

76 Prudhomme 1997: p. 136, quoting Heidegger in his later work, *Humanismusbrief.*

77 Elders 1990: pp. 48–9.

78 *īśvaraprasādanimittajñāna.*

79 *jñānayajñena cāpyanye yajanto māmupāsate/ekatvena pṛthaktvena bahudhā viśvatomukham.*

80 Patton 2008: 105.

81 *viśvarūpaiśvare cetaḥsamādhānalakṣaṇaḥ.*

82 *apṛthagbhūtāḥ paraṃ devaṃ nārāyaṇamātmatvena gatāḥ santaḥ*; p. 143.

83 Fiorenza and Kaufman 1998: 146. For the relevant passage in Augustine, see Augustine 1993.

84 Williams 1999; Kerr 2002: 149–61.

85 Hemming 2003: 88.

86 *bhagavatsvarūpātmaikatvaśaraṇānāṃ.*

87 *tasmāt sarvabhūtaiḥ vailakṣaṇyamatyantameva parameśvarasya siddhaṃ nirviśeṣatvamekatvaṃ ca.*

88 *ekamavibhaktaṃ yathoktamātmānaṃ yaḥ paśyati saḥ vibhaktānekātmaviparītadarśibhyaḥ viśiṣyate saiva paśyatīti.*
89 *yadā bhūtapṛthagbhāvamekasthamanupaśyati/ tataiva ca vistāraṃ brahma sampadyate tadā.*
90 *ye bhajanti tu māṃ bhaktyā mayi te teṣu cāpyaham.*
91 I have slightly altered the translation Marion gives; Civ. 8.11 (BA 34.270–2) Quoted by Jean-Luc Marion (2008: 171).
92 *brahmano hi pratiṣṭhāhamamṛtasyāvyayasya ca/ śāśvatasya ca dharmasya sukhasyaikāntikasya ca.*
93 *amṛtādisvabhāvasya paramātmanaḥ pratyagātmā pratiṣṭhā samyagjñānena paramātmatayā niścīyate.*
94 *yayā ca īśvaraśaktyā bhaktānugrahādiprayojanāya brahma pratitiṣṭhate pravartate sā śaktiḥ brahmaivāhaṃ śaktiśaktimatorananyatvāt.*
95 *athavā brahmaśabdavācyatvāt savikalpakaṃ brahma. tasya brahmaṇaḥ nirvikalpako'hameva nānyaḥ pratiṣṭhā"śrayaḥ.*
96 *imaṃ … dharmaṃ niḥśreyasaprayojanaṃ paramārthatattvaṃ ca vāsudevākhyaṃ parabrahmābhidheyabhūtaṃ viśeṣata abhivyañjayat viśiṣṭaprayojanasambandhābhidheyavat gītāśāstraṃ*; p. 3.

Chapter 2

1 My claim in such a project would be that the elaborate architectonic of a *brahman* at once the abstract principle of the *Brahmasutras* (and the *Upaniṣads*) as well as the richly charactered Nārāyaṇa of Śrī Vaiṣṇavism is simply set aside in the *Gītā* commentary. Freed of having to talk of Nārāyaṇa through *brahman*, Rāmānuja here offers a daring reworking of *brahman* that perhaps would not or should not count as Vedānta at all, in the sense in which the Vedānta is understood as meditation on the ultimate explanatory power of *brahman*. To bring out this overwhelmingly important feature of the *Gītā* commentary (without contrast to the *brahman*-oriented texts) is the task of this chapter.
2 I thank Krishnan Ram-Prasad for alerting me to this possibility.
3 Rāmānuja n.d./2004 have both been consulted and page references follow that order; all translations are my own.
4 Śaṅkara 1950. Any further references to Śaṅkara's commentary will be to this edition.
5 *nāsate vidyate bhāvo nābhāvo vidyate sataḥ/ubhayorapi dṛṣṭo'ntastvanayosta ttvadarśibhiḥ //*
6 *asato dehasya sadbhāvo na vidyate sataścātmano nāsadbhāvaḥ*; p. 69/43.
7 *vināśasvabhāvo hyasattvam; avināśasvabhāvaśca sattvam.*
8 *dehātmasvabhāvājñānamohitasya tanmohaśāntaye hyubhayornāśitvānāśitva rūpasvabhāvavivekaiva vaktavyaḥ*; p. 70/44.
9 *karma brahmodbhavaṃ viddhi brahmākṣarasamudbhavam/.*

10 *brahmaśabdanirdiṣṭaṃ prakṛtipariṇāmarūpaṃ śarīram... brahmākṣarasamudbhavamityatrākṣaraśabdanirdiṣṭo jīvātmā; annapānādinā tṛptākṣarādhiṣṭhitaṃ śarīraṃ karmaṇo prabhavatīti karmasādhanabhūtaṃ śarīramakṣarasamudbhavam*; p. 130/115–16.
11 *prakṛtisaṃsargadoṣaviyuktayā samamātmavastu hi brahma*; p. 203/194.
12 *māyāṃ tu prakṛtiṃ vidyānmāyinaṃ tu maheśvaram.*
13 *asyāḥ kāryaṃ bhagavatsvarūpatirodhānam svasvarūpabhogyatvabuddhiśca. ato bhagavanmāyayā mohitaṃ sarvaṃ jagat bhagavantamanavadhikātiśayā nandasvarūpaṃ nābhijānāti*; p. 253/246.
14 Prudhomme 1997: 107.
15 E.g., Westphal 2001: 258–9.
16 Clayton 2006: 101–32.
17 Ricœur 1998: 352–3.
18 Westphal 1998: 151.
19 Westphal 2001: 7.
20 Westphal 1998: 152.
21 Marion 1991.
22 Derrida 1982: 6.
23 Derrida 1992; 77.
24 *ibid.*; p. 137.
25 See for example, Kearney 2001 who, incidentally, criticises Marion's argument that the God without Being is revealed in the privileged mystical experience of the liturgical authority, the bishop; and Carlson 1999, who offers a clear analysis of the Marion-Derrida controversy.
26 Ricœur 1998: 356.
27 Schrijvers 2010: p. 237.
28 *kṣetrajñaṃ cāpi māṃ viddhi sarvakṣetreṣu.../*
29 *acidvastunaścidvastunaḥ parasya brahmaṇo bhogyatvena bhokṛtvena ceśitṛtvena ca svarūpavivekamāhuḥ kāścana śrutayaḥ*; p. 416/417.
30 *ata sthūlasūkṣmacidacitprakāraṃ brahmaiva kāryaṃ kāraṇam ceti brahmopādānaṃ jagat*; p. 418/421–2.
31 For a sustained study of the symbolism and use of the body metaphor in Rāmānuja, with a comparison with Augustine, see Barua 2009.
32 Lipner 1984: 38–9.
33 In other words, instead of a material *brahman* and a sentient *brahman*, the language changes to a material *prakrti* and a sentient *prakṛti.*
34 *athā sarvakāraṇasyāpi prakṛtidvayasya kāraṇatvena sarvācetanavastuśeṣaścetanasyāpi śeṣitvena kāraṇatayā śeṣitayā cāhaṃ parataraḥ, tathā jñānaśaktibalādiguṇayogena cāhameva parataraḥ. matto'nyat madvyatiriktaṃ jñānabalādiguṇāntarayogi kiṃcidapi parataraṃ nāsti*; p. 248/240.
35 *ātmaśarīrabhāvenāvasthanaṃ ca jagadbrahmano*; p. 248/240.
36 *bhāvayitā dhārayitā niyanta ca.*
37 *sarvamātmavastu maccharīratayā madādhāraṃ maccheṣabhūtaṃ*

madekapravartyam; p. 146/130. The term 'actuation' is in Swami Adidevananda's translation.

38 *na tadasti vinā yat syānmayā bhūtaṃ carācaram.*

39 *anena sarvasyāsya sāmānādhikaraṇyanirdeśasyātmatayāvasthitireva heturiti prakaṭayati; ibid.*

40 Lipner 1984: 29–31; 43–7.

41 *sarvaṃ vastujātaṃ sarvāvasthaṃ mayā ātmabhūtena yuktaṃ syādityarthaḥ*; p. 351/355.

42 *nāmarūpavyākaraṇavacanāḥ.*

43 *acijjīvaviśiṣṭaparamātma*; p. 418/421.

44 Ricœur 1998: 348.

45 For a systematic defence of Thomistic science, see te Velde 2006.

46 *mayi sarvāṇi karmāṇi saṃnyasyādhyātmacetasā/nirāśīrnirmamo bhūtvā yudhyasva vigatajvaraḥ//.*

47 *ato maccharīratayā matpravartyātmasvarūpānusandhānena sarvāṇi karmāṇi mayaiva kriyamāṇānīti mayi paramapuruṣe saṃnyasya tāni ca kevalaṃ madārādhanānīti kṛtvā tatphale nirāśīḥ; tataiva tatra karmaṇi mamatārahito bhūtvā vigatajvaro yuddhādikaṃ kuruṣva*; p. 143/128.

48 *vāsudevaśeṣataikaraso'haṃ tadāyattatvasvarūpasthitipravṛttiś ca*; p. 259/252. A similar point on Kṛṣṇa being the principal (*śeṣi*) is made under 9.27, p. 316/314.

49 *…brahmaiva tena gantavyaṃ brahmakarmasamādhinā//.*

50 *brahmātmakatayā brahmabhūtamātmasvarūpaṃ gantavyam. mumukṣuṇā kriyamāṇaṃ karma parabrahmātmakamevetyanusandhānayuktatayā jñānākāraṃ sākṣādātmāvalokanasādhanaṃ na jñānaniṣṭhāvyavadhānenetyarthaḥ*; p. 176/167

51 *tava manniyāmyatāpūrvakamaccheṣataikarasatām ārādhyādeś caitatsvabhāvakagarbhatām atyarthaprītiyukto 'nusandhatsva*; p. 316/314–5.

52 Clooney, 2008b.

53 *yo māṃ paśyati sarvatra sarvaṃ ca mayi paśyati/tasyāhaṃ na praṇaśyāmi sa ca me na praṇaśyati//.*

54 *tato vipākadaśām āpanno mama sādharmyam upāgataḥ "nirañjanaḥ paramaṃ sāmyam upaiti" (Muṇḍaka Upaniṣad 3.1.3) ity ucyamānaṃ sarvasyātmavastuno vidhūtapuṇyapāpasya svarūpeṇāvasthitasya matsāmyaṃ paśyan yaḥ sarvatrātmavastuni māṃ paśyati, sarvam ātmavastu ca mayi paśyati; anyonyasāmyād anyataradarśanena anyatarad apīdṛśam iti paśyati, tasya svātmasvarūpaṃ paśyato 'haṃ tatsāmyān na praṇaśyāmi nādarśanam upayāmi; mamāpi māṃ paśyato matsāmyāt svātmānaṃ matsamam avalokayan sa nādarśanam upayāti.*

55 *paramaṃ puruṣaṃ divyaṃ yāti…anucintayana//.*

56 Carmen 1974: 88–97.

57 *ibid.*, pp. 90–1.

58 Footnote 11, p. 286.

59 *avyaktaṃ vyaktam āpannaṃ manyante mām abuddhayaḥ/paraṃ bhāvam ajānanto mamāvyayam anuttamam//*
60 *vāḍmanasāparicchedyasvarūpasvabhāvaḥ.*
61 For a study of the relationship between Kṛṣṇa as God and Kṛṣṇa as the descent of God Viṣṇu, see Matchett 2001.
62 On the developed doctrine of Nārāyaṇa-with-Śrī as expounded a few centuries later by Vedānta Deśika, see Clooney 2008a: chapter 4, pp. 149–66.
63 *ajo 'pi sann avyayātmā bhūtānām īśvaro 'pi san/prakṛtiṃ svām adhiṣṭhāya sambhavāmy ātmamāyayā.*
64 *ato 'pahatapāpmatvādisamastakalyāṇaguṇātmakatvaṃ sarvam aiśaṃ svabhāvam ajahat svam eva rūpaṃ devamanuṣyādisajātīyasaṃsthānaṃ kurvann ātmasaṅkalpena devādirūpaḥ sambhavāmi*; p. 160/148.
65 *yadā yadā hi dharmasya glānir bhavati bhārata/abhyutthānam adharmasya tadā "tmānaṃ sṛjāmy aham// paritrāṇāya sādhūnāṃ vināśāya ca duṣkṛtām/ dharmasaṃsthāpanārthāya sambhavāmi yuge yuge//* (4.7–8).
66 *sarve manuṣyāḥ madanuvartanaikamanorathā mama vartma matsvabhāvaṃ sarvaṃ yogināṃ vāṅmanasāgocaram api svakīyaiś cakṣurādikaraṇaiḥ sarvaśaḥ svāpekṣitaiḥ sarvaprakārair anubhūyānuvartante*; comm. on 4.11; p. 165/153–4.
67 See Young 1988 on Rāmānuja on this verse, regarding the forms of worship.
68 p. 300/299.
69 Śaṅkara's commentary, p. 133.
70 *acitsaṃsargaviyuktaṃ svarūpeṇāvasthitaṃ muktasvarūpaṃ*; p. 285/282–3.
71 *avyaktaṃ vyaktimāpannaṃ manyante māmabuddhayaḥ/paraṃ bhāvamajānanto mamāvyayamanuttamam//*; p. 124.
72 *manuṣyatvasaṃsthāna*; p. 264/258.
73 *māṃ sarvasamāśrayaṇīyatvāya manuṣvatvasaṃsthānam āsthitaṃ*; comm. on 7.25; p. 264/258.
74 18.66, p. 598/599.
75 *anādikālasañcitānantākṛtyakaraṇakṛtyākaraṇarūpebhyaḥ sarvebhyaḥ; ibid.*
76 Tillich 1959; p. 10.
77 For a relatively simple comparative analysis of the doctrine of *avatāra*, in the light of Christian belief in the Incarnation, see Carmen 1994: chapter 10.
78 *yoginām api sarveṣāṃ madgatenāntarātmanā/śraddhāvān bhajate yo māṃ sa me yuktatamo mataḥ//* (6.47).
79 *matpriyatvātirekeṇānanyasādhāraṇasvabhāvatayā madgatena antarātmanā manasā – bāhyābhyantarasakalavṛttiviśeṣāśrayabhūtaṃ mano hy antarātmā, atyarthaṃ matpriyatvena mayā vinā svadhāraṇālābhān madgatena manasā – śraddhāvān atyarthamatpriyatvena kṣaṇamātraviśleṣāsahatayā matprāptipravṛttau tvarāvān yo māṃ bhajate... bhajate sevate upāste*; p. 239 [wrongly done]/ 230.
80 *kalayati gaṇayatīti kālaḥ*; p. 376/378.
81 'The mythic-poeticized God figuratively portrays the meaning of the world by focusing in himself the inaugural openness of being within which

everything can be present...God...presents the meaning of the world in a concrete figure', writes Summerell of Heidegger's 'last God' or the 'godly God'; Summerell 1998): pp. 127–9.

82 Westphal 2001: p. 269. Compare too, perhaps even more illegitimately from the author's point of view: 'In the presence of the icon, that which awakens and lures the gaze beyond what it can see, one feels oneself in the presence of that which is extraordinarily good' (Barron 2007: 62).

83 *ahaṃ sarveśvaro nikhilajagadudayavibhavalayalīlo 'vāptasamastakāmaḥ satyasaṅkalpo 'navadhikātiśayāsaṅkhyeyakalyāṇaguṇagaṇaḥ svābhāvikānavadhikātiśayānandasvānubhave vartamānaḥ*; p. 315/313.

84 *tatra kṣaraśabdanirdṛṣṭaḥ puruṣo jīvaśabdābhilapanīya brahmādistambaparyantakṣaraṇasvabhāvācitsaṃsṛṣṭasarvabhūtāni. atrācitsaṃsargarūpaikopādhinā puruṣa ityekatvanirdeśaḥ. akṣaraśabdanirdiṣṭaḥ kūṭasthaḥ; acitsaṃsargaviyuktaḥ svena rūpeṇāvasthito muktātmā. sa tv acitsaṃsargābhāvād acitpariṇāmaviśeṣabrahmādi dehāsādhāraṇo na bhavatīti kūṭasthetyucyate. atrāpyekatvanirdeśo 'cidviyogarūpaikopādhinā 'bhihitaḥ. nahītaḥ pūrvam anādau kāle muktaikaiva*; p. 498/489-90.

85 *sarvāsu śrutiṣu paramātmā iti nirdeśād eva hy uttama puruṣo baddhamukta puruṣābhyāmarthāntarabhūta ity avagamyate. katham?*; p. 499/490.

86 Carmen says that this relationship, where God is dependent on his devotees is 'somewhat surprising' (Carmen: 191).

87 Introduction; p. 42/13.

88 See, especially, Introduction and Chapter 1 of Caputo 2006.

89 *tena vinā mama'pyātmadhāranaṃ na saṃbhavati*; p. 258/251.

90 So Caputo artfully reads St Paul's saying of the weakness of God revealed on the cross – 'for whenever I am weak, then I am strong' (2 Corinthians 12:10) – as being part of a larger economy of power; Caputo 2006: 42.

91 *tadviyogamasahamāno'hameva taṃ vṛṇe*; p. 279/276.

92 *manorathapathadūravarti priyaṃ prāpyeva*; p. 315/313.

93 Carmen 1974: 192–3.

94 Deleuze and Guattari 1987.

95 Tillich 1959: 16.

96 'My critique of Tillich is that he claims to be a Christian theologian but then opts for a view of the divine that seems to me not Christian at all but more nearly at home with certain neoplatonisms, or Hindu or Buddhist thought. He is, of course, entitled to such an ontology, but not, it seems to me, to call it Christian'; Westphal, personal communication. My thanks to him for this discussion.

97 Westphal 1998: 169.

98 *ahaṃ madvyatiriktāt samastacidacidvastujātān nikhilaheyapratyanīkatayā nānāvidhānavadhikātiśayāsaṅkhyeyakalyāṇaguṇagaṇānantamahāvibhūtitayā ca viviktaḥ*; comm. on 7.2; p. 224–5/236.

99 p. 380/381.

100 This uncertainty haunts the movement of these ideas through medieval

Christianity. Without endorsing the actual conclusion that Aquinas and others accepted an ontological notion of *hyperousios* through the Latin *essentia*, see Jones 2008 for the difficulties with reading Dionysius the Aeropagite's Neoplatonic use of 'hyperbeing' in *The Divine Names* as other than being.

101 p. 438/434.

102 *brahmano hi pratiṣṭhāhamamṛtasyāvyayasya ca/ śāśvatasya ca dharmasya sukhasyaikāntikasya ca.*

103 Clooney 2008a: chapter 4, on Vedānta Deśika. For a detailed survey, see Raman 2007.

104 *bhagavato niraṅkuśaiśvaryādikalyāṇaguṇagaṇānantyaṃ, kṛtsnasya jagatas taccharīratayā tadātmakatvena tatpravartyatvaṃ ca*; comm. on 10.1; p. 325/324.

105 *manmanā bhava madbhakto madyājī māṃ namaskuru/ mām evaiṣyasi yuktvaivam ātmānaṃ matparāyaṇaḥ//* (9.34).

106 Derrida 1992.

107 Merold Westphal says that a Tillichian commitment to ontology is xenophobic, afraid of the other; Westphal 1998: 160.

Chapter 3

1 *yasmād evaṃ nityo 'vikriyaś ca ātmā tasmāt yudhyasva, yuddhāt uparamaṃ mā kārṣīḥ ity arthaḥ. na hy atra yuddhakartavyatā vidhīyate, yuddhe pravṛtta eva hi asau śokamohapratibaddhaḥ tūṣṇīṃ āste. ataḥ tasya karta vyapratibandhāpanayanamātraṃ bhagavatā kriyate. tasmāt 'yudhasva' iti anuvādamātraṃ, na vidhiḥ*; 2.18, p. 19.

2 *ekasvarūpatvena anupacayātmakatvāt pramātṛtvād vyāpakatvāc ca ātmā nityaḥ. dehastūpacayātmakatvāt śarīriṇaḥ karmaphalabhogārthatvād anekarūpatvād vyāpyatvāc ca vināśī. tasmād dehasya vināśasvabhāvatvād ātmano nityasvabhāvatvāc ca ubhāv api na śokasthānam iti śastrapātādiparuṣasparśānavarjanīyān svagatānanyagatāṃś ca dhairyeṇa soḍhvāmṛtatvaprāptaye anabhisaṃhitaphalaṃ yuddhākhyaṃ karmārabhasva*; 2.18, p. 49–51/72.

3 Larson 1979 is the standard contemporary introduction to Sāṃkhya; on the specific aspects of the relationship between consciousness and experience in the Sāṃkhya theory of *puruṣa*, see Burley 2007.

4 The contrast is clear in Greek thought, where the possibility of rebirths is entertained only rarely. Having committed himself to it, Plotinus has to consider the unintelligible possibility that Socrates might be the reincarnation of Pythogoras, if he also accepts the general Greek idea (presupposed in modern Western philosophy) that the soul of Socrates is also the person of Socrates. But Plotinus, almost alone in his tradition, approaches the notion of an *ātman*, saying that each soul contains the

principles of all the individuals as which it will incarnate; Sorabji 2006: 122–3. Sorabji recognises that the Indian systems might handle this problem more efficiently. But I must add that the price that has to be paid is to de-link personal individuality from the soul – which is normal in India and baffling to the West.

5 Cary 2003.

6 Locke, John. *An Essay Concerning Human Understanding*. P. Nidditch (ed.). Oxford: Clarendon Press, 1979; especially p. 335ff.

7 Allison 1983, 138.

8 See the papers in Siderits, Thompson and Zahavi 2011.

9 *nāśakaṃ hi śastrajalāgnivāyvādikaṃ nāśyaṃ vyāpya śithilīkaroti*; 2.17; p. 71/46.

10 *yena sarvaṃ idaṃ jagat tataṃ vyāptaṃ sadākhyena brahmaṇā sākāśaṃ, ākāśeneva ghaṭādayaḥ*; 2.17, p. 18.

11 *vedāvināśinaṃ nityaṃ ya enam ajam avyayam, kathaṃ sa puruṣaḥ pārtha kaṃ ghātayati hanti kam*; 2.21.

12 *viduṣo 'tmatvāt. na dehādisaṅghātasya vidvattā. ataḥ pāriśeṣyāt asaṃhata ātmā vidvān avikriya iti tasya viduṣaḥ karmāsambhavādākṣepo yuktaḥ 'kathaṃ sa puruṣaḥ' iti. yathā buddhyādyāhṛtasya śabdādyarthasyāvikriya eva san buddhivṛttyavivekavijñānenāvidyayā upalabdhātmā kalpyate, evam eva ātmānātmavivekajñānena buddhivṛttyā vidyayāsatyarūpayaiva paramārthato 'vikriya eva ātmā vidvān ucyate*; 2.21, pp. 21–2.

13 Advaitins generally make a distinction between the 'mind' (*manas*), which is an internal organ, any state (*vṛtti*) of which represents a conceptual experience, and the 'intellect' (*buddhi*), a specific instrument of conceptualisation, which generates judgements regarding mental states. There is also another special cognitive function, the *ahaṃkāra* or 'I-maker', which ascribes an idiosyncratic perspective to the experience of a bodily locus. While there are interesting issues to explore here, and intra-Advaitic debates, I have chosen to ignore Śaṅkara's own rather loose use of '*buddhi*' and talked about mental states, because it more accurately captures the idea presented so cryptically here.

14 On these characterisations of Kant and Husserl, see Zahavi 2005: chapter 5.

15 Lewis and Staehler 2010: 18.

16 On Śaṅkara and Husserl on conscousness and self, see Maharana 2009; on Rāmānuja and Husserl, see Gupta 1982. These are relatively preliminary explorations, and much more ought to be done to offer mutual cross-cultural illumination.

17 *upadraṣṭānumantā ca bhartā bhoktā maheśvaraḥ, paramātmeti cāpy ukto dehe 'smin puruṣaḥ paraḥ*; 13.23.

18 *samīpasthaḥ san draṣṭā svayam avyāpṛtaḥ*; 13.23, p. 205.

19 *kāryakaraṇapravṛttiṣu svayam apravṛtto 'pi pravṛtta iva tadanukūlo vibhāvyate; ibid.*

20 On *sākṣī* – the concept of *ātman* as 'witness' – in Śaṅkara and later Advaitins, see Chatterjee and Dravid 1979.

21 *bharaṇaṃ nāma dehendriyamanobuddhīnāṃ saṃhatānāṃ caitanyātmapārārthyena nimittabhūtena caitanyābhāsānāṃ yat svarūpadhāraṇaṃ taccaitanyātmakṛtam eveti bhartātmety ucyate; ibid.*
22 *agnyuṣṇavan nityacaitanyasvarūpeṇa buddheḥ sukhaduḥkhamohātmakāḥ pratyayāḥ sarvaviṣayaviṣayāś caitanyātmagrastā iva jāyamānā vibhaktā vibhāvyante; ibid.*
23 *asmin dehe 'vasthito 'yaṃ puruṣo dehapravṛttyanuguṇasaṅkalpādirūpeṇa dehasyopadraṣṭānumantā ca bhavati, tathā dehasya bhartā ca bhavati; tathā dehapravṛttijanitasukhaduḥkhayor bhoktā ca bhavati*; p. 450/446.
24 For a thoughtful exploration (if in terminology that can now seem dated) of how Rāmānuja and his successors seek to distinguish between the impersonal self's attributive yet intrinsic consciousness, and the intentional consciousness that the human subject has towards objects, see Raju 1964.
25 I am taking the risk of relying on a largely intuitive sense of what '*guṇa*' means here, for understanding its many specific usages can become a task in itself; see Narain 1961. For the Sāṃkhya origins of this theory, on which the *Gītā* draws so heavily, see Wezler 1999.
26 *sukhasaṅgena: 'sukhyaham' iti viṣayabhūtasya sukhasya viṣayiṇy ātmani saṃśleṣāpādanaṃ mṛṣaiva sukhe sañjanam iti*; p. 215.
27 *jñānasukhayoḥ saṅge hi jāte tatsādhaneṣu laukikavaidikeṣu pravartate, tataś ca tatphalānubhavasādhanabhūtāsu yoniṣu jāyate*; p. 465/462.
28 *brahmabhāvayogyo bhavati, yathāvasthitam ātmānam amṛtam avyayaṃ prāpnotīty arthaḥ*; p. 479/473.
29 *ye śāstravidhim utsṛjya yajante śraddhayānvitāḥ, teṣāṃ niṣṭhā tu kā kṛṣṇa ! sattvam āho rajas tamaḥ*; 17.1.
30 *devādipūjāvidhiparaṃ kiñcic chāstraṃ paśyanta eva tad utsṛjyāśraddadhānatayā tadvihitāyāṃ devādipūjāyāṃ śraddhayānvitāḥ pravartanta iti na śakyaṃ kalpayituṃ yasmāt*; p. 240.
31 *bhagavānaśāstravihitaśraddhāyās tatpūrvakasya ca yāgāder niṣphalatvaṃ hṛdi nidhāya śāstrīyasyaiva yāgāder guṇatas traividhyaṃ pratipādayituṃ śāstrīyaśraddhāyās traividhyaṃ tāvad āha*; 17.2; p. 524/516.
32 *sattvānurūpā sarvasya śraddhā bhavati…*
33 *śraddhāmayo 'yaṃ puruṣo ye yacchradhaḥ sa eva saḥ.*
34 Malinar 2007; p. 216.
35 As Hans Schmid explains Heidegger's notion of 'falling' (Schmid 2005).
36 Lewis and Staehler 2010, 92.
37 Russon 2008, 101–2.
38 Russon 2008, 99.
39 Interestingly, Richard Cohen says of the Jewish thinker Franz Rosenzweig (Cohen 1993, p. 116): 'Escape from the *personality* means a deeper enrootedess in what Rosenzweig calls *character*, an inalienably ownmost non-relational and almost timeless selfhood. Breaking out of everyday selfhood in Heidegger means a deeper appreciation for *Dasein's* embrace of the world and world-time. For Rosenzweig it means the opposite: a greater detachment from the world owing to a harder, firmer, and nearly

impenetrable self-attachment. Here is the detachment of the hero, so fully grounded in his own resources, in his own self, as to be able to make a stand, to defy the world unto death.' This might be an obvious way to read Kṛṣṇa's teaching to Arjuna, but neither Śaṅkara nor Rāmānuja takes up such a line of thought. For them the heroic is still erroneous, cognitively and emotionally.

40 *'iha' iti karmādhikārabhūmipradarśanārtham iti*; p. 240.

41 Patton's translation perhaps most fluently captures the relevant sense of this polysemic word; Patton 2008, p. 184.

42 *kāmyānāṃ karmaṇāṃ nyāsaṃ sannyāsaṃ kavayo viduḥ, sarvakarmaphalatyāgaṃ prāhus tyāgaṃ vicakṣaṇāḥ*; 18.2.

43 For an exploration of Śaṅkara's critique of action, and his limited concession to its role, see Ram-Prasad 2007: chapter 3.

44 *tad viśuddhaṃ prasannam ātmālocanakṣamaṃ bhavati*; p. 253.

45 *tasya 'śeṣakarmaparityāgasyāśakyatvāt*; p. 254.

46 *tad dhi vastubhūtāḥ guṇāḥ yadi vāvidyākalpitās taddharmaḥ karma. tadātmany avidyādhyāropitam evety avidvān 'nahi kaś cit kṣaṇam apy aśeṣatas tyaktuṃ śaknoti' (3.5) ity uktam. vidvāṃs tu punar vidyayāvidyāyāṃ nivṛttāyāṃ śaknoty evāśeṣataḥ karma parityaktuṃ, avidyādhyāropitasya śeṣānupapatteḥ*; commentary on 18.48, p. 271.

47 *na hi karma dṛṣṭadvāreṇa manaḥprasādahetuḥ, apitu bhagavatprasādadvāreṇa*; commentary on 18.8, p. 550/545.

48 For a detailed study of Rāmānuja on the relationship between ritual action for the removal of consequentiality (which Sawai calls 'evil action' (*karman*)), see Sawai 1993. He looks not only at the *Gītābhāṣya* but also the *Śrībhāṣya* and the *Vedārthasaṃgraha*. I am in agreement with Sawai's argument that action is an auxiliary and not direct means of attaining God, 'a prerequisite for the origination of meditation on the Lord, but also for the acquisition of perfect knowledge of Him' (p. 27).

49 That, at other points, Rāmānuja makes the much more lavish point about the gift of God's gracious love does not necessarily count against this line of thought. For Rāmānuja, it is the case both that God loves all and that only some gain the competence to earn God's love.

50 *idānīṃ bhagavati puruṣottame antaryāmiṇi kartṛtvānusandhānena ātmany akartṛtvānusandhānaprakāram āha – tata eva phalakarmaṇor api mamatāparityāgo bhavatīti*; p. 555/549.

51 For the classic exploration of *līlā*, see Kinsley 1979.

52 *asmin karmaṇi mama kartṛtvābhāvād etat phalaṃ na mayā saṃbadhyate.*

53 *paramātmanā dattais tadādhāraiś ca karaṇakalevarādibhis tadāhitaśaktibhiḥ svayaṃ ca jīvātmā tadādhāras tadāhitaśaktiḥ san karmaniṣpattaye svecchayā karaṇādyadhiṣṭhānākāraṃ prayatnaṃ cārabhate, tadantaravasthitaḥ paramātmā svānumatidānena taṃ pravartayatīti jīvasyāpi svabuddhyaiva pravṛttihetutvam asti*; pp. 558/555–8.

54 Going back to the seminal collection of essays in Matilal 1989, there have

been many sophisticated studies of the ethical challenges in the *Gītā* itself; see Brodbeck 2004, a response in Kuznetsova 2007, and more recently, Sreekumar 2012 on the interpretation of the moral philosophy of the *Gītā* as rule-consequentialism. Sreekumar argues that Kṛṣṇa teaches a form of consequentialism that takes liberation (*mokṣa*) and the welfare of the world (*lokasaṃgraha*) as intrinsically valuable.

55 *tac ca sarvakriyāsv api samānaṃ kartṛtvāder avidyākṛtatvaṃ, avikriyatvāt ātmanaḥ. vikriyāvān hi kartā ātmanaḥ karmabhūtam anyaṃ prayojayati 'kuru' iti. tadetadaviśeṣeṇa viduṣaḥ sarvakriyāsu kartṛtvaṃ hetukartṛtvaṃ ca pratiṣedhati bhagavān vāsudevo viduṣaḥ karmādhikārābhāvapradarśanārthaṃ 'vedāvināśinaṃ... kathaṃ sa puruṣaḥ' ityādinā*; p. 23.

56 *atas tvayi vipratiṣiddham idam upalambhyate; yad etān haniṣyāmīty anuśocanam, yac ca dehātiriktātmajñānakṛtaṃ dharmādharmabhāṣaṇam. ato dehasvabhāvaṃ ca na jānāsi, tadatiriktam ātmānaṃ ca nityam; tatprāptyupayabhūtaṃ yuddhādikaṃ dharmaṃ ca. idaṃ ca yuddhaṃ phalābhisandhirahitam ātmayāthātmyāvāptyupāyabhūtam*; p. 60–1; 32.

57 *vidyamānair avidyamānaiś ca guṇair ātmany adhyāropitair viśiṣṭam ātmānaṃ 'ahaṃ' iti manyate so 'haṅkāro 'vidyākhyaḥ kaṣṭatamaḥ*; pp. 237–8.

58 Note here that Śaṅkara is not saying that the mind ascribes a set of attributes and then identifies the bearer as the 'I'. Rather, in talking of the 'I' formally, the mind cannot but talk of that 'I' in terms of attributes. In Kantian terms, Śaṅkara takes the mind to operate with an essential indexical for itself, the 'I', which he does not think is the result of ascription; but he does think that to talk about an 'I' is to do so only in terms of ascription. But whereas Kant would say that the formal 'I' refers not-ascriptively to the self – the Nyāya position (Ram-Prasad 2012: 135–7) that later Viśiṣṭādvaitins would hold too – Śaṅkara's view is that the self's non-ascriptive reflexivity is precisely not a reference to an 'I' (Ram-Prasad 2011: 229–32).

59 Śaṅkara does not give a philosophically elaborate account of his position in this commentary. For a more thoroughgoing analysis of the Advaitic position, starting with Śaṅkara, see Ram-Prasad 2001: pp. 180–8; and Ram-Prasad 2011: 226–35.

60 *'ananyāpekṣo 'ham eva sarvaṃ karomi' ity evaṃrūpam ahaṅkāram āśritāḥ tathā 'sarvasya karaṇe madbalam eva paryāptaṃ' iti ca balam, ato 'matsadṛśo na kaś cid asti' iti ca darpam; 'evam bhūtasya mama kāmamātreṇa sarvaṃ sampatsyate' iti kāmaṃ, 'mama ye aniṣṭakāriṇas tān sarvān haniṣyāmi' iti ca krodham*; p. 518/510.

61 *yadi hi jñeyasya dehādeḥ kṣetrasya dharmāḥ sukhaduḥkhamohecchādayo jñātuḥ (ātmanaḥ) bhavanti, tarhi jñeyasya kṣetrasya dharmāḥ kecanātmano bhavanty avidyādhyāropitāḥ jarāmaraṇādayas tu na bhavantīti viśeṣahetur vaktavyaḥ*; p. 187.

62 *yady ātmano dharmo 'vidyāvattvaṃ duḥkhitvādi ca kathaṃ bhoḥ pratyakṣam upalabhyate? kathaṃ vā kṣetrajñadharmaḥ? 'jñeyaṃ ca tatsarvaṃ kṣetraṃ,*

jñātaiva kṣetrajñaḥ' ity avadhārite 'vidyāduḥkhitvādeḥ kṣetrajñaviśeṣaṇatvaṃ kṣetrajñadharmatvaṃ tasya ca pratyakṣopalabhyatvam iti viruddham ucyate 'vidyāmātrāvaṣṭambhāt kevalam; p. 191.

63 *na hi tava jñātur jñeyabhūtayāvidyayā tatkāle sambandho grahītuṃ śakyate, avidyāyā viṣayatvenaiva jñātur upayuktatvāt*; p. 192.

64 The Kantian resonances here cannot be pursued, and Śaṅkara remains cryptic even in his longer Upaniṣadic commentaries on this matter. It becomes important in the work of later Advaitins. For a succinct exploration of the Kantian debate in recent times via a critique of the view (propounded by Qassim Cassam) that the body is in fact the necessary condition to think oneself as subject, see Longuenesse 2006.

65 For standard discussions on error theory in two major areas, in arithmetic, see Wright 1983: chapter 3; on morals, see J. L. Mackie 1977, chapter 1.

66 *dehātmasvabhāvājñānamohitasya tanmohaśāntaye hy ubhayor nāśitvānāśitvarūpasvabhāvaviveka eva vaktavyaḥ*; p. 70/44.

67 *mama yo bhāvaḥ svabhāva asaṃsāritvam, asaṃsāritvaprāptaye upapanno bhavatīty arthaḥ*; commentary on 13.19, p. 446/441.

68 *niṣkriyabrahmātmasambodhāt saḥ niṣkarmā tasya bhāvaḥ naiṣkarmyaṃ*; p. 271.

69 *naiṣkarmyasiddhiṃ paramāṃ prakṛṣṭāṃ karmajasiddhivilakṣaṇāṃ sadyomuktyavasthānarūpāṃ*; p. 272.

70 *paramapuruṣakartṛtvānusandhānenātmakartṛtve vigataspṛhaḥ*; p. 584/582.

71 *tāni sarvāṇi saṃyamya yukta āsīta matparaḥ.*

72 *ahaṃ vāsudevaḥ sarvapratyagātmā paro yasya sa matparaḥ, 'nānyo 'haṃ tasmāt' ity āsīta ity arthaḥ*; p. 39.

73 *manasi madviṣaye sati nirdagdhāśeṣakalmaṣatayā nirmalīkṛtaṃ viṣayānurāgarahitaṃ mana indriyāṇi svavaśāni karoti. tato vaśyendriyaṃ mana ātmadarśanāya prabhavati*; p. 106/91.

74 *māṃ śaraṇam upagatānāṃ matprasādād evaitāḥ sarvāḥ pravṛttayaḥ suśakāḥ siddhiparyantā bhavanti*; p. 489/482.

75 *sarvadharmān parityajya mām ekaṃ śaraṇaṃ vraja, ahaṃ tvā sarvapāpebhyo mokṣayiṣyāmi mā śucaḥ.*

76 *ātmajñānasya tu kevalasya niśśreyasahetutvaṃ bhedapratyayanivartakatvena kaivalyaphalāvasānatvāt*; p. 281.

77 *ayam aham asmi, kevalo 'kartā 'kriyo 'phalaḥ, na matto 'nyo 'sti kaś cit; ibid.*

78 *sarvadharmādharmabandhanarūpebhyaḥ.*

79 *anādikālasaṃcitānantākṛtyajaraṇakṛtyākaraṇarūpebhyaḥ sarvebhyaḥ pāpebhyaḥ*; p. 598/599.

80 *sarvapāpavinirmuktātyarthabhagavatpriyapuruṣanirvartyatvād bhaktiyogasya*; p. 598/600.

Bibliography

Allison, Henry (1983), *Kant's Transcendental Idealism, An Interpretation and Defense*. New Haven: Yale University Press

Augustine (1993), *Free Choice of the Will*. Thomas Williams (trans.). Indianapolis: Hackett

Barron, Robert (2007), *The priority of Christ: toward a postliberal Catholicism*. Grand Rapids, MI: Brazos Press

Barua, Ankur (2009), *The Divine Body in History. A comparative study of the symbolism of time and embodiment in St Augustine and Rāmānuja*. Bern: Peter Lang

Bradley, Malkovsky (ed.) (2000), *New Perspectives on Advaita Vedānta. Essays in Commemoration of Professor Richard De Smet, S.J.* Leiden: Brill

Brockington, John (1998), *The Sanskrit Epics*. Leiden: Brill

Brodbeck, Simon (2004), 'Calling Krishna's bluff: non-attached action in the Bhagavadgītā', *Journal of Indian Philosophy* 32.1, pp. 81-103

van Buitenen, J. A. B. (1956), *Rāmānuja's Vedārthasaṃgraha. Introduction, Critical Edition and Annotated Translation*. Poona: Deccan College Postgraduate and Research Institute

—(1966), 'On the Archaism of the Bhāgavata Purāṇa', in Milton Singer (ed.) *Krishna: Myths, Rites and Attitudes*. Chicago: Chicago University Press; pp. 23–40

—(1981), *The Bhagavadgītā in the Mahābhārata. Text and Translation*. Chicago: Chicago University Press

Burley, Michael (2007), *Classical Sāṃkhya and Yoga: An Indian Metaphysics of Experience*. London: Routledge

Caputo, John D. (2006), *The Weakness of God. A Theology of the Event*. Bloomington: Indiana University Press

Caputo, John D., Mark Dooley and Michael J. Scanlon (eds) (2002), *Questioning God*. Bloomington: Indiana University Press

Carlson, Thomas A. (1999), *Indiscretion. Finitude and the Naming of God*. Chicago: The University of Chicago Press

Carmen, John (1974), *The Theology of Rāmānuja. An Essay in Interreligious Understanding*. New Haven: Yale University Press

—(1994), *Meekness and Majesty. A Comparative Study of Contrasts and Harmony in the Concept of God*. Grand Rapids, MI: Eerdmans

Cary, Phillip (2003), *Augustine's Invention of the Inner Self: The Legacy of a Christian Platonist*. New York: Oxford University Press

Chari, S. M. S. (2005), *The Philosophy of the Bhagavadgita*. Delhi: Munshiram Manoharlal

Chatterjee, A. K. and R. R. Dravid (1979), *The Concept of sākṣī in Advaita Vedānta*. Varanasi: Benares Hindu University Press

Clayton, John (2006), *Religions, Reasons and Gods. Essays in Cross-Cultural Philosophy of Religion*. Cambridge: Cambridge University Press

Clooney, F. X. (1996), *Seeing Through Texts: Doing Theology among the Srivaisnavas of South India*. New York: State University of New York Press

—(2000), 'Śaṃkara's Theological Realism: the Meaning and Usefulness of Gods (devatā) in the Uttara Mīmāṃsā Sūtra Bhāṣya', in B. J. Malkovsky (ed.) *New Perspectives on Advaita Vedānta. Essays in Commemoration of Professor Richard De Smet, S.J.* Leiden: Brill; pp. 30–50

—(2008a), *Beyond Compare. St Francis de Sales and Śrī Vedānta Deśika on Loving Surrender to God*. Washington DC: Georgetown University Press

—(2008b), 'Imago Dei, Parama Samyam: Hindu Light on a Traditional Christian Theme', *International Journal of Hindu Studies* 12.3; pp. 227–55

—(2008c), *The Truth, the Way, the Life: Christian Commentary on the Three Holy Mantras of the Srivaisnavas*. Leuven: Peeters Publishing

Cohen, Richard A. (1993), 'Authentic selfhood in Heidegger and Rosenzweig', *Human Studies* 16: 111–28

Colledge, Edmund and Bernard McGinn (transl. and intro.)(1981), *Meister Eckhart. The essential sermons, commentaries, treatises and defense*. London: SPCK

Coward, Harold and Toby Foshay (eds) (1992), *Derrida and Negative Theology*. Albany: State University of New York Press

De Smet, Richard (2010), *Brahman and Person*. Ivo Coelho (ed.). Delhi: Motilal Benarsidass

Deleuze, Gilles and Felix Guattari (1987), *A Thousand Plateaus*. Brian Massumi (trans.). Minneapolis: University of Minnesota Press

Demacopoulos, G. E. and A. Papanikolaou (eds) (2008), *Orthodox Readings of Augustine*. New York: St Vladimir's Seminary Press

Derrida, Jacques (1982), 'Differance', in *Margins of Philosophy*. Alan Bass (trans.). Chicago: Chicago University Press

—(1992), 'How to Avoid Speaking: Denials', Ken Frieden (trans.) in Harold Coward and Toby Foshay (eds) *Derrida and Negative Theology*. Albany: State University of New York Press

Eckhart, Meister (1974), *Meister Eckhart. Parisian Questions and Prologues*. Armand Maurer (trans.). Toronto: Pontifical Institute of Mediaeval Studies

—(1979–81), Sermon 28, in *German Sermons and Treatises*, M. O'C. Walshe (trans.) London: Watkins.

Elders, L. J. (1990), *The Philosophical Theology of St. Thomas Aquinas*. Leiden: Brill; chapter 6

Fiorenza, Francis S. and Gordon D. Kaufman (1998), 'God', in Mark C. Taylor (ed.) *Critical Terms for Religious Studies*. Chicago: Chicago University Press, pp. 136–59.

Gilson, Etienne (1936), *The Spirit of Medieval Philosophy*. A. H. C. Downes (trans.). New York: Charles Scribner's Sons

Grant, Sara (1991), *Towards an Alternative Theology: Confessions of a Non-dualist Christian*. Bangalore: Asian Trading Corporation
—(2000), 'The Contemporary Relevance of the Advaita of Śaṅkarācārya', in Bradley Malkovsky (ed.) *New Perspectives on Advaita Vedānta. Essays in Commemoration of Professor Richard De Smet, S.J.* Leiden: Brill; pp. 148–63
Greisch, Jean (2001), '"Idipsum". Divine Selfhood and the Postmodern Subject', in John D. Caputo, Mark Dooley and Michael J. Scanlon (eds) *Questioning God*. Bloomington: Indiana University Press; pp. 235–62
Grimes, John (2007), *Śaṅkara and Heidegger: Being, Truth, Freedom*. Varanasi: Indica Press. First published 1989, Peter Lang: New York
Gupta, Bina (1982), 'Phenomenological analysis in Husserl and Rāmānuja: A comparative study', *International Studies in Philosophy*, 14.2: 19–32
Hacker, Paul (1965), 'Relations of Early Advaitins to Vaiṣṇavism, in Philology and Confrontation' in Wilhelm Halbfass (ed.) *Paul Hacker on Traditional and Modern Vedanta*. Albany: State University of New York Press; pp. 33–40
—(1995), 'Distinctive Features of the Doctrine and Terminology of Śaṅkara: Avidyā, Nāmarūpa, Māyā, *Īśvara*', in Wilhelm Halbfass (ed.) *Philology and Confrontation: Paul Hacker on Traditional and Modern Vedānta*. Albany: State University of New York Press, chapter 4
Heidegger, Martin (1975), *Early Greek thinking*. David Farrell Krell and Frank A. Capuzzi, (eds, trans.). New York: Harper & Row
Hemming, Laurence Paul (2003), 'In Matters of Truth: Heidegger and Aquinas' in Fergus Kerr, (ed.) *Contemplating Aquinas. On the Varieties of Interpretation*. London: SCM Press; pp. 85–104
Isayeva, Natalia (1993), *Shankara and Indian Philosophy*. Albany: State University of New York Press/ Delhi: Sri Satguru Publications
Jones, John D. (2008), 'The Divine Names in John Sarracen's Translations', *American Catholic Philosophical Quarterly* 82. 4. pp. 661–82
Kearney, Richard (2001), 'The God Who May Be' in John D.Caputo, Mark Dooley and Michael J. Scanlon (eds) *Questioning God*. Bloomington: Indiana University Press, pp. 153–85
Kerr, Fergus (2002), *After Aquinas. Versions of Thomism*. Oxford: Blackwell
—(ed.) (2003), *Contemplating Aquinas. On the Varieties of Interpretation*. London: SCM Press
Kinsley, David R. (1979), *The Divine Player: a study of Kṛṣṇa līlā*. Delhi: Motilal Benarsidass
Kumarappa, Bharatan (1934), *The Hindu Conception of the Deity as Culminating in Rāmānuja*. London: Luzac and Co.
Kuznetsova, Irina (2007), *Dharma in Ancient Indian Thought: Tracing the Continuity of Ideas from the Vedas to the Mahabharata*. London: Hardinge Simpole
Larson, G. J. (1979), *Classical Sāṃkhya: An Interpretation of its History and Meaning*. (2nd edn), Delhi: Motilal Benarsidass
Lester, Robert C. (1966), 'Rāmānuja and Śrī-Vaiṣṇavism: the Concept of Prapatti or Śaraṇāgati', *History of Religion* 5.2. pp. 266–82

Lewis, Michael and Tanja Staehler (2010), *Phenomenology*. An Introduction. London: Continuum

Lipner, Julius (1984), *The Face of Truth*. Basingstoke: Macmillan

Longuenesse, Beatrice (2006), 'Self-Consciousness and Consciousness of One's own Body. Variations on a Kantian Theme', *Philosophical Topics* 34.1–2. pp. 283–309

Mackie, J. L. (1977), *Ethics: Inventing Right and Wrong*. Harmondsworth: Penguin

Maharana Surya Kanta (2009), 'Phenomenology of Consciousness in Ādi Śaṃkara and Edmund Husserl', *The Indo-Pacific Journal of Phenomenology* 9.1, May: 1–12

Malinar, Angelika (2007), *The Bhagavadgītā. Doctrines and Contexts*. Cambridge: Cambridge University Press

Malkovsky, B. J. (ed.) (2000), *New Perspectives on Advaita Vedānta. Essays in Commemoration of Professor Richard De Smet, S.J.* Leiden: Brill

Marion, Jean-Luc (1991), *God Without Being*. Thomas A. Carlson (trans.). Chicago: University of Chicago Press

—(2008), 'Idipsum: The Name of God According to Augustine' in Demacopoulos, G. E. and A. Papanikolaou (eds) *Orthodox Readings of Augustine*. New York: St Vladimir's Seminary Press; pp. 167–90

Matchett, Freda (2001), *Kṛṣṇa, Lord or avatāra?: the relationship between Kṛṣṇa and Viṣṇu in the context of the avatāra myth as presented by the Harivaṃśa, the Viṣṇupurāṇa and the Bhāgavatapurāṇa*. Richmond: Curzon

Matilal, Bimal Krishna (ed.) (1989), *Moral Dilemmas in the Mahābhārata*. Shimla: Indian Institute of Advanced Study

Mayeda, Sengaku (1965), 'The Authenticity of the Bhagavadgītābhāṣya Ascribed to Śaṅkara', *Wiener Zeitschrift für die Kunde Süd-und Ostasiens*, IX; pp. 155–94

Milton Singer (ed.) (1969), *Krishna: Myths, Rites and Attitudes*. Chicago: Chicago University Press

Minor, Robert N. (ed.) (1986), *Modern Interpreters of the Bhagavad Gītā*. Albany: State University of New York Press

Narain, Harsh (1961), 'Finding an English Equivalent for 'Guṇa'', *Philosophy East and West* 11.1/2, pp. 45–51

Otto, Rudolf (1970), *Mysticism East and West: a comparative analysis of the nature of mysticism*. Bertha L. Nracey and Richenda C. Payne (trans.). New York: Macmillan (Lectures delivered in 1923–4)

Owen, H. P. (1971), *Concepts of Deity*. London: Macmillan

Patton, Laurie (trans.) (2008), *The Bhagavad Gītā*. London: Penguin

Prudhomme, Jeff Owen (1997), *God and Being. Heidegger's Relation to Theology*. Atlantic Highlands, NJ: Humanities Press

Raju, P. T. (1964), 'The Existential and the Phenomenological Consciousness in the Philosophy of Rāmānuja (Svarūpajñāna and Dharmabhūtajñāna)', *Journal of the American Oriental Society* 84.4: pp. 395–404

Raman, Srilata (2007), *Self-Surrender (prapatti) to God in Śrīvaiṣṇavism*. London: Routledge

Ram-Prasad, Chakravarthi (2001), *Knowledge and Liberation in Classical Indian Thought*. Basingstoke: Palgrave
—(2002), *Advaita Epistemology and Metaphysics*. Routledge Curzon: London
—(2011), 'Situating the Elusive Self of Advaita Vedānta', in Mark Siderits, Evan Thompson and Dan Zahavi (eds) *Self, No Self? Perspectives from Analytical, Phenomenological, and Indian Traditions*. Oxford: Oxford University Press; pp. 217–38
Ricœur, Paul (1998), 'From Interpretation to Translation', in André Le Cocque and Paul Ricœur *Thinking Biblically. Exegetical and Hermeneutical Studies*, David Pellauer (trans.). Chicago: Chicago University Press: pp. 341–55
—(1998), *Thinking Biblically. Exegetical and Hermeneutical Studies*, David Pellauer (trans.). Chicago: Chicago University Press
Russon, John (2008), 'The Self as Resolution: Heidegger, Derrida and the Intimacy of the Question of the Meaning of Being', *Research in Phenomenology* 38; pp. 90–110
Sawai, Yoshitsugu (1993), 'Rāmānuja's Theory of Karman', *Journal of Indian Philosophy* 21: pp. 11–29
Schmid, Hans Bernhard (2005), 'The Broken "We"', *Topos* 11/2; pp. 16–27
Schrijvers, Joeri (2010), 'Marion, Levinas, and Heidegger on the question concerning ontotheology', *Continental Philosophy* 43.1; pp. 207–39
Sharma, A. (1986), *The Hindu Gītā*. London: Duckworth
Siderits, Mark, Evan Thompson and Dan Zahavi (eds) (2011), *Self, No Self? Perspectives from Analytical, Phenomenological and Indian Traditions*. New York: Oxford University Press
Singer, Milton (ed.) (1996), *Krishna: Myths, Rites and Attitudes*. Chicago: Chicago University Press
Sorabji, Richard (2006), *Self. Ancient and Modern Insights about Individuality, Life and Death*. Oxford: Clarendon Press
Sreekumar, Sandeep (2012), 'An Analysis of Consequentialism and Deontology in the Normative Ethics of the Bhagavadgītā', *Journal of Indian Philosophy* 40.3; pp. 277–315
Summerell, Orrin F. (ed.) (1998), *The Otherness of God. Charlottesville*: University of Virginia Press
—(1998), 'The Otherness of the Thinking of Being: Heidegger's Conception of the Theological Difference', in Orrin F. Summerell (ed.) *The Otherness of God*. Charlottesville: University of Virginia Press, pp. 111–34
Taylor, Mark C. (ed.) (1998), *Critical Terms for Religious Studies*. Chicago: Chicago University Press
Te Velde, Rudi (2006), *Aquinas on God: The Divine Science of the Summa Theologiae*. Aldershot: Ashgate
Thomson, Iain (2000), 'Ontotheology? Understanding Heidegger's Destruction of Metaphysics', *International Journal of Philosophical Studies* Vol.8(3), 297–327
Tillich, Paul (1959), 'The Two Types of Philosophy of Religion' in *Theology of Culture*. New York: Oxford University Press
Westphal, Merold (1998), 'Faith as the Overcoming of Ontological Xenophobia',

in Summerell, Orrin F. (ed.) *The Otherness of God. Charlottesville*: University of Virginia Press; pp. 149–72
—(2001), *Overcoming onto-theology: towards a postmodern Christian faith*. New York: Fordham University Press
Wezler, Albrecht (1999), 'On the origin(s) of the Guṇa theory. Struggling for a new approach,' *Asiatische Studien* 53, pp. 537–51
Wilhelm Halbfass (ed.) (1965), *Philology and Confrontation. Paul Hacker on Traditional and Modern Vedanta*. Albany: State University of New York Press
Williams, A. N. (1999), *The Ground of Union: Deification in Aquinas and Palamas*. Oxford: Oxford University Press
Wright, Crispin C. (1983), *Frege's Conception of Numbers as Objects*. Aberdeen: Aberdeen University Press
Young, Katherine K. (1988), 'Rāmānuja on Bhagavad*gītā* 4:11: The issue of arcāvatāra', *Journal of South Asian Literature* 23.2; pp. 90–110
Zaehner, R. C. (1969), *The Bhagavad Gītā*. Oxford: Oxford University Press.
Zahavi, Dan 2005 *Subjectivity and Selfhood. Investigating the First-Person Perspective*. Cambridge, MA: Bradford, MIT Press

Gītābhāṣya Texts:
Rāmānuja n.d. *Śrī Rāmānuja Gītā Bhāṣya. With Text in Devanagari and English Rendering and Index of First Lines of Verses*. Svāmī Ādidevānanda (trans.). Madras: Sri Ramakrishna Math/2004 *Śrīmad Bhagavad Gītā with Śrī Bhagavad Rāmānuja's Bhāṣya and Śrī Vedānta Deśika's Tātparyacandrikā*. Uttamur Viraraghavacharya (ed.) Chennai: Sri Uttamur Viraraghavacharya Centenary Trust
Śaṅkara (1950), *The Bhagavad-Gītā with the Commentary of Śrī Śaṅkarācārya*. Dinkar Vishnu Gokhale (ed.). Poona: Oriental Book Agency
Also consulted: (1935), *Śrīmad Bhagavad-Gītā with Eleven Commentaries*. Shastri Gajana Shambu Sandhale (ed.). Bombay: The Gujarati Printing Press

Index

This index covers the Introduction, chapters and endnotes. Concepts are categorised primarily in English, where there is a standard translation from the original language, and principal terms in Sanskrit are included. An 'n.' after a page number indicates an endnote.